The Ugly Frontier

THE
UGLY
FRONTIER

David Shears

ALFRED A. KNOPF

NEW YORK

1970

Contents

MAP AND DIAGRAM

Illustrations

following page 140

Preface

THIS book is the result of curiosity, a desire to know more about the hard physical facts of German division. So little has been written, even in Germany, from this standpoint. Only the Berlin Wall has been extensively described and even here there are gaps in our knowledge. Much of the available literature is too propagandistic, too narrowly confined to shootings and escapes.

What follows is not another Cold War treatise—although the Cold War is still being waged in Germany. It is an attempt to describe as factually as possible just how the frontier operates, to put the Wall in perspective as just a small section of the border fortifications. Even many Germans know remarkably little about the workings of the few links that still remain between East and West, the confrontations over the years and the way the border is watched and guarded. It is these gaps that this book is intended to fill, and I have deliberately relegated to the last chapter any discussion of the 'German Question'.

Most of the book was researched and written in the spring and summer of last year. Some updating of the text was made down to the turn of the year, but the broad picture has remained so stable that there has been no need for radical revision. The advent of the Brandt–Scheel coalition of Social Democrats and Free Democrats in Bonn has done nothing to change East Germany's demand for full diplomatic recognition as the precondition of any relaxation in travel and communications. Rightly or wrongly—the case is arguable—this is a price that neither Herr Brandt nor any other foreseeable West German Chancellor is willing to pay. The only hope of any significant reduction in the barriers and restrictions dividing Germany is in the wake of a general thaw in East–West relations. At the time of writing the prospects of this look uncertain at best, and East Germany's capacity for acting as a brake on any budding *rapprochement* should not be underestimated.

It would be impossible to list all the people who helped in the preparation of this book: local officials and ordinary citizens in communities up and down the border and in Berlin. All the

PREFACE

Western border-guarding agencies proved most co-operative, arranging among other things trips by helicopter, jeep and boat along the land and water frontier. Numerous Bonn government officials gave generously of their time and knowledge without attempting to inject their political views into the book.

I want to thank *The Daily Telegraph* for granting me an extended leave to undertake the task. My secretary, Gabriele Hemken, devoted much of her spare time to the typing. But most of all I owe a debt of gratitude to my wife for her help with the historical research and in the laborious tasks of revision, proof-reading and indexing.

David Shears

Bad Godesberg
January, 1970

The Ugly Frontier

1

The Ugly Frontier

LIKE a duelling scar across the face of Germany, the world's ugliest frontier cuts a swath from the Baltic to Czechoslovakia. With its minefields, watchtowers and other fortifications, it divides Europe more effectively than the Alps or the Pyrenees and constitutes perhaps the most daunting man-made obstacle since the Great Wall of China. Vagaries of war and rivalries of power have created a monstrous anomaly in the mid-twentieth century. When Churchill coined the term Iron Curtain in his Fulton speech of 1946 he was being prophetic. It was not until six years later that East Germany began stringing barbed wire along her border with the Federal Republic, the line separating the post-war Soviet occupation zone from the Western Allied zones. Even then, the East Germans left a loophole in Berlin which remained open until the Wall went up on August 13, 1961. The name Iron Curtain has fallen into disuse in recent years, like the barbed wire along the original ten-metre ploughed strip now overgrown with weeds. Even in Bonn, where official documents still describe East Germany as the 'Soviet Zone', Churchill's term is seldom heard. Yet it was never more fitting than it is today, when new and more sophisticated barriers are constantly being devised to hinder movement between the two parts of Germany.

Even a statesman of Sir Winston's prescience could hardly have foreseen the full scope of these fortifications. Mines laid in double or triple rows extend today along more than half the land border, enclosed between twin wire fences. Ditches, trip-wires, flood-lights, dogs and over 2,000 watchtowers, observation posts and dugouts manned by 50,000 soldiers complete the frontier obstacles.

Consider the staggering dimensions of this undertaking. The Berlin Wall is thirty miles long; the entire border between isolated West Berlin and surrounding East Germany (including the Wall) measures just 100 miles. The East–West German frontier, with all its salients and indentations, covers precisely 858 miles: the road distance from New York to Chicago or from Land's End to John o' Groats. Villages and farms, sometimes even

houses, have been divided between East and West, families torn
asunder. Seventeen million East Germans are separated from
fifty-eight million fellow-Germans in the Federal Republic and
2·2 million in West Berlin.

Citizens of the German Democratic Republic wishing to cross
this frontier to the West have three choices. They can wait until
they reach pensionable age—sixty-five for men, sixty for women—
when they automatically become entitled to exit visas. For by
that time the East German government has no further interest in
keeping them; they are 'useless mouths'. Secondly, they can pose
as devout Communists in the hope of securing permission to
travel abroad in some official delegation. But this is a chancy
business, a method which in any case is open only to small groups
of intellectuals, sportsmen, trade officials and so on. Thirdly, they
can try to cross illegally, either by means of forged documents or
by braving the hazards of the border. In the past, until at least the
year 1967, East German refugees were able to get false passports
and other assistance from private Western escape organizations,
which naturally set a price for their services. Sometimes a refugee
was charged £1,000 or more and paid instalments for years after
his arrival in the West. Whether this kind of activity continues
today is a well-kept secret: if it does, it is probably on a small
scale since the East German frontier guards have become adept
at detecting counterfeit papers and secret hiding-places.

So the only recourse for the average would-be escaper is to run
the gauntlet of the obstacle course itself with all its deadly dangers.
As the lethal efficiency of the frontier security system increases,
so the number of successful escapes is dropping. Most East Germans know that the penalty of failure is a mine underfoot, a
bullet in the back or a fifteen-month jail term for attempted 'flight
from the Republic'. Virtually the only escapers to cross the so-called
'green frontier' today are people living close to the border,
familiar with its twists and turns. Nobody knows how many
would-be fugitives are rounded up in the five-kilometre 'forbidden zone' on the Communist side of the border before they
ever get close to the minefields and wire. Western officials and
refugee organizations warn East Germans that the risks of escape
make illegal border-crossing an almost suicidal undertaking. Yet
a number of fugitives still get through; nearly every day the West
German newspapers carry a paragraph reporting a new escape by
one, two or three refugees. Sometimes there are astounding

stories of whole families crossing the minefields unscathed, or heartrending accounts of groups in which one parent or one child has been wounded by a Communist mine or bullet and urges his companions to leave him behind.

Only one in nine of the 255,790 East German refugees who fled to West German camps during the eight years following the building of the Berlin Wall in 1961 came across the frontier fortifications. The rest crossed by less hazardous means. Half the total came legally, by East German standards, as pensioners or otherwise supplied with exit visas. Others defected while travelling abroad, or were smuggled out by the Scarlet Pimpernel methods of the escape organizations. Of those who assayed the border fortifications, at least 137 lost their lives, half of them on the East–West German border and the rest on the perimeter surrounding West Berlin.

To outflank the minefields and barbed wire is not easy: the Baltic Sea is patrolled by armed East German craft, and minefields bar access to GDR beaches within swimming range of the West. Nevertheless, in the summer months a few hardy fugitives succeed in escaping by sea, sometimes to be picked up by Danish and Swedish ferries. The West German *Bundesgrenzschutz* (Federal Frontier Defence Force) maintains a flotilla of patrol craft in the Baltic, but it does not intervene within the three-mile limit claimed as East German territorial waters. Once a refugee is outside the three-mile limit, however, he is fair game for both sides. Sometimes Communist and Western vessels have rammed each other in racing towards a fugitive boat or swimmer.

Dismayed by adverse world reaction to the horrors of this frontier with its frequent incidents, the East German government has set up an 'information centre' inside the massive Brandenburg Gate on the Unter den Linden in Berlin. Here a privileged visitor may sit in the plush blue armchairs of a briefing-room as a polished Major of the East German National People's Army tries to pretend that the Wall and the border are normal frontier fortifications 'typical of those existing between sovereign states'. He claims that their purpose is to keep out Western spies and 'provocateurs'. As to the shootings, he contends that East German frontier guards are under orders to shoot 'illegal' border crossers only as a last resort, and then only to aim low. But he will concede under pressure that fatalities may occur, since 'our machine carbines tend to rise as they are fired'.

Illegal border crossers are mostly the younger generation. Well over half the illicit refugees from East Germany in 1961–68 were less than twenty-five years old: youths yearning to escape from the monotony of the 'workers' paradise', to savour the bright lights, opportunities—and fleshpots—of the West, that they had watched on television programmes from Berlin and the Federal Republic. Some, of course, were disillusioned or homesick after a few weeks or months of job-hunting in the West, and returned to the East. But the majority stayed, settled and married in the West, leaving their parents and other relatives on the other side of the frontier.

The continuing trickle of refugees includes deserters from the East German Army, sentries and patrols who skip across the border when their comrades' backs are turned. In one celebrated case some years ago, one of the two East German guards on duty in the watchtower overlooking the Helmstedt Autobahn checkpoint made a particularly daring escape in broad daylight. First he quietly pocketed the bolt from his machine carbine. Then, taking his companion's live carbine unobserved from the rack and leaving his own, he calmly climbed down the watchtower ladder, pretending he needed to visit the latrine. On reaching the ground he simply walked to the West, a distance of only a few yards, while his fellow-sentry vainly tried to shoot him with the dud weapon. Since then, the East German Army has erected a high wire fence around the base of the tower to prevent a repeat performance.

But in most cases the East German guards, of whom 2,350 fled to the West between 1961–68, come across by simply making a dash for it. To minimize these desertions the East German Army normally requires men on patrol to move in pairs. Communist watchtowers closest to the border are usually empty. East German officers do not trust their soldiers to resist the temptation to throw away their weapons and run for the West. Often the minefields along the land border are laid not by troops stationed locally but by pioneer units based elsewhere, so that the frontier guards are kept in ignorance of the precise mine patterns. Work gangs of the National People's Army (NVA) are supervised by armed sentries to discourage any sudden bids for freedom. Listening to Western broadcasts is forbidden in NVA barracks, and soldiers are subjected to intensive Communist indoctrination.

Any Western visitor approaching the border must remember

one key fact: that all the fortifications are on the eastern side. Many casual tourists stroll unwittingly into East German territory because they imagine that the fences and minefields follow the actual border. But this is not so: the wire and the mines are set back at distances varying from 50 to 500 yards behind the demarcation line. The border itself is marked only by *Halt! Zonengrenze* (zonal boundary) signs erected by the West German Frontier Defence Force. Here and there, often partially hidden by long grass, one will find innocent-looking white marker stones planted by the East German guards, and occasionally a tall, striped post shaped like an obelisk and bearing a plaque with the East German national emblem. Unless, of course, the plaque has been torn off by souvenir-hunters prepared to risk an East German bullet.

To wander across this line into the no-man's-land between it and the fences is to court trouble. One may be arrested and held for days of interrogation by Communist authorities. One's foot might be blown off by an old mine that has washed out of its resting-place. One might conceivably be shot; but people coming into East Germany from the West run fewer risks than refugees trying to leave the German Democratic Republic. For the elaborate paraphernalia of Communist border 'defence' is designed to keep East Germans in rather than Westerners out. Militarily, the minefields and fences are useless against a Western invasion. There are no tank traps, no artillery emplacements; the wooden watchtowers and flimsy prefabricated pillboxes could be reduced to a shambles by a single shell. True, a deep ditch runs along sections of the border, but it is so designed as to offer no obstacle to tanks or other tracked vehicles heading eastward. It serves only to trap cars or trucks trying to charge the border from East to West.

Late in 1968 the East Germans began replacing wooden watch-towers with concrete ones symbolizing the permanency of the frontier. Old Russian-type wooden box mines are being super-seded by compact plastic mines which are more durable and less likely to wash out in case of flooding. Old and rusty barbed wire is giving way to wire mesh screens which are harder to negotiate and less unsightly. Rotting wooden posts are being replaced by concrete supports. Infra-red detectors and other modern warning devices are being installed. Communist patrol boats on the River Elbe are being renewed: at the end of 1968 there were at least twenty-seven Communist patrol craft along the sixty-mile stretch of river frontier, including sixteen of the latest type, capable of thirty knots.

To fly in an American army helicopter along the border, to drive with British military patrols or to sail along the Elbe in a West German Customs launch is an eerie experience. One looks across at the peaceful farms and fields on the other side, thinking of the innumerable family and business ties ruptured by this unnatural barrier. Occasionally, but only occasionally, one sees a couple of East German guards on patrol, trudging along their side of the border in fatigue dress carrying carbines and cameras. Sometimes, too, one will see a working party of Communist troops repairing fences, building patrol roads or replacing mines. When one sets out in a launch on the Elbe an East German patrol boat manned by armed troops will cast loose from the eastern bank and follow in close pursuit, cameras levelled at the Western craft.

There is no fraternization and virtually no contact between patrols on either side of the border, although they are often within hailing distance of one another. Sometimes an argument arises as to the exact line of the border, and this, as we shall see, can lead to tense confrontations. West German Customs men sometimes exchange a few pleasantries with an East German officer on the other side who is known to them. But in general there is not much love lost between the frontiersmen of East and West.

Everywhere the border presents a bleak and depressing spectacle. Mile after mile the mined strip runs over hill and dale, zigzagging through woodland and meadow. Trees and undergrowth have been cut down to minimize cover and provide a wide field of fire. It often takes sharp eyes or binoculars to spot the less obvious East German observation platforms in trees and to pick out the low pillboxes. Most West Germans have never been to the border; they know it only from pictures or from newspaper accounts of escapes. And they accept it as a fact of life. It may separate them from cherished relatives, but it scarcely affects their daily lives unless they happen to live in the so-called Zonal Border Region where the frontier has cut off their traditional markets and sources of supply.

The gulf between the two parts of Germany is steadily widening, not just because the fences are getting higher and the mine-fields deadlier. Politically, socially and economically the German

Democratic Republic and the Federal Republic are growing further apart despite all the efforts of well-meaning West German organizations bearing such titles as *Unteilbares Deutschland*— Germany Indivisible. Burgomasters of villages on either side of the border have virtually no contact with one another. Public utility links have been cut. When Duderstadt, a small Western town near Göttingen, asked the local authorities on the other side to clear the springs on which it had long depended, the East refused and Duderstadt had to dig wells for an independent supply. Water connections exist only on a very localized basis, and there are virtually no electric power links across the border. At one time there used to be joint lignite mining in one locality, but now the barbed wire runs right through the opencast workings straddling the frontier. In short, the border has been tightly sealed, each part of Germany belonging to a different world. With every passing year the outlook for German reunification appears dimmer.

Given this rigid division, the loopholes in the border become all the more intriguing. Three Autobahns, two main roads, eight railway crossings and two waterways are still 'open' under Communist control. These are the sluice-gates through which more than 2·5 million Germans still contrive to exchange visits between East and West every year; through which West Berlin is supplied and the entire flow of intra-German trade is conducted.

The 'legal' German travellers across the border include, of course, the East German pensioners mentioned above. East Germans sometimes say that theirs is 'the only country in the world where people actually look forward to growing old'. Nearly 1,500,000 elderly East Germans were allowed to visit the Federal Republic and West Berlin in 1968. Most of them returned to their homes in the East when their permits expired, but a few stayed behind to live with Western relatives. Then there are the privileged travellers such as Communist officials and businessmen, sports teams and delegates to scientific congresses. In the reverse direction 1,260,000 West Germans visited the GDR in 1968, somewhat less than in the previous year. For West Germans are permitted by East Germany's Communist rulers to cross the border at prescribed checkpoints for annual visits lasting up to a month. While Bonn puts no constraint upon such journeys, Herr Ulbricht's government in East Berlin issues entry visas on strict conditions. There is no blanket authorization for tourist travel by West Germans to the East, despite the GDR's efforts to attract tourists from other Western countries. A West German may only visit East Germany if he has parents, grandparents, brothers or sisters living there. Even then, the application for a permit must come from the East German relatives, not from the intending visitor himself. Seldom is permission granted for a West German to enter East Germany by car; normally he must go by rail. Evidently the East German government fears the 'propaganda' effect of thousands of shiny West German cars roaming the otherwise thinly-populated roads of the German Democratic Republic. It is one thing for a Cologne bricklayer to tell his East German relatives that he has a car; it is quite another for him to drive it to his brother's house in Leipzig so that car-hungry East Germans can see it and be envious.

Through the border checkpoints, too, flows all the road, rail and canal traffic serving West Berlin. In 1968 there were 3·7 million travellers each way on the Berlin Autobahns and railways. Altogether some 6·5 million travellers, then, cross the East–West German land border annually on return trips. It is an enormous figure considering the obstacles in the shape of permits, visas and checkpoint formalities that the East Germans put in the way. Apart from the problem of permits already discussed, Western visitors to East Germany now have to produce passports and buy visas at the border. Under new regulations laid down in June 1968, even travellers between Berlin and the Federal Republic must buy transit visas at DM 5 apiece for a one-way journey, but the cost is refunded by the Bonn government. Until 1968, travellers on the Berlin Autobahns could go through the checkpoints on production of their ordinary identity cards, but now they have to show passports. All these annoyances can be avoided by flying to West Berlin; it is not surprising that more than two million of the travellers between Berlin and the Federal Republic annually choose to go by air, and the proportion is increasing.

For there are other harassments at the border checkpoints besides red tape. Certain kinds of travellers are barred altogether from East Germany, including the Berlin Autobahns. A motorist or lorry-driver alleged to belong to the 'neo-Nazi' National Democratic Party is liable to be turned back at the border. Bonn government officials are also generally banned from visiting Berlin, although the rule is rarely enforced.

Cars and trucks, like trains and barges, are closely examined at

the checkpoint. For example, at Wartha, on the Frankfurt–
Dresden Autobahn, mirrors set in the roadway reveal any would-
be fugitive clinging to the underside of cars leaving East Germany. Communist border guards invariably open car boots and
hoods and lift up seat cushions before allowing motorists to
proceed. Western newspapers may be confiscated. Cameras and
foreign currency holdings must be declared before a visitor is
admitted to the GDR. A minimum amount of currency must be
changed into East German marks at the border; at the time of
writing the figure is DM 10 for each day's intended stay in the
GDR. Every document received on entering the GDR must be
retained for the return journey. Once I was held up for five hours
at Wartha on my way home from the Leipzig Fair because I had
mislaid a special press pass for the Fair. The Communist guards
at the checkpoint were polite but firm; they explained that they
had to telephone all the other checkpoints to warn them that the
pass might have fallen into unauthorized hands. Woe betide the
desperado who tries nowadays to crash the border by force. Even
a truck hung with bulletproof plating is unlikely to succeed.
Apart from heavy booms and 'slalom' concrete barriers (as at
Checkpoint Charlie in Berlin), some of the border crossings are
equipped with a new refinement: wagons loaded with stones are
parked on ramps beside the road, ready to roll into the path of
an oncoming vehicle at the touch of a switch from the guardhouse.

Of course the vast majority of the old East–West links are
closed. According to Western figures, the East Germans barricaded thirty-two railway lines, three Autobahns, thirty-one main
roads, eighty primary roads, about sixty secondary roads and
thousands of lanes and cart tracks when they closed the East–
West German border. These once-busy intersections may be seen
all along the frontier today, neglected and decaying in a mass of
weeds and rusty metal. Railway tracks are torn up, bridges are
down. Tall fences and anti-tank barriers stand starkly astride the
thoroughfares.

Airline connections are totally lacking. West Germany's
Lufthansa flies to Prague, Bucharest, Budapest and Belgrade in
Eastern Europe but it does not cross East Germany or land any-
where in the GDR. It cannot even fly the three air corridors to
Berlin, which are reserved almost—but not quite—exclusively
for planes of the three wartime Western Allies. In the reverse

direction, the East German airline Interflug may not touch down in West Berlin or anywhere in the Federal Republic.

Other communications, too, are hamstrung by the political division of Germany. Telephoning from one side of the border to the other is difficult and time-consuming because of the acute shortage of lines. Often there is a twenty-hour delay for a normal call and the only way to obtain a quick connection is to book a special call at ten times the usual rate. Telex communications operate more normally, but are also hampered by a lack of lines. Mail moves freely across the border but letter-writers on both sides work on the cautious assumption that every envelope is liable to be opened by Communist censors. Gift parcels from West Germans to relatives in the East are allowed, but only subject to strict Communist regulations as to the type and amount of each commodity involved. Western publications are severely restricted in East Germany. Non-Communist Western newspapers are rigidly excluded. Although the Bonn Parliament tried in 1968 to get a newspaper exchange arrangement started, by removing restrictions on the sale of East German publications in West Germany, the Communist government did not reciprocate. So the gulf in reading-matter between the GDR and the Federal Republic remains almost complete. The only form of communication that flourishes despite the barriers and the censorship is airborne: broadcasts or, to a limited extent, leaflet-carrying balloons and rockets launched across the border.

Almost all of East Germany can receive television from West Berlin and the Federal Republic, as well as radio. Similarly, the GDR beams transmissions to the West. Less openly, the two halves of Germany engage in short-range leaflet warfare, with the Federal Republic floating balloon-borne propaganda eastward and the GDR shooting leaflets westward in small rockets and papier mâché balls fired from primitive mortars.

The patchwork of barriers and loopholes that has developed in this divided nation offers an absorbing study. Rife as it is with absurdities and paradoxes, it nevertheless has come to be taken pretty much for granted. The risk in attempting a description is that the kaleidoscope is constantly changing. Yet the changes are mostly peripheral: a new glint here, a new shadow there. Basically the scene stays static, and seems likely to remain so as long as the confrontation persists between East and West Germany.

2

Drawing the Border

WHEN the Big Three wartime Allies sat down in early 1944 to chart the boundaries of their respective post-war occupation zones, probably none of the diplomats involved realized that the Soviet zone border would endure as the dividing-line through Germany for the indefinite future. Certainly the Americans and the British had no such intention. The startling fact in retrospect is that the present East–West line, giving Russia forty per cent of Germany and leaving Berlin marooned from the West, was accepted almost without demur. Indeed, it was proposed not by the Russians but by the British, and the Americans never raised any serious objection.

Recommendations for the allocation of occupation zones were drafted at meetings of the Anglo-American-Russian European Advisory Commission, which convened in Lancaster House, London, on January 14, 1944, for its first formal session. On the following day the British delegation, led by Sir William (later Lord) Strang, circulated a plan which placed the Soviet zone's western border almost exactly where it is today. The British were well prepared, in contrast to their American colleagues who were hamstrung by a complete lack of instructions from Washington. Strang wrote later that John G. Winant, the American Ambassador to London who was chief United States delegate, was 'placed in an embarrassing position by cross-currents of opinion and unresolved disagreements as to policy or jurisdiction among governmental agencies in Washington'.[1] Mr. Winant's successive political advisers on the E.A.C., George F. Kennan and Philip E. Mosely, have described these frustrations in graphic terms.

The British having been first off the mark with their proposal on zonal boundaries, the American delegation forwarded it to Washington and waited for a reaction. Mr. Kennan writes:

> Several weeks went by. No word from Washington. Repeated telegraphic appeals for instructions went unanswered.

[1] Lord Strang, *Home and Abroad*, London: André Deutsch, 1956.

Our British colleagues became restive, ourselves acutely embarrassed.[1]

On February 18, roughly a month after the British memorandum had been circulated, the Russians accepted Britain's suggested zonal borders practically without change. Again, the American delegation informed Washington. It was like talking to a brick wall. Kennan was irked to hear, years later, that the British proposals came as no surprise to either the White House or the American Joint Chiefs of Staff; that they had been discussed at the end of 1943 in the Combined (Anglo-American) Chiefs of Staff meeting at Cairo without the State Department being told. So the American delegation in London remained completely in the dark.

The problem in Washington was that the Civil Affairs Division of the War Department considered that the delimitation of future occupation zones was a purely military matter which was no concern of the European Advisory Commission. It argued that the zones would be determined by the location of troops at the time of Germany's defeat.[2] The War Department thus blocked the transmittal of any instructions to Winant; indeed, according to Mosely it even vetoed draft telegrams telling Winant that he could not expect an early reply to his urgent appeals for guidance. But the War Department was not devoid of ideas. On March 8 Winant received what Kennan calls a 'most curious communication' from Washington. This was a brief memorandum with accompanying sketch-maps which had been produced by the American Joint Chiefs of Staff. It showed a very much reduced Soviet zone: smaller, in fact, than either the British or the American zone. An enormous United States zone in north-west Germany would have reached as far as Stettin on the Baltic, roughly 150 miles eastward of the present division at Lübeck. From there the line was to reach southward to Berlin and thence by way of Cottbus and Leipzig to Bayreuth.

Coming at this late stage, three weeks after the Russians in the E.A.C. had accepted the original British proposal, the Washington memorandum caused consternation in the American delegation. Kennan felt that the Joint Chiefs' borderline proposal made no sense at all. It cut across geographic and administrative

[1] George F. Kennan, *Memoirs 1925–1950*, London: Hutchinson and Boston: Atlantic-Little, Brown, 1967, p. 167.

[2] See Philip E. Mosely, 'The Occupation of Germany', *Foreign Affairs*, XXVIII (July 1950), p. 588.

boundaries, and it did not even link up with the Czechoslovak frontier, thus leaving a gap. It was clear, writes Kennan, that the American delegation would need some very strong and well-founded arguments, probably coupled with some tangible means of pressure, to persuade the Russians to accept a line so far east of the one they had already agreed with the British. 'But we had not even been given any arguments to offer, not to mention any means of pressure. We had no idea what the line proposed by the Joint Chiefs of Staff represented, what its rationale was supposed to be, why we wanted just this line and no other.'[1]

The embarrassing military directive was never presented at the meetings of the E.A.C. Strang does not mention it in his memoirs, and there is no reason to suppose that either the British or the Russian delegation ever heard of it. Nor was there any reason why they should, since in sending the Chiefs of Staff memorandum to Winant the State Department had merely attached a note: 'This document is transmitted to you for your consideration and for your recommendations in regard to it.' At no time was Winant instructed to press for a reduction in the size of the proposed Soviet zone. Not that the American delegation was keen, at this late stage, to try anything of the sort. Kennan wired the Department in April: 'If we were to come forward now with the Joint Chiefs' proposal the Russians would only conclude that we had decided to cut down their zone by nearly fifty per cent over what they themselves had asked for. This would cause them to be highly suspicious of our motives. . . .'[2]

To try to straighten out the confusion, Kennan flew to Washington. Finding the State Department no help, he went to the White House, where he recalls that President Roosevelt received him 'graciously' but was far more interested in the issue of whether Britain or the United States should get the coveted north-western zone than in the borderline of the Soviet zone. When Kennan finally showed him the Joint Chiefs' map and explained the confusion, Roosevelt laughed and said: 'Why that's just something I once drew on the back of an envelope.' Actually it was not the back of an envelope; the President had sketched his concept of the zonal boundaries in pencil on a National Geographic Society map while on his way to the Cairo Conference at the end of 1943.

---

[1] Kennan, *op. cit.*, p. 168.
[2] U.S. Department of State, *Foreign Relations of the United States 1944*, Vol. 1, Washington: G.P.O., 1966, p. 209.

General George C. Marshall, chairman of the American Joint Chiefs, had handed it to his staff who took it back to Washington and developed it into the subsequent directive.

'I asked him,' Kennan says, 'whether he would himself see to the removal of the confusion, or whether there was something more I should do about it. He said I could relax—he would see to it that the mix-up was straightened out.'[1] Indeed, on May 1, 1944, Cordell Hull, the Secretary of State, sent Winant instructions approved by the President and the Joint Chiefs to accept the Soviet zone boundaries as proposed by the British and endorsed by the Russians.

From then on, there was no further serious argument, although Strang does recall one amusing sidelight. 'When we were discussing the boundaries of the zones of occupation in Germany,' he says,

> Gusev tried for a couple of months to secure the allocation of the island of Fehmarn in the Baltic to the Soviet zone. According to the text of our draft, this island clearly fell within the British zone as part of the province of Schleswig-Holstein to which it belonged; but the draughtsman who had prepared the accompanying map had left its allocation somewhat ambiguous. Gusev seized on this. He fought stubbornly— albeit with an occasional twinkle in his eye, for he knew he was being naughty—to gain this further advance of Soviet influence in the Baltic towards Denmark. I no less stubbornly resisted, though the Foreign Office authorized me to give way. I continued to stand out, and one day Gusev blandly, as though it had never meant anything to him, dropped his demand.[2]

This was, in the light of subsequent history, just as well. For Fehmarn Island, now linked to the Schleswig-Holstein mainland by a splendid bridge, has become the jumping-off point for a major road–rail ferry on the way to Copenhagen.

The London Protocol of September 12, 1944, based on the British plan, specified that the Soviet zone should comprise:

> The territory of Germany (including the province of East Prussia) situated to the east of a line drawn from the point on Lübeck Bay where the frontiers of Schleswig-Holstein and Mecklenburg meet, along the western frontier of Mecklenburg

---

[1] Kennan, *op. cit.*, p. 171.   [2] Strang, *op. cit.*, p. 207.

to the frontier of the province of Hanover, thence along the eastern frontier of Hanover, to the frontier of Brunswick; thence along the western frontier of the Prussian province of Saxony to the western frontier of Anhalt; thence along the western frontier of Anhalt; thence along the western frontier of the Prussian province of Saxony and the western frontier of Thuringia to where the latter meets the Bavarian border; thence eastwards along the northern border of Bavaria to the 1937 Czechoslovakian frontier . . . with the exception of the Berlin area, for which a special system of occupation is provided below.[1]

Strang in his memoirs has tried to explain why the line was drawn so far to the West (within about 100 miles of the Rhine at one point). He recalls that the E.A.C. planners were meeting before the Normandy landings of June, 1944, when it could not be foreseen how deeply the Western Allied forces would penetrate into Germany. Mosely writes that the American War Department believed at the time that the Russians would eventually control all of Germany up to the Rhine. Strang says it was felt that if there were to be three zones there must be broad equality between them, taking account of area, population and productive resources, and respecting as far as possible existing provincial boundaries for the sake of administrative convenience. He adds:

Taking all these criteria into consideration, the sub-division proposed [by Britain] seemed as fair as any, and if it perhaps erred somewhat in generosity to the Soviet zone (the Soviet zone included 40 per cent of the area, 36 per cent of the population and 33 per cent of the productive resources), this was in line with the desire of our military authorities, who had pre-occupations about post-war shortages of manpower, not to take on a larger area of occupation than need be. There was also the consideration that the Soviet zone might be subject to reduction if the boundaries of Germany were altered in favour of Poland. If we had tried to thrust the limits of the Soviet zone very far eastwards, there would then almost certainly have been no agreement. Had there been no agreement by the time the Western forces met the Soviet forces at Torgau on the Elbe in 1945, we and the Americans might then have negotiated a

[1] U.S. Department of State, *Foreign Relations of the United States: The Conferences of Malta and Yalta 1945*, Washington: G.P.O., 1955, pp. 118f.

settlement fixing the eastern boundary of our zones on the Elbe, over 100 miles to the East of the line actually agreed upon; but Berlin, of which the Russians were in occupation, would then assuredly have remained a part of the Soviet zone and would not have come under joint administration. The moral effect in Germany as a whole of the undivided control of their capital by the Soviet forces is not easily measured, but would have been far-reaching; and the free world would have lost the asset, uneasy and precarious though it may be, of having a foot in Berlin and of establishing an oasis of freedom in the middle of the desert of the Soviet zone.[1]

So much, then, for the original drawing of the border by the E.A.C. As it turned out, of course, the Western planners had been much too pessimistic as to the relative positions of the Anglo-American and Soviet forces on VE-Day. When the war ended on May 8, 1945, it was the Western forces that had penetrated deeply into the Soviet zone, not the reverse. President Truman and Marshal Stalin agreed in an exchange of telegrams on July 1 that the Western Allies should pull back their troops from Mecklenburg, Saxony–Anhalt, Thuringia and Saxony to the zonal border so that the Russians could occupy the whole of their zone.

Before examining post-war adjustments in the line, it is relevant to ask whether this boundary was likely to 'encourage rather than prejudice any separatist or particularist tendencies which may develop in Germany after her defeat', as stated in the original British memorandum to the E.A.C. The British plan drew the zonal boundaries so as not to cut across 'areas in which local autonomous movements are likely to take place'. It said no one could foretell whether any such spontaneous movements tending to divide the *Reich* might develop after the war. 'Any such movements will, however, almost certainly be based on the revival of old loyalties to States and Provinces within certain natural internal boundaries dictated by geography, history and economic considerations ... an anti-Prussian bias may well develop in certain areas, and there are strong grounds for weakening the present preponderance of Prussia.'[2]

Was it reasonable to suppose that the line dividing the Soviet zone from those of the Western Allies, purposefully following

[1] Strang, *op. cit.*, p. 214.
[2] U.S. Dept. of State, *Foreign Relations 1944*, Vol. 1, pp. 150ff.

old provincial borders, would in fact enhance genuine political, religious or ethnic distinctions within Germany? Seen in historical perspective, it might be argued that it was.

Even in the Middle Ages, roughly the same line divided Germans who looked to their Latin neighbours to the west, whose higher civilization they absorbed, from Germans who looked down on their Slav neighbours in the east, into whose lands they sought to expand. The contacts of Germans with Western culture on the one hand, with an alien eastern people on the other, left different marks on the peoples of West and East Germany. The Holy Roman Empire, which loosely united them, was important to its Western subjects as their representative in political dealings with Western powers; in their relations with the eastern peoples, characterized by mutual threats rather than diplomacy, the Germans of the East acted not on behalf of the Holy Roman Empire but of their own states which lay astride the Empire's eastern borders. Ethnic considerations were unimportant in determining eastern or western orientation: tribal and territorial divisions did not coincide—in fact tribal connections were often as remote as in the case of Prussia, which took its name from a tribe it exterminated in the process of its creation. Sectional religious differences, however, became deeply entrenched after the Reformation and remain even today largely the same as at the end of the Thirty Years' War. Golo Mann writes: 'Since the eastward-looking, newly German or colonial parts of Germany—Brandenburg, Pomerania and Prussia—became Protestant while the old Empire to the South and West remained predominantly Catholic, the Reformation once again strengthened the dividing line between the two regions of Germany.'[1]

Politically, of course, Germany in the waning days of the Holy Roman Empire was divided into countless mini-states, not into a clearly defined western and eastern region. But when Napoleon stepped in, today's dividing line became somewhat discernible. The Holy Roman Empire was dissolved and, in the area under French control, Church lands and smaller territories were incorporated into the larger states which in turn were joined in the Confederation of the Rhine. And when the Congress of Vienna again redrew the map, creating the German Confederation as a successor to the Holy Roman Empire, a Germany consisting of

[1] Golo Mann, *The History of Germany since 1789*, London: Chatto and Windus and New York: Praeger, 1968, p. 10.

three distinct components emerged: Austria, Prussia and the *Mittelstaaten*. Leaving aside the fate of Austria—an integral part of the former Empire, for many years to come the greatest influence in the new Confederation, but ultimately excluded from the German *Reich*—two elements remained in the territory which we now call Germany: Prussia, the giant in the East, and the smaller states, most of them former members of the Confederation of the Rhine, in the West.

Prussia had suffered defeat and loss of territory at the hands of Napoleon, sensed a rising tide of national feeling culminating in the 'Wars of Liberation' against France, and finally came out of the war not only with its western lands restored but with the Rhineland and half of Saxony added in compensation for Polish areas ceded to Russia. For the first time Prussia, which previously had included as many Poles as Germans, became a primarily German state. Its outlook was necessarily different from that of the smaller states which, though always purely German, had been pervaded by French ideas in the years of dependence on (or, as in the Rhineland, occupation by) France, and had sided with Napoleon till the last year of the war. The smaller states were by no means united, but their individual and collective relationship with Prussia forms the history of German unification in the nineteenth century. The relationship was not a happy one. It was mainly characterized by fear: fear of having their sovereignty swallowed up by Prussia, of seeing their nascent liberalism nipped in the bud by Prussian conservatism, of being forced by Prussian strength to abandon their traditional links with Austria. For economic reasons the *Mittelstaaten* one by one were forced to join the Prussian-led *Zollverein* (customs union). Their hopes in 1848 to transform the German Confederation into a genuine nation-state, even at the price of Prussian instead of Austrian leadership, were scotched; popular uprisings in support of the federal constitution drafted at the Frankfurt *Paulskirche* were put down by Prussian arms.

When, in the 1860s, Bismarck set out to find an answer to German national feeling, he had in mind an answer only in the interests of Prussia, an expanded Prussia including all of Germany except Austria. Despite their yearning for national unity, this was not what the *Mittelstaaten* wanted. Bavaria, Württemberg and Baden, in the south, might have accepted Prussian leadership of a liberal federation, but since a Prussian-led Germany was not likely

to be either liberal or truly federal, they supported maintenance of
the German Confederation led by Austria. Nassau and the Elec-
torate of Hessen, almost surrounded by Prussian lands, were more
divided in their sympathies, as were the Grand Duchy of Hessen,
Hanover, Brunswick and Oldenburg, but all of them hoped to
guard their sovereignty against Prussian incursion. Support for
Prussian leadership in this western area came only from the
Hanseatic city-states, Bremen, Hamburg and Lübeck.

The picture was only slightly different in the states farther to
the east. Saxony, having lost half of its territory to Prussia in 1815,
leaned to Austria in self-defence. But, densely populated and industrialized early, its economic interests lay with Prussia; its
Protestantism, too, linked it with Prussia rather than Austria;
culturally it differed from both, partly because of its location at the
crossroads between Germans and Slavs. Feelings were likewise
divided in Thuringia, a collection of eight small states not particularly united, and the two Mecklenburgs, but economically all
three were dependent on Prussia and ultimately had not much
choice but to go along with it. Nevertheless, clear support for
Prussia in the eastern area came only from Anhalt and the
smallest states.

The 1866 war was to settle whether Prussia or Austria would
lead Germany. While it was brewing, the smaller members of the
Confederation mobilized. In response, Prussia declared the Confederation dissolved, and its armies marched against the dis-
united smaller states. The settlement following the subsequent
defeat of Austria provided for the annexation by Prussia of all
German territories North of the Main River (except Saxony)
whose troops had fought against it, and the inclusion of the remaining states in this area in the North German Confederation.
The states South of the River Main, though left free to form their
own Confederation, neither had the will nor was it realistic for
them to do so. Eventually they were forced to elect delegates to
the North German Parliament by Bismarck's threat to dissolve the
Zollverein, on which they were economically dependent, unless
they joined in reforming it. By 1870, none were left with any real
choice but to join Prussia in the war against France.

Thus came into being the German *Reich*: by Prussian conquest
or coercion of its reluctant fellow-Germans. A creature of the
Prussian state, founded without or even against the wishes of
the German people, ostensibly providing representation for its

the provincial frontiers on their maps. Frequently they got together over a glass of vodka and agreed on local changes to simplify administration. For instance, at Schlutup close to Lübeck
travellers through the road checkpoint may see a house which was
'given' to the British zone by the local Russian commandant after
the war. The house and its red brick outbuilding belonged to the
Soviet zone province of Mecklenburg, but was handed over in
response to a British officer's request to use it as a guardroom for
British military police. The buildings and adjacent land have remained in the West ever since 1945, more by usage than by right.
Frau Ellen Breest recalls with a wry smile that when she was born
in the house it belonged to Mecklenburg and when her son was
born in the selfsame house after the war it belonged to Schleswig-
Holstein. She and her family get their gas and electricity from the
West and her policeman husband pays his income taxes in Lübeck.
But they have never received a rate demand, and Frau Breest is
far from happy. 'I wish we *could* pay property taxes to the West,'
she says. 'Then we would know we really belonged.' But evidently East Germany lacks the power to collect the tax and West
Germany does not feel legally entitled to do so.

A much bigger adjustment in the zonal border occurred some
sixteen miles south of Lübeck in the neighbourhood of Ratzeburg.
Here in a marshy region of lakes and streams roughly 12,000
acres of the British zone were exchanged for about 6,500 acres of
the Soviet zone. The purpose was to rationalize the border where
communication was difficult. The areas ceded to the Soviet zone
were already isolated from the West. But Ratzeburg officials
claim today that the deal was a 'poor swap' because of the difference in area involved, even though it pushed back the
Soviet zone border from the immediate environs of Ratzeburg
itself.

Further south, Lord Montgomery made over to the Russians a
slab of the British zone lying beyond the River Elbe which could
not be easily administered from the West since the bridges were
down. In return, the Russians handed over to the British some
tracts of land on the western bank. In the Harz Mountains almost
three-quarters of the county of Blankenburg, an enclave of the
British zone's Brunswick province lying east of the continuous
provincial border, went to the Soviet zone. An information
kiosk placard outside the Western border village of Hohegeiss
states that the county has shrunk from 182 square miles to forty-

eight square miles. 'All cultural, economic and personal links with the towns and villages now in the East have been broken', it reports. Farther southward again lies another enclave of interest, the oblong area embracing the villages of Ostheim, Sondheim, Stetten, Urspringen and Lichtenburg in northern Bavaria. This little island of territory originally belonged to the province of Thuringia which now is part of East Germany. In the summer of 1945 the villagers of Ostheim feared that the Americans would withdraw and hand them over to the Russians. There was great excitement when a jeep-load of Russian officers appeared, but the American commander awarded the enclave to the United States zone with a stroke of the pen. Neither the Russians nor the East Germans have ever laid claim to it since.

The trouble with these 'strokes of the pen' is that they tended to be imprecise. It is widely believed that British and Russian officers occasionally sketched agreed changes on beermats, giving rise to the headline in one London newspaper, 'The Beermat Border'. But the tale that one such beermat is still to be seen in the hands of a local German official seems unfounded. In fact, the whole beermat story must be doubted since beermats were lacking in Germany at the end of the war. Nevertheless it is certainly true that the military authorities of both sides, still tinged with the rosy flush of victory, were easy-going in their methods. The lines they drew in soft pencil on maps with a 1 : 100,000 scale were up to two millimetres wide, causing endless trouble when the East Germans started to spread barbed wire along the border years later. Obviously the officers of 1945 did not foresee the complications that their casual cartography would create for the future.

Berlin, too, has its border anomalies. Ten enclaves of West Berlin territory, ranging in size from less than eight acres to 110 acres lie beyond the fringes of the Western sectors, surrounded by East German territory. Steinstücken, an area of thirty acres just outside the American sector, contains 180 inhabitants and three American soldiers who symbolize United States power. In October 1951 the East German People's Police occupied Steinstücken and announced its incorporation in the GDR county of Potsdam. But the community was 'freed' a few days later and its people may travel to West Berlin, less than a mile away, through the fortifications surrounding the city. Nearby, at Wüste Mark, there is at the time of writing only a lone septuagenarian inhabitant.

Two small enclaves adjoining the British sector are deserted except in the summer months when West Berliners are allowed through the barbed wire to tend their allotments. East German troops open the gates in the fencing only at certain hours, and keep sentries on guard. Eiskeller is a special case: jutting out like a peninsula from Spandau in the British sector, it is connected with West Berlin by a half-mile track. It became famous when, after the building of the Berlin Wall in August 1961, the East Germans tried to stop a twelve-year-old boy from using the path to cycle to school, and the British provided an armoured car to escort him to classes.

Even more important as a source of future trouble than the cavalier drawing of boundaries was the lack of precision concerning Allied access to Berlin. The assumption in the E.A.C. had been that the occupation zones would not be sealed off from each other, and that arrangements for transit to Berlin could safely be left to the military commanders to arrange after Germany's defeat. Strang concedes in his memoirs that it might have been a mistake not to try to get a clause on Berlin access inserted into the final E.A.C. protocol. But he recalls that neither the British nor the American delegation was ever instructed to raise the question, and in any case the Russians would have maintained that these were 'self-evident matters which it would be for the military commanders to settle'.[1]

When the war ended, the Western Allies could have tried to get firm commitments on Berlin access during their negotiations with the Russians over the withdrawal of American and British troops to their occupation zones. General Lucius D. Clay, who was then deputy American military governor, later confessed that it may have been unfortunate not to have insisted on free access to Berlin as a condition of the Western pullback. Instead, agreement was reached at a meeting with Marshal Zhukov of the Soviet Union on June 29, 1945, on the withdrawal of Western forces, but the issue of access was only provisionally settled. The Russians were willing to grant access only by means of one road, one railroad and two air corridors; since the West wanted unrestricted right of access by all routes, no hard and fast guarantee of specific routes was set down in writing pending renewed discussion in the Allied Control Council. It was only orally agreed at the meeting that all military road, rail and air traffic to and from Berlin would

[1] Strang, *op. cit.*, p. 216.

be free from border search or control.[1] Both Clay and Strang agree that it is doubtful whether anything in writing would have made much practical difference, since the Russians always found technical reasons for violating undertakings. This may be true enough, but the lack of explicit guarantees has hampered the Western position ever since.

[1] See Lucius D. Clay, *Decision in Germany*, Garden City, N.Y.: Doubleday and Co., Inc., 1950, pp. 24ff.

3

Building the Barricades

IT takes an effort of the imagination for any present-day visitor to the Wire and the Wall to conceive the borders dividing Germany and Berlin in former days. Today all is quiet on the Eastern front: incidents are extremely rare, as the sheer technical efficiency of the East German frontier fortifications has imposed an unearthly, sinister peace. The task of guarding the border is tedious and depressing. Pioneer troops and work gangs are still to be seen at intervals along the line, replacing old mines and wire or building concrete watchtowers, but much of the work is routine maintenance. Broadly speaking, the fortifications are complete, and they convey an impression of permanence.

During the first post-war decade things were very different along the zonal border. Legally the Soviet zone boundary was just like the lines dividing the American, British and French zones; administrative borders which today are quite forgotten. Germany was in ruins, a defeated nation paying penance for the crimes of the Third Reich. Across the boundaries of its occupation zones flowed a westbound tidal wave of refugees, Germans uprooted from their homes in Poland, Hungary and Czechoslovakia or the 'lost provinces' beyond the Oder–Neisse Line. Nearly twelve million of these so-called 'expellees' were to resettle in what was left of Germany after the frontier readjustments; over two million more died of hunger, exposure and illness. In addition there were millions of refugees from the Soviet zone seeking sanctuary in the West from the excesses of the Red Army. Exact numbers were impossible to count; the East–West border was wide open in the immediate post-war months to all comers. By the time of the 1961 West German census there were 3·1 million people from the area we now call East Germany who had fled to the Federal Republic. The figure does not include expellees from territories further East who halted and settled for a while in the Soviet zone before continuing their emigration to the West.

Obviously this enormous exodus threw a heavy burden upon

the scarce resources of the Western zones: food, housing and transport were already overstrained. In June 1946 the governing Allied Control Council issued at Soviet request an order 'closing' the zonal borders. It was estimated that within the preceding nine months 1·6 million people had crossed into the British zone alone. Soon afterwards the Allies introduced thirty-day passes which allowed Germans to visit other zones for urgent personal reasons. But the restrictions had little effect. Still the westbound trek continued as refugees and expellees dodged through woods and fields to elude Allied military patrols. Here and there signs nailed to forest trees pointed to the 'green border'. Sometimes German police in Soviet zone border areas would quietly advise travellers on the best route to escape Russian guards. When one was caught, a bottle of schnapps or vodka often persuaded Russian soldiers to turn a blind eye. In the Helmstedt area alone, astride the main Autobahn leading from Berlin, no fewer than five million people came across the border to the West during the years 1945–47, including two million 'illegal' crossers.

Crime and black marketeering were rife in those days. In this same period Helmstedt police registered 17 murders, 200 robberies and 100 frontier incidents involving Russian troops. People in border areas offered to guide refugees along unguarded woodland trails from East to West—for a substantial fee. Often these 'guides' turned out to be crooks who robbed and killed once the forest was reached. Sometimes Western policemen were abducted to the Soviet zone. There was no Customs Service on the zonal border until 1949; it was patrolled in the immediate post-war years by local police and troops of the victorious powers. Fish was a favourite black market commodity. Helmstedt people remember the stench in trains used by smugglers to bring in fish from Bremen which could then be carried in rucksacks across to the Soviet zone and sold for a profit. In the first three years after the war Helmstedt police seized 150,000 lbs of fish, 100,000 lbs of meat, 60,000 tins of meat products and 10,000 bottles of spirits from illegal border-crossers. It was a wild frontier, and not only at Helmstedt.

In the shattered city of Berlin there was no restriction on movement between the Eastern and Western sectors, or between the Western sectors and the surrounding Soviet zone. But the early unity of Berlin had its drawbacks, notably the opportunities it presented to the Soviet authorities for political kidnappings. By November 13, 1947, when the city parliament finally voted its lack of confidence in the Soviet-backed police chief, no fewer than 5,413 people had been arrested and disappeared. Many of them vanished from the Western sectors.

Within the Allied Control Council there was no agreement on fostering the economic unity of Germany. More and more, the Russians and the West went their different ways until the Western currency reform in the summer of 1948 suddenly gave the East–West border economic significance. Introduction of the new Western Deutsche Mark into the Western sectors of Berlin not only posed serious monetary problems in the undivided city; it also touched off the Berlin blockade. For eleven long months, until May the following year, the road, rail and canal lifelines connecting Berlin to the West were cut off and the 2·2 million inhabitants of the Western sectors had to be supplied by air. The siege was worsened by the Soviet ban on deliveries of food, milk, electricity and lignite from the Russian zone to West Berlin. The wild scenes of jubilation that greeted the lifting of the blockade could not disguise the widening gulf between East and West, a schism which proceeded to tear asunder the once-proud German nation and its erstwhile capital.

Russia promised in the New York agreement of May 4, 1949, to lift all the restrictions it had imposed since March 1 of the previous year upon communications, transport and trade between Berlin and the Western zones and between the Eastern zone and the Western zones. Cars, trucks, trains and barges moved normally again, bringing to Berliners all the good things of life they had missed during the blockade, from fish to shaving soap, from coal to darning wool. But when the foreign ministers of Russia and the West met in Paris later that month they could only confirm that the old deadlock remained as firm as ever. German unity was out of the question; nothing could prevent the creation of separate German governments in East and West. After elections in the three Western zones on August 1, the Federal Republic was founded in the following month. Across the border, the German Democratic Republic was born on October 7, 1949.

But on the dividing-line there were still no minefields or barbed wire. People crossing zonal boundaries were still supposed to show interzonal passes but the tide of refugees and expellees continued to flow westward without serious hindrance. Many people commuted across the East–West zonal border to work; in Berlin over 100,000 inhabitants of the Western sectors had jobs in the East in 1949, and 45,000 East Berliners commuted every day to the West. As West Berlin's economy picked up momentum more and more workers came over from the Eastern sector until by 1952 the numbers commuting in each direction were balanced. Roads and railways linking West Berlin with the surrounding East German countryside were still open. Both around Berlin and on the zonal border, farmers tilled their fields astride the lines of demarcation, villages and towns kept up their traditional contacts. Football teams arranged fixtures across the East–West border; people visited relatives on family occasions, municipalities co-operated in maintaining water supplies and sent fire engines across the border when barns burned in neighbouring communities. But these contacts were doomed to gradual extinction. Already by the early 1950s Otto Grotewohl, premier of the GDR, could discern the dangers posed for his fledgeling state by the drain of refugees to the West. People were fleeing the 'workers' and peasants' state' at the rate of between 10,000–20,000 a month, according to official Bonn statistics. These figures covered only those refugees who had chosen to register at the official reception centres where they were given food, lodging and medical care until they could find homes and jobs. There was no compulsion to register and the total outflow of refugees from East Germany was probably twice as large as the government figures showed. If they all had been pensioners there would have been no cause for Herr Grotewohl to worry: his 17 million population was overloaded with people outside working age. But the disturbing truth was that East Germany was losing the very people it could least afford to spare: the skilled, professional and educated classes. If the GDR was ever going to surmount its acute economic problems, its lack of raw materials and its immense losses through war damage and Soviet reparations, it would need all the productive skills it could muster. For a while, according to officials of the Marienfelde refugee camp in West Berlin, as many as one quarter of East Germany's entire output of high-school graduates possessing the *Abitur* school-leaving certificate were fleeing to the West.

So it was not surprising that on May 26, 1952, Grotewohl's government announced its drastic decision to barricade the border. It was from this fateful date onward that the zonal boundary became an ugly frontier; all the cold-blooded apparatus of watchtowers, mines, ditches and killings, all the horrors of the Berlin Wall, were only refinements and logical consequences of this announcement. It is worth examining in some detail for this reason. Essentially it provided for the creation of a ten-metre ploughed strip alongside the entire length of the border. This was to be backed to the east by a 500-metre 'protective strip' and a three-mile 'forbidden zone' which could be entered only with a special pass. There was no mention in the announcement of any kind of fence, but East German border guards promptly started spreading barbed wire along the border. Residents of the forbidden zone had to have a special stamp in their identity cards. Local border-crossing traffic was halted, and fields in the 500-metre protective strip could only be worked between sunrise and sundown. Work in the immediate vicinity of the ploughed strip could only be performed under police supervision.

'Crossing the ten-metre control strip is forbidden for all persons', the decree said. 'Persons who attempt to cross the control strip either in the direction of the GDR or West Germany will be arrested by the border control patrols. Weapons will be used in case of failure to observe the orders of the border patrols.'

The decree was timed to coincide with West Germany's signature of the ill-fated European Defence Community treaty, and Grotewohl contended that it was designed to protect the GDR from 'spies, diversionists, terrorists and smugglers' who were allegedly being sent across the border in ever-increasing numbers. (It is noteworthy that at this time the Communist government was still referring to the border as the 'demarcation line'—as the Federal Republic does to this day—instead of the 'State Frontier of the GDR'.)

But the true purpose of the directive was plain: it was primarily designed to keep East Germans from fleeing to the West. If East Germans could be trusted not to defect, why should they be barred from crossing the ploughed strip, why should they have to observe a curfew and work next to the border under police supervision? Why, furthermore, should an estimated 8,000 allegedly 'unreliable' residents of the East German border areas have been evicted from their homes in May–June 1952, to be resettled further back in the GDR? West German sources say that riots ensued in a number of the villages affected and hundreds of People's Police had to be used to quell them. Remaining border inhabitants had to be pacified with extra rations, pay and pensions.

The Grotewohl decree made no mention of the border dividing West Berlin from East Germany but here, too, restrictions were applied. As early as April 1949 telephone links between the Schöneberg district of West Berlin and the Soviet zone had been cut off; bus and tram services across the zonal boundary had been subjected to increasing harassment culminating in arrests of transport workers, which finally brought this traffic to an end in October 1950. Less than a week after the Grotewohl decree the East German government ordered that travellers to the GDR must show permits, obtainable in the Soviet sector. From July 1952 the 35,000 West Berliners owning houses or land in the surrounding GDR were barred from visiting their property. Roads leading to West Berlin were barricaded or guarded; a start was made with barbed wire and ploughed 'death strips' around the Western sectors. Travellers from East Germany to East Berlin were interrogated on their trains or at the city limits on the reasons for their journeys. The aim was to check emigration to the West, but despite all these measures the flow of refugees through Berlin continued at redoubled pace. While in the years 1949–51 the number entering West Berlin had remained fairly stable at around 60,000 annually, the intake rose dramatically to 129,000 in 1952 and 297,000 in 1953.

Berlin's open East–West sector boundary became the sole safe channel of escape to freedom. Refugees came over from the East on the U-Bahn (underground railway) or the S-Bahn (elevated railway), or walked across carrying bundles and shepherding their children. Although the East Berlin authorities reduced the number of street crossing-points from 227 to 100, it was not difficult for refugees to merge with the daily stream of commuters across the sector border. But they often arrived destitute, hungry and exhausted. They were bedded down in makeshift quarters including disused factories and air raid bunkers. Then they began the tedious round of checks and interviews to determine whether they rated as 'recognized' refugees. To pass the test they had to prove that they were fleeing for political reasons: that they had been subject to persecution in the East. The laws and regulations in the West were—and still are—rigid and precise. Neither West Germany nor West Berlin was prepared to spend money and resources on refugees who came over merely because of the higher living standard in the West. These people—and they were numerous—were not sent back to the East. But they were denied unemployment assistance, government aid in finding homes and jobs; they were left to shift for themselves. Almost all the recognized refugees were flown out of Berlin to the Federal Republic at government expense. Tens of thousands of un-recognized fugitives elected to stay in West Berlin despite all the difficulties of overcrowding and job-hunting rather than return to the Communist East.

A typical unrecognized refugee was a girl who had moved to West Berlin simply because, as she put it, 'the clothes in the shops are so much prettier'. She found a job as a maid in the Dahlem suburb of the city, and stayed. A plea of political persecution did not require proof of time served in an East German jail, but this helped. For instance, there was the case of a fifty-eight-year-old inn-keeper who had been jailed in 1948 for allowing non-Communist political parties to hold meetings on his premises. He had only secured his release by signing a pledge to work for the Russian secret service, which had demanded that he spy on a friend in West Berlin and entice anti-Communist propagandists to his pub where he would betray them to the police. This man had no difficulty in passing the test as a recognized refugee. Nor did a woman farmer who testified in 1952 that she was forced to flee because she could not get enough labour to fulfil her milk and pork production quotas, and therefore faced legal prosecution.

Rising discontent in East Germany boiled over on June 17, 1953, a date revered in German history, when angry East Ger-mans staged their brief revolt. Shocked by the stoning of Soviet tanks, the burning of Communist propaganda kiosks, the tearing down of the Red Flag from the Brandenburg Gate and protest marches by thousands of workers, the Communist régime had to make concessions. It cancelled its ten per cent forced increase in working norms (quotas), the move which had touched off the outburst.[1]

A period of relative calm ensued; the refugee count dropped sharply in 1954 after its peak of the previous year, only to rise again. But the East German government announced no new drastic measures to check the exodus. The commuters—and the refugees—still crossed the Berlin sector border. In 1957 no fewer than 2,720,000 East Germans visited relatives in the Federal Republic. Nobody could force them to return against their will. But then the screws began to tighten: on December 11 of that year the East German Passport Law was amended to provide that any unauthorized departure from the GDR—'flight from the Republic'

[1] See Chapter Ten, pp. 156ff.

—was an offence punishable by three years' jail. Penal terms were also imposed on persons caught making preparations to leave the GDR, and exit permits were henceforth denied to whole categories of the population including schoolchildren, students and relatives of refugees.

Meanwhile the East German border guards and pioneers along the East–West frontier were not idle. Slowly but surely they continued to raise new obstacles, new hazards to trap would-be escapers. By May 1959 Western border guards counted 500 watchtowers along the line. In that year the village of Obersachswerfen in Thuringia, just on the Communist side of the border, was turned into a so-called 'Border Police Supporters' Village'. East German press reports said that the village councillors had reached an agreement with the Communist National Front whereby all 182 inhabitants would help police by reporting suspicious persons, observing the border constantly while working in the fields and aiding police patrols as necessary. In return, the local police unit would help the villagers with the harvest. The arrangement was made, these reports said, after thirty 'West German provocators' had tried to enter the GDR in the area. A local woman named Gunkel was held up as an example: she was said to have thwarted the flight to the West of two strange youths by reporting their presence to police. But other border villages were less loyal to the Communist line. One of the more congenial stories of those days is that the village of Niedergandern, near Göttingen, brought its brass band to the border one summer day in 1959 to serenade the neighbouring village of Kirchgandern on the Communist side of the wire. Smiling and waving, the people of Kirchgandern flocked to the barriers to enjoy the music—until the People's Police drove them away.

Elise Becker, aged eighty-four and living in the Western border village of Kleinensee close to the Bad Hersfeld–Eisenach Autobahn, had always taken the direct route to visit her seventy-eight-year-old cousin in the nearby village of Grossensee. The fact that Grossensee was now on the other side of the border did not worry her; she proceeded at Whitsun, 1959, to take her usual path. She got across undetected but on her way back she was stopped by a People's Police patrol. Exactly what she said to them is not recorded, but can be imagined. In any event the determined old lady got her way; she was allowed to return home unmolested, by the direct route. On another occasion three years earlier the two villages had co-operated in defiance of Communist regulations. Kleinensee drew its water supply from Grossensee, but one day the pipe burst in the East. Grossensee authorities agreed to make repairs but lacked the necessary material. After long negotiations the requisite sections of pipe were simply pushed through the barbed wire fence from the West. But the Grossensee officials were not always so complaisant. A few weeks after the pipe incident an elderly Grossensee woman travelled fifty miles by way of an authorized frontier crossing-point to visit her daughter in Kleinensee whose house she could see from her own. During the visit the mother died. Since she had expressed a wish to be buried in a family plot at Grossensee, the Kleinensee villagers suggested that her coffin be simply pushed through the wire in the same way as the pipe. But this the GDR officials refused, and the casket had to be taken the long way round.

In the late 1950s it was still possible for people in neighbouring border communities to pay group visits to songfests, concerts and sporting events, provided they were willing to put up with the red tape and expense involved in taking the long detour to the official border checkpoints. As late as October 1959, a West German newspaper could still write: 'Fortunately the zonal border is not to be compared with the Iron Curtain on the Czech frontier. Only at "key points" are there observation towers. Barbed wire only exists in places . . . elsewhere one can get across. But a few hundred metres behind the ten-metre strip in the Zone comes the second line of defences in the forbidden zone.' The clampdown was not yet complete. Town officials at Duderstadt in the West co-operated with nearby communities across the border on such matters as controlling rabies and foot-and-mouth disease, regulating streams and drainage, exploiting woods in no-man's-land areas, returning strayed animals and sharing fire brigades in time of need.

One curious event in 1959 was the sudden removal by the People's Police of all wire and road barriers on a stretch of the extreme North end of the frontier close to the Baltic Sea. Local Western communities were astounded, but the explanation was not long in coming. It transpired that the East Germans wanted to improve the scenery for the benefit of a group of visiting diplomats from Bonn. When the V.I.P.'s arrived in their column of black limousines a fortnight later—they included a dozen ambassadors, the Minister of the Soviet Embassy and about forty-five other diplomats—there was not a strand of barbed wire to be seen. Ditches had been filled in and the ploughed strip disguised. Needless to say, the People's Police (known as *Vopos* from their German title, *Volkspolizei*), had simply moved the fortifications further back out of sight. Did the East Germans perform this cosmetic operation on Russian orders? It is quite possible: certainly the Russians regard the Wire and the Wall as a tremendous propaganda liability to the entire Communist bloc. It is widely believed in East Berlin that the Russians delayed the building of the Berlin Wall for two years before it finally went up in August 1961.

Embarrassing or not, the Wall was inevitable. To the East German régime, Berlin was an open sore. Their country was being bled white. Ordinary East Germans awoke each morning to find another essential supplier gone: the butcher, the baker, the plumber, the milkman. Three out of every five refugees were productive workers; roughly half of them were young people aged less than twenty-five. Many were professional men who were hard to replace. For instance, in the years 1954–61 the GDR lost nearly 5,000 doctors, dentists and veterinary surgeons, over 800 judges and lawyers, nearly 17,000 schoolteachers and roughly the same number of qualified engineers and technicians. Between 1945 and the time of the Wall at least 2,691,270 refugees had fled from East Germany to register in West Berlin and the Federal Republic. Yet this was not all: as we have seen, the total of registered refugees leaves out of account those people who emigrated without visiting the official reception centres; these are estimated to number roughly a million since the war. So the aggregate loss to East Germany from 1945–61 was at least 3·6 million people, roughly equal to the entire population of Norway. Over the years there had been an average daily outflow of 500 people, equal to the population of a small village. Most of them in the later stages came through Berlin.

There were other reasons for the building of the Wall. West Berlin was a constant thorn in the flesh of the GDR because of its separate currency and the unfavourable exchange rate between East- and West-marks. Its growing prosperity and bright lights stood in marked contrast to the lower living standard and monotony of the East. From the Communist standpoint, the fewer East Germans allowed to sample the delights of West Berlin the better. Furthermore, the open sector boundary gave full scope to clandestine activities on both sides. The Russians and the East Germans exploited the opportunities for spying, abduction and propaganda, but both sides could play these games. In West Berlin the Allied occupation forces maintained—and still maintain—substantial intelligence and security branches. In addition there was no lack of German undercover groups and organizations in West Berlin engaged in helping fugitives to escape, gathering information and spreading anti-Communist propaganda.

But these were minor irritants compared to the compelling need to halt the refugee exodus. With increasing fervour the Communist press began in the late 1950s to accuse the West German government of deliberately enticing East Germans to the West. Ernst Lemmer, Federal Minister for All-German Affairs, made repeated broadcasts to the East German population denying these charges. Speaking on March 7, 1961, over RIAS[1] radio in West Berlin, he said the enticement allegation was false, and added:

> The responsible spokesmen of the Federal Government and also of the major parties have appealed in innumerable statements to our unfortunate compatriots in [East Germany] with suitable tact to hold out as long as possible and not to come to us as refugees except under the most dire compulsion. . . . We have constantly expressed our deep anxiety that the human resources of the Zone would be bled away eventually by the continued outflow of refugees. . . . The restoration of [German national unity] will not be advanced by further reductions in the population of the Communist-ruled part of Germany. This is unfortunately already the case to a frightening degree.

But still they came. Many emigrated for economic reasons, in search of better jobs and housing. But countless others fled from collectivization, from pressures to perform political and propaganda services for the régime or from refusal to accept Communist indoctrination in the schools. In July 1961 they were coming across at the rate of 1,000 a day. Harold Macmillan, the British Prime Minister, spoke in the United Nations General Assembly of people 'voting with their feet'. There was an air of tension in Berlin and East Germany, although nobody knew exactly what was coming. Nikita Khrushchev, the Soviet leader, denied at a press conference soon after his Vienna meeting with

[1] See Chapter Ten, pp. 156ff.

President Kennedy that he knew of any plans to build a wall through Berlin. Walter Ulbricht, who had succeeded Grotewohl in the seat of power of the GDR, also declared: 'Nobody intends to build a wall.'

Tension nevertheless rose further as increasing numbers of People's Army troops poured into East Berlin. The Communist press lambasted 'frontier crossers' and continued to agitate against West German 'enticement'. Commuters from East Berlin who had jobs in the Western sectors were harassed by Communist police, and many were forced to alight at underground and elevated railway stations before entering the West. More and more decided to emigrate before it was too late. Marienfelde refugee camp in West Berlin registered over 1,700 arrivals daily on August 8, 9 and 10. The exchange rate dropped to a new low of more than five East-marks for every West-mark. Willi Stoph, the GDR premier, forecast new 'protective measures' in a speech to the East German parliament which would involve 'certain inconveniences' for citizens. As a result, the Marienfelde refugee count rose the following day, August 12, to 2,400. Police interference with travellers on the U-Bahn and S-Bahn became so acute that trains were only lightly filled. Travellers wishing to cross West Berlin from Potsdam to the Soviet sector were told to take the 'outer ring' on the S-Bahn, a detour of fifty miles.

Typical of the refugees who came across in those last hectic days was a man we will call Emil Schmidt, a building supervisor from Leipzig, with his wife and child. He had been under pressure for years to join the Communist party and had seen his former boss falsely accused of tax evasion. When Ulbricht dropped a hint in mid-June that something would be done before the end of the year to halt the refugee outflow, Schmidt resolved to flee. It was a heart-rending decision for him to leave his home, his friends and relatives in Leipzig. It meant abandoning all his property, including his one-third share in a sixteen-unit block of flats, all that he had scrimped and saved to buy. 'I dared not sell a stick of furniture,' he says. 'That would have been reported by the informers who lived in every apartment building, and I would have come under suspicion.' He knew also that travellers on trains to Berlin were closely checked. So he sent his wife and thirteen-year-old son ahead, carrying only holiday suitcases. They managed to cross to West Berlin on the U-Bahn. Next day, August 11, Schmidt himself set out from Leipzig also carrying only a small suitcase and a letter from his firm claiming that he had to go to Berlin on business. He crossed to the West on the S-Bahn the same day and went with his family to Marienfelde, where after days of standing in queues he was accepted as a recognized refugee. Everything he left behind in Leipzig was impounded. His share of the apartment building and the proceeds of the forced sale of his furniture and effects are credited to his name in case he should ever return. Schmidt has heard that people who fled East Germany before the Wall are not punished when they decide to return. But after a sticky start he managed to find a job and a modest flat in Munich. He says today: 'I have never for a moment considered going back —for me it is simply a matter of living in freedom.'

Then at 2 a.m. on August 13 the last great loophole in the barriers encircling East Germany slammed shut: police and troops blocked all but thirteen of the remaining eighty crossing points between West and East Berlin. They spread barbed wire, tore up paving blocks and erected street barricades in a desperate effort to present the West with a *fait accompli*. By daybreak all intersections were guarded by armed police, People's Army troops and reservists. Except for one or two controlled checkpoints, all U-Bahn and S-Bahn links between the two halves of Berlin were severed. Desperate East Berliners made a last rush to get across; by the afternoon of the 13th six thousand had reached Marienfelde. The roads and lawns around the refugee centre were black with fugitives, and the British Army lent tents to give them shelter. From now on, East Berliners could cross legally to the West only with special passes. All commuting from East to West was halted; the number of East Berliners with jobs in the West had dwindled in any case to 13,000. But West Berliners were still in those days allowed to visit East Berlin merely on production of their identity cards. Residents of the Federal Republic, on the other hand, needed to obtain one-day entry permits from GDR officials in order to cross the sector boundary.

Next day a furious demonstration erupted as West Berliners vented their wrath and frustration in front of the Brandenburg Gate. They were dispersed by tear gas and water cannons from Communist trucks drawn up, along with tanks, before the triumphal arch. The West protested; Willy Brandt, the governing Mayor of West Berlin, wrote his famous letter to President Kennedy. But nothing short of physical force in the shape of tanks and bulldozers could have destroyed the Wall. Rightly or wrongly

—the question has been debated ever since—the Western Allies hesitated to take this risk. During the night of August 17–18 Communist 'shock workers' erected a concrete barrier up to six feet high through the Potsdamer Platz. Ugly sections of wall appeared elsewhere along the sector boundary, made of concrete blocks messily cemented and topped with barbed wire. Around the perimeter of West Berlin other Communist forces were busily strengthening the border with East Germany. On the night of August 22 the GDR authorities announced that henceforth West Berliners as well as West Germans would have to acquire special visas to enter East Berlin, that the number of crossing-points would be reduced to seven; they warned people 'in the interests of their own safety' to keep 100 metres back from the Wall on both sides. This last point was promptly denounced by the British, American and French commandants as 'effrontery' and next day 1,000 Allied troops patrolled right up to the sector boundary with tanks, armoured cars and anti-tank guns.

Berliners are a tough, resilient breed and they regarded the Wall as an outrage, a challenge to their ingenuity and courage. Westerners set explosive charges to blow it up, Easterners tried to knock it down with trucks, bulldozers and power shovels. Refugees jumped from windows in the Bernauer Strasse houses along the border while Western firemen stretched safety nets beneath. Even with the hasty, jerry-building methods at first employed, it took time to replace barbed wire with masonry. East Berliners probed for weak spots by daylight and then returned with their families under cover of darkness to wriggle through the wire to the West. Bombed sites, narrow alleys and ruined buildings often provided sufficient cover to enable them to reach the border undetected. But in the ensuing weeks and months these loopholes were closed. Windows in the Bernauer Strasse were walled up, houses and ruins abutting on the border were torn down. Direct escape across the Wall by all the obvious means became increasingly risky. To this day there are still refugees who manage to climb across: as recently as September 1969 a building worker named Eberhard Grzyb succeeded in bringing a ladder and scrambling over. But he was working in the immediate vicinity of the Wall and he was lucky in that the shots fired by East German sentries missed. Such exceptions apart, flight by conventional methods soon became rare as the East Germans raised the hazards. From the autumn of 1961 onward, would-be refugees had to invent more subtle methods than a frontal assault on the Wall. They obtained forged papers, they tunnelled, they swung across the Wall on high wires. They swam canals and lakes, they seized a pleasure steamer. They posed as Russian or American soldiers and walked brazenly through the checkpoints. On one celebrated occasion an East German engine-driver seized an entire train and drove it across from Albrechtshof in East Germany to Spandau in the British sector of Berlin. More of this later; the saga of escapes since 1961 is a gripping adventure story.

As each escape route was uncovered, the Communist guards blocked it off. Slalom concrete barriers were installed at road crossings such as Checkpoint Charlie to foil attempts to crash the border. East German guards became adept at spotting secret hiding-places under car seats. Sophisticated forgery detectors were installed to expose false passports. Secret underground microphones were buried close to the Wall to overhear clandestine tunnelling. More lights and watchtowers were erected, more houses demolished to provide a clear field of fire. By the mid-1960s escape to West Berlin by almost any method had become a fiendishly perilous undertaking. More and more refugees fell to Communist bullets. Between the building of the Wall and the end of 1966 at least seventy-four people were killed or died of injuries as a result of Communist action around West Berlin. Cruel and inhuman though it was, the Wall achieved its purpose. By closing the last escape hatch for refugees it completed the framework for East Germany's remarkable economic recovery in the 1960s. From the global viewpoint, it stabilized by draconian means an area of Central Europe which had threatened to spark off a Third World War. The fact that it cemented the division of Germany was not viewed with unalloyed dismay by countries which had suffered under German hegemony during the Third Reich.

But the 17 million people of East Germany could not regard the Wall with such Olympian detachment. They were trapped, imprisoned, cut off from the West by the ugliest barrier in the world. Would-be refugees, their easy escape route gone, turned their eyes to the long western border. As a result, tension rose all along the line from Lübeck to Hof. The GDR authorities moved rapidly to tighten the noose: on August 17, 1961, they imposed a temporary ban on all travel to the Federal Republic. Very few travel permits were issued in subsequent years; in 1963 only 50,000 East Germans were allowed to visit relatives in the West, less than two per cent of the number in 1957. This travel ban, following hard upon the building of the Wall, made discontented East Germans all the more determined to flee. The East German Interior Ministry responded by drafting its Secret Order No.39/61 of September 14, 1961, which laid down an elaborate system of border control. A further 2,000 inhabitants of the forbidden zone were expelled from their homes and the old 1952 frontier control regulations made more rigorous and watertight. Henceforth only such persons 'who through their previous behaviour provide a guarantee that security in the forbidden zone will not be endangered' were allowed to remain in this three-mile strip. They were compelled to register and their residence permits were valid for only three months at a time. Foreigners, West Germans and other travellers were barred without exception from entering the forbidden zone. Workers inside the zone had to show permits issued by the local border guard commander. All roads and paths leading into the 500-metre protective strip had to be barricaded, except those needed for access to houses and farms; these had to be guarded by sentries with movable booms. Similar roadblocks and guard-poles were to be installed at entrances to the forbidden zone. Other detailed regulations called for the clearing of trees, undergrowth and tall vegetation standing less than 100 metres from the ploughed control strip, and banned hunting, boating, fishing and even the keeping of carrier pigeons close to the border. At this time, too, the 50,000-strong Border Police which had hitherto been under the East German Interior Ministry were absorbed into the National People's Army and renamed the Frontier Command. A subsequent decree and a further set of regulations were promulgated on March 19, 1964, to codify these directives and adapt them to local conditions.

Escape across the Baltic Sea—the so-called 'blue border'—was restricted by placing armed Transport Police guards aboard East German ferries to Scandinavia. They were ordered to watch for passengers who seemed likely to defect, and prevent them from going ashore. The Danish port of Gedser was the scene of a notorious incident on August 24, 1961, when these armed guards seized and beat up an East German passenger who tried to jump to the quayside from the ferry *Seebad Warnemünde*. There was some shooting in which several East German bullets hit a Danish fishing boat. The harbourmaster of Gedser protested to the East German captain, and three days later 3,000 Danes demonstrated on the quayside next to the ship under banners inscribed 'No *Vopo* Methods Here'. After a similar incident on September 7 which prompted Danish government protests the GDR government decreed that henceforth no East German be allowed to go ashore at either Gedser or Trelleborg in Sweden. Regulations were laid down in June and July 1962, to hamper Baltic escapes in small boats and on air mattresses. A three-mile forbidden zone was established along the entire seacoast of East Germany, subject to control on the pattern of the East–West border. Special restrictions were enforced along the western end of the coast nearest Lübeck Bay, reaching back as far as Bad Doberan. Canoes, rowing and paddle boats were banned at the seaside; motorboats and yachts with seagoing permits were permitted to put out only between sunrise and sunset, and then only after notification to the People's Police. Holidaymakers could only stay in the coastal resorts with the permission of local authorities.

Nevertheless, refugees continued to overcome these obstacles and elude East German patrol craft on the high seas. On October 10, 1963, Captain H. H. Justesen of the Danish ship *Gedser* saw an East German naval craft bearing down on a family of refugees rowing for their lives in international waters towards the Federal Republic. He placed his ship between the East German warship and the rowboat, forcing the former to throw its engines full speed astern to avoid a collision. By the time the People's Navy craft had circumvented the *Gedser* the refugees had been hauled aboard the Danish ship. This was only one of the more dramatic rescues: throughout the 1960s there was a constant stream of refugees into Scandinavia. Many were picked up half-frozen from the sea; many more jumped ship—literally jumped—in Danish and Swedish ports. So frequent were the defections that the harbourmasters at Gedser and Trelleborg felt obliged to provide liferafts and lifebelts beside the piers used by East German ferries. When the GDR trade union vacation ship *Völkerfreundschaft* visited Stockholm in July, 1965, eleven of her passengers and crew stayed behind in the Swedish capital. Others jumped ship in the Kiel Canal, through which Communist vessels frequently travel.

But in the Baltic as elsewhere the number of successful defections is constantly dropping. Only thirty-eight East German refugees managed to cross the 'blue border' by all these means combined in the sixteen months ending in April 1969. Five years earlier the number was three times as large. Of the thirty-four Baltic escapers in 1968, only four were picked up from the sea. One of these was the man who towed himself to the Gedser lightship behind a home-made submersible motor. On February 2, 1968, the body of a young East German was washed ashore in Schleswig-Holstein. Nobody knows how many others died in attempting to flee across the water.

Herr Ulbricht's Wire and Wall had become by the late 1960s almost totally effective. Without such redoubtable physical barriers the political contrast between the two Germanies could not have been maintained; the economic viability of East Germany would never have been achieved. Without the Ugly Frontier, the GDR would have become depopulated, demoralized and depressed; a monumental failure of the Communist system. To Moscow as to East Berlin, the Wire and the Wall were lesser evils.

4

Running the Gauntlet

IT was about 1 a.m. on August 13, 1969, the eighth anniversary of the building of the Wall. Two families, four adults and five children, were crouching in the cab of a works locomotive. They were in an opencast mine just east of the border, travelling along the crest of an embankment toward the tip at the end of the line, the spot where loose soil covered a few of the frontier mines.

Suddenly the outline of a woman signalman loomed out of the darkness ahead. Eckhard Oborny stopped the engine as the woman called: 'You are driving without lights!' While Oborny hesitated his sixteen-month-old daughter began to cry and everybody felt a clutch of fear. The sleeping drug had worn off—would the baby give them away? Oborny had the presence of mind to switch on the compressor and its whine drowned the child's whimpers. Simultaneously he leaned from the cab window and shouted with all his authority as the mine's engineer in charge of transport: 'I'm making a secret inspection trip—I don't need lights.'

Without waiting for her answer he started the locomotive again and it rumbled slowly around the long curve toward the watchtower. Oborny's brother Horst, a Commander in the East German People's Navy, knew that his fate lay in Eckhard's hands. They had secretly plotted the escape together, using code messages to avoid arousing suspicion. This was their last opportunity, for the next day they expected workmen to start moving the tracks to another part of the mine. Horst's wife Liane was pale with fear and excitement. If anything should happen to her three children, she had told Horst earlier, she could never forgive herself.

Half a mile ahead the single track began, and Eckhard had to halt and wait for another train coming the other way. At 1.18 it passed, and the light changed to green. The westbound locomotive, with its tense passengers, moved cautiously ahead, passing the foot of the watchtower with its armed guards. But the sentries suspected nothing; they did not turn on their searchlight, and the engine rumbled safely onward. There was another hazard still to come, a brightly-lit conveyor machine with its crew of three. Eckhard called to the workmen as he passed: 'As soon as I am gone tell Signalbox 3 that the next train can come.' Still there were 500 yards to go before they could dismount, and an unexpected obstacle occurred. Eckhard saw that one of the rails was buried eighteen inches deep in loose earth. But it was too late to hesitate: he pulled the lever to full power and ploughed on in desperation, holding his breath, and fortunately the engine stayed on the tracks.

Reaching the top of the tip at the end of the embankment, the locomotive halted and the four adults jumped out. Eckhard and Horst Oborny each clutched a sleeping child in their arms, Liane took her two older boys Leif, twelve, and Sören, ten, by the hand and Eckhard's wife Brigitte took the remaining toddler. Half running, half sliding, they scrambled in the darkness down the loose scree of the tip and finally found the safe spot where the mines were covered. Three fences had still to be negotiated: the men tore their trousers on the barbed wire. Then they saw the playing-field of Neu Büddenstedt ahead and they knew for sure that they were in the West. Behind them the guards in their watchtower on the Harbke mine had not fired a shot. Exhausted with running and fear, the two Oborny families roused a local resident. 'We have come across from the other side—help us, call the police!'

Later they told their story to *Bild Zeitung*, the popular German newspaper. By any standards they had been well off in East Germany, with cars, television sets, comfortable flats and good incomes. But the strain of living in constant dread of informers, of having to disguise their true beliefs even from their children for fear of betrayal: this was the reason for their decision to abandon everything and flee to the West. When Horst and Liane watched Western television programmes their older children would eavesdrop through the keyhole of the living-room door. And when the boys began whistling the theme tune of 'Bonanza' the parents were horrified. As a naval officer Horst was afraid that someone might discover his home-made converter built to enable his TV set to pick up the second as well as the first West German channel.

Now both Oborny families are living somewhere in West Germany. They fear that Horst, especially, might be followed by

East German agents if his whereabouts were known. Their escape succeeded because Eckhard had the right to drive his locomotives up to the border any time he chose. The episode is another proof of the adage that most escapes nowadays are made by people who live close to the border and know the lie of the land.

The Oborny adventure reminded many Germans of another famous railway escape, Harry Deterling's seizure of an entire East German train on the night of December 5, 1961, less than four months after the Berlin Wall went up.

Seven families totalling twenty-five people came across in this daring train ride to freedom, beginning at Oranienburg in East Germany and ending at Spandau in West Berlin. Contrary to the sensational account given in a subsequent German film, the Communist border guards were so taken aback that they did not shoot.

Deterling, then twenty-eight, had been an engine driver on the East German Railways since 1955 but he was not allowed to bring trains to the immediate vicinity of the border. As soon as the Wall was built he resolved to flee, and originally planned to make his escape between Christmas and New Year's Day. But then he heard that the line he was planning to use, from Albrechtshof in the East to Spandau–West in Berlin, was to be blocked within the next few days. He realized that he must act fast. The first problem was to get himself assigned to the Oranienburg–Albrechtshof line. He applied for permission to drive the stretch just once, on his normal day off, saying he wished to broaden his knowledge of the railway network. His superiors were surprised that he volunteered to serve an extra shift, since Deterling had never been noted for his devotion to the Communist cause. But he got his permission. Then another problem arose—how could he get rid of the strange fireman who normally worked this line? Deterling sent him home with the explanation that his own fireman, Hartmut Lichy, also wanted to familiarize himself with the route. Lichy was one of the trusted friends whom Deterling had let in on the plot during weeks of secret preparation.

On the eve of the escape Deterling told his wife Ingrid to be ready with their four children on the platform at Oranienburg Station the following night. He cycled through the neighbourhood to other relatives and friends, spreading the same message. Lichy's parents and sister were also aboard when the train with

its eight coaches pulled out of Oranienburg with Deterling and
Lichy on the footplate of engine 234, an old pre-war steam locomotive. The fugitives brought thirty suitcases, two prams, shop-
ping bags and even radios in their baggage. Children were told
that they were going to a party in Albrechtshof, the border
station just 500 yards from West Berlin territory. But the train
did not stop in Albrechtshof. It roared through at nearly 50
m.p.h. past the astonished station-master. There was no barrier
across the track and the Communist guards did not have time
to open fire. Deterling and Lichy had feared the worst and prepared themselves a hiding-place from Communist bullets behind
the cab. They instructed their wives to throw themselves to the
floor with the children as the train passed Albrechtshof. But by
the time the sentries had woken up to what was happening the
train was vanishing into West Berlin.

The only person with the presence of mind to react was the
conductor. He pulled the emergency brake lever, but nothing
happened. Deterling and Lichy had taken care to lower the steam
pressure in the circuit so as to put the brake out of action. So the
train rattled unhindered past the barbed wire and no-man's-land
of Berlin's perimeter. Shortly before reaching Spandau station
Deterling brought the line of coaches to a halt. Twenty-five
overjoyed refugees jumped down beside the tracks, hugging each
other in relief and delight. Deterling, the hero of the hour, won
everybody's fervent thanks. None of the passengers was more
grateful to him than a seventeen-year-old girl. She had known
nothing of the escape plot and boarded the train unwittingly on
her way home in East Germany. When she told Spandau police
that her parents had fled to West Berlin before the Wall they were
summoned for a tearful reunion. Neither the parents nor the girl
had thought they would ever see each other again.

No less surprised to find himself in the West was the *Trans-
portpolizist* assigned to the train. This armed guard seemed
totally confused. 'He didn't even know where we were,' passengers reported. As the train rumbled through Albrechtshof the
'*Trapo*' had groused and said he would complain to the railway
authorities. Even when the passengers alighted in the West he still
did not realize what had happened. At first he yelled: 'Alighting
between stations is forbidden!' Then he demanded that everyone
follow him back along the tracks to East Germany. The refugees
just laughed. Deterling's rescue operation had brought out eight

men, ten women and seven children. Four of them only caught the train by sheer luck. They missed it when it left Oranienburg at 7.33 p.m. because they spent too much time in last-minute packing. Chasing it from station to station by car, they finally caught up with it in Falkensee, the last scheduled stop before Albrechtshof.

Ingrid Deterling could not bear to watch the film based on the escape when it was shown on West German television in June 1969. 'For me it's certainly not a beautiful memory,' she said. 'I was constantly afraid we would be shot. Only my four children were not scared. I still remember how the oldest one, then just six, said: "Papi is driving fast today." '

Besides Deterling's group and the seventeen-year-old girl, two other East Germans had cause to be grateful to the engine-driver that night. They were standing on the platform at Albrechtshof waiting for the train to take them aboard on the return trip to Oranienburg. When they saw it make its dash for the border, these two young men took advantage of the general confusion to sneak across behind it, following the tracks. They, too, made it safely to the West. Two hours after the escape the West allowed the East German State Railways to send another engine to haul the train back to East Germany. Aboard it were a few passengers and the railway guard, who had no desire to seek asylum in the West. They returned to their families in the GDR. Deterling himself is happily employed today as an engine-driver in West Germany. He is unlikely ever to return to his old home in Oranienburg: a Communist court at Potsdam has since sentenced him to death.

Those who could not seize trains or locomotives to break out to the West could sometimes leap aboard unobserved. In January and February of 1964 seventeen people escaped singly or in pairs by jumping on to westbound trains leaving Friedrichstrasse Station in East Berlin. Ten of them, aged sixteen to nineteen, were from the Max Planck School in the Eastern sector. They climbed the metal viaduct carrying the elevated track beside the River Spree bridge, then waited for the 8.53 p.m. train to Aachen or the 10.27 p.m. Moscow–Paris express to pull out of the station only 100 yards away. By the time the trains drew level they were moving at 15 m.p.h. and the youngsters had to run full tilt along the brightly-lit track to catch a passing handle and swing themselves up. Then they had to open a door and disappear inside the train before being seen by foot patrols. As Frank Thomascheidt, one of the schoolboys, pushed his way into the toilet after climbing aboard, an irate passenger called through the door: 'Open up at once!' Frank realized that the man could pull the emergency brake before the train was safely into Western territory. He came out and the stranger demanded: 'Where do you come from?' Frank considered pushing the man, who was smaller than himself, into the toilet. But just then the train passed over the Humboldt Harbour bridge and Frank knew he was in the West. 'I'm a refugee,' Frank said. 'Then get off immediately at the Zoo Station,' the man insisted in peremptory tones. 'Did you think I wanted to go further?' Frank responded, and left the man standing.

But this escape route, too, was discovered after one of the boys lost his nerve, dropped off the viaduct and broke both legs and an arm. This boy did not, as later reported, fall immediately into the hands of the dreaded *Stasi*, the East German State Security Service. He was picked up and carried out of the danger zone by a man who himself had been waiting to flee by the same method, and later succeeded. It was only a week later after two further schoolboy escapes that the injured boy was arrested, the secret having leaked out at school. True to form, the *Stasi* moved quickly to close the unsuspected loophole, posting hidden guards and installing alarm wires. But still there was one more member of the depleted Max Planck School to come—a girl named Christel John. She came through the ring around West Berlin by crawling and climbing through the obstacles one by one, partly in full view of two sentries. Holger Klein, one of the train-jumpers, said at a subsequent reunion in West Berlin: 'She had more courage than the rest of us put together.'

Most attempts to bring out refugees in groups followed tracks more secret, however, than those of the railways. Tunnels under the fortifications ringing West Berlin were the favoured means of mass escapes in the first three years after the building of the Wall. On January 24, 1962, West Berlin officials announced that twenty-eight refugees had escaped by cutting a hole in the barbed-wire fence on Berlin's western border. But soon an American news agency uncovered the true story by interviewing some of the fugitives in a refugee camp: they had dug a tunnel from the basement of an East German house to a garden in the French-sector suburb of Frohnau. It was, in fact, the first major tunnel escape. When the truth began to leak out the Berlin Senate tried to hush it up, having received word that at least 100 other East Germans still hoped to use the tunnel. But the Senate's efforts failed, the tunnel's existence was betrayed and East German border guards promptly occupied the house from which the thirty-yard tunnel began. German newspapers erupted in furious attacks on the American agency for the 'tragic indiscretion'.

Max Thomas, aged eighty-one, lived just four doors down the road from the house in which this first big tunnel escape originated. He had known about the plot, but the tunnellers refused to take him or his elderly friends along. 'You are too old and your wives are too fat,' the plotters said. Herr Thomas was stung to action. He decided to build a tunnel of his own, and marshalled his friends. Most of them were too old to dig, so a fifty-seven-year-old truck driver helped by two seventy-year-old men excavated the shaft and removed 4,000 buckets of soil. The tunnel began under the chicken coop, passed beneath the Oranienburger Chaussee and ended in West Berlin territory a few yards beyond the last wire obstacles. During the sixteen days and nights of digging Herr Thomas kept in the background, pretending to be pottering in his garden. Every fifteen minutes a Communist border patrol passed and Herr Thomas would switch off the light in the tunnel, which ran off an extension flex from his kitchen. This was the signal for all activity to cease. They had the usual problems that beset all Berlin tunnellers: the air grew worse as the shaft lengthened, soil conditions varied and there was a scarcity of wood to support the tunnel walls and roof. But the men did their work well. When finished, the tunnel measured 102 feet long and up to five feet six inches high. Asked why they had bothered to build the tunnel with so much headroom, the gallant diggers replied: 'We wanted to take our wives to freedom in comfort—and upright.' In the end eight men and four women, all of ripe age, walked through the Thomas tunnel on May 5, 1962.

Berlin's most famous escape tunnels were dug beneath the Bernauer Strasse in the French sector, the street in which the roadway is in the West but the houses on one side belong to the East. First there was the tunnel through which twenty-nine East Berliners came across in September 1962. A second, even larger group of refugees had been due to follow, but the shaft became flooded and impassable. This tunnel was filmed and partly financed by an American television network.

Even more publicity, not all of it favourable, attended the most celebrated tunnel of all, known as Tunnel 57 because it brought fifty-seven East Berliners to the West. This was dug mostly by student volunteers from Berlin's Technical University, using theodolites, fresh-air pumps and hoses, hoists and a wheeled trolley for transporting the soil to the surface. Tunnel 57, code-named Operation Tokyo, was both the biggest and the last significant escape tunnel in Berlin. It took six months to dig, from April to October 1964, with thirty-five men working shifts. Starting from a disused bakery in the Bernauer Strasse, it led beneath the roadway to a ramshackle outdoor lavatory in the backyard of a house on the East Berlin side. It was 140 yards long and just big enough for a person to crawl through. From the outset the project was fraught with difficulty and danger. The diggers wanted to keep away from another tunnel which had been dug from the same basement at the turn of the year 1963–64 and followed a parallel course. Although the eastern end of this old shaft had been blown up by Communist guards, one could never be sure that they would not open it up again and send men down with listening instruments.

While they were still digging a vertical well beneath the bakery they suffered their first setback, when water unexpectedly flooded in and threatened to collapse the sides. Not daring to bring timber from elsewhere for fear of arousing suspicion, the young tunnellers tore doors from hinges and planks from the floor of the rented basement to shore up the threatened pit. Then they resumed digging, this time horizontally, carefully scattering the excavated sand in other rented rooms of the bakery. So as not to attract attention from the watchful guards across the street, the students stayed in the house for ten days at a stretch. They posted a lookout on the roof of a nearby house to warn the diggers by means of a field telephone if the guards began to test the ground with sound detectors.

The tunnel was only wide enough for one man to dig at a time. He pushed the sand back to another, who loaded it into the trolley which plied to and fro to the foot of the shaft. The rope kept breaking, and as the work progressed the men needed more and more timber to support the roof. There was a constant danger of hitting a water pipe which might flood the shaft again. Close to their goal they did in fact hit a drainpipe seventeen feet underground, but luckily they struck a joint and the pipe held.

The most dangerous moment, as in all such tunnel projects, was the breakthrough to the surface. Had they calculated right? Had their project been detected or betrayed? On one previous occasion the Communist guards had set a trap. They had waited in hiding until the first tunneller was out, then overpowered him and ordered him to call to his comrades below ground: 'Come here—there is a sick man.' Instead he yelled: 'Go back!' and was beaten up.

To lessen these risks the builders of Tunnel 57 sent an accomplice across to the back yard where their shaft would emerge. He signalled to the diggers below by stamping on the ground to indicate their position. The first man to push his forefinger carefully to the surface found that the privy shack was right overhead. The hole was enlarged, and by Saturday October 3 all was ready for the escape. Telegrams went out to the East Germans selected for the flight: 'Mother-in-law having her silver wedding, we will celebrate the occasion today or tomorrow.' The would-be refugees had to move fast. They had been told in advance that when they got the code telegram they should assemble at the secret rendezvous, Strelitzer Strasse 55, at prearranged times. Some of them were at dinner when the message arrived, others received it when they were already in bed. Leaving almost everything, they hastened to the meeting-place. One Dresden citizen who missed the last train to Berlin took a taxi all the way from Leipzig. Completely exhausted, he reached the tunnel in time and made his escape. It took half an hour to crawl through the long tunnel. In places the water was so deep that there was only just enough space to breathe. By midnight on Saturday twenty-eight people had been brought through, then operations were stopped. On the following night twenty-nine came West. All the fugitives were shaking with fright. They had been told to cross the yard to the shack one by one, without shoes. One family did not want to be separated at this critical moment. Some walked as if in a trance, they were so afraid. One fat woman got stuck in the tunnel and began to weep. Would she have to turn back? The hole could not be widened without making a noise which might betray the escape route. The escape helpers gave a hefty final push and she, too, was safely on her way.

For the tunnellers who had toiled for six long months the longest moments were in the first hour on Saturday when the fugitives failed to reach the rendezvous at the appointed time. But then they had the exhilaration of hauling up the fifty-seven refugees—twenty-three men, thirty-one women and three children—to a tearful reunion in the bakery. The oldest was seventy and the youngest, a child of three and a half, said on reaching the West: 'There were no wild animals in the cave.' The story is told of one mother who crawled right past her son in a widened section of the tunnel. He was a tunneller, and he did not give a sign of recognition. Only later, when she had been safely pulled to the surface in the improvised bosun's chair, was she told that her own son had been one of those responsible for her rescue. She almost collapsed with emotion.

Discovery sooner or later was inevitable. Just after midnight on the night of Sunday to Monday two men entered the disused house where the refugees had gathered. One turned a flashlight on the escape helpers. Thinking the two were refugees, one of the students snapped: 'Are you crazy? Turn off the light and get going.' One of the men said he wanted to fetch a friend outside. Minutes later a flying squad of East German soldiers roared to the scene on trucks and motor cycles. The lookout on the Western rooftop telephoned: 'Everybody come back immediately!' None of the four escape helpers outside the East Berlin end of the tunnel panicked. The man detailed to watch the tunnel entrance stood back and let his comrades from the rendezvous house plunge down the hole first. While the sub-machine-guns fired some 120 shots, the four students made it back into the tunnel and escaped safely. They were saved by the confusion. For the Communist guards thought at first that the tunnel entrance must be in the basement of the house. They fired wildly downstairs and did not discover the hole in the floor of the shack until the escape helpers had made their get-away.

Tunnel 57 had been a tremendous success. But it left two controversial after-effects. One Egon Schulz, an East German corporal, was killed in the mêlée, and the Communist government blamed the escape helpers. To this day it is unclear whether Schulz was accidentally shot by his fellow guards or died from a Western bullet. The escape helpers are claimed by the West to have been unarmed. But there have been reports that one of them fired a pistol, and probably nobody will ever know exactly what happened.

The financing of Tunnel 57 has also been criticized. Herr Wolfgang Fuchs, the twenty-six-year-old leader of the undertaking, told me that the tunnel cost about DM 50,000 (£4,500 or $12,500).[1] He denied most emphatically reports that he had mulcted the refugees of a sum several times as large. In fact he said he had obtained affidavits to the contrary from all of them. His funds, he claimed, had come from the Christian Democratic Union party in Berlin and from the sale of story and picture rights to magazines. Fuchs ceased his Scarlet Pimpernel activities after Tunnel 57. A refugee from East Germany himself, he had started in the escape business by bringing over the girl he later married and her mother. He and his trusty band of students started seven tunnels, of which three were successful. He estimates that altogether as many as 100 tunnels were started in Berlin but all except a dozen failed because of betrayal, detection or physical difficulties such as flooding.

Mass escapes by means of trains and tunnels were the exception rather than the rule. Many of the most perilous and original stratagems for outwitting the frontier guards were devised by individuals such as Heinz Meixner, a twenty-year-old Austrian, who wanted to get his fiancée Margit across to West Berlin in May 1963. He surreptitiously measured the height of the Checkpoint Charlie booms and found that an Austin-Healey Sprite could just squeeze underneath if he took off the windscreen and let some air out of the tyres. So he rented the car in West Berlin, drove legally across to the East, loaded Margit into the covered passenger seat and his future mother-in-law into the boot, and drove back through Checkpoint Charlie at 50 m.p.h., ducking his head to avoid the closed booms. All three reached the West unscathed. It was not until Norbert Konrad, an Argentinian, emulated this feat seven weeks later, using the very same car to rescue his East German bride, that the border guards hung metal bars from the booms to prevent a further repetition.

There were many other motorized escapes, notably the famous occasion in September 1964 when two families came across in a refrigerated meat truck, hidden under chilled sides of pork. Erich Ross, thirty-two, was the driver who brought across his wife, their eight daughters and his brother- and sister-in-law with their three children. Ross was trusted to drive his truck regularly into West Berlin since nobody thought he would abandon his large family in the East. He doped the children with sleeping pills but

[1] All conversions are at the DM rate preceding revaluation in October 1969.

most of them were awake and coughing or whimpering with cold when the truck reached the Heinrich–Heine–Strasse checkpoint. Ross gave the signal from the cab, flashing the light on and off inside the closed truck to warn the occupants that this was the critical moment. The adults snuffed out the childen's cries with coats and blankets. The border guards did not bother to break the seal and open the door. They waved the truck through after a brief halt. 'If they had tried to hold me up I would have simply charged the barriers,' Ross said.

East German guards soon learned to detect secret compartments and double floors in cars. But for a long time there was one vehicle they never suspected of carrying stowaways: the tiny two-seater Isetta. By removing the petrol tank and replacing it with a small canister the owner of one Isetta was able to create a secret compartment beside the engine just big enough to hold a refugee. Five women and four men were brought singly out of East Berlin by this means before the trick was discovered. The tenth refugee, a fifty-nine-year-old woman, moved while the car was standing at Checkpoint Charlie. Seeing the apparently empty vehicle rock, an alert border guard examined it more closely. The woman and the car driver, an Algerian, were arrested.

Berlin's lakes and canals were favourite routes of escape in the early days. Many refugees swam to freedom: one family is said to have pushed a baby ahead of them in a bathtub. As late as October 1962 a group of eight men and four women managed a mass swim through chilly water to West Berlin. But such feats became steadily more hazardous as guards installed underwater barriers and kept a close watch for bobbing heads. The most celebrated river escape was the seizure of the pleasure steamer *Friedrich Wolf* in early June, 1962. The plotters began their escape by the classical method of getting the captain and engineer drunk —on a bottle of brandy and a bottle of German champagne apiece, followed by five or six glasses of beer. Then the ship's cook and steward locked them up and took command, bringing the rest of the would-be fugitives aboard. At 4.30 a.m. they cast off on to the River Spree from Treptow in the Eastern sector, then swung sharply to port into the Landwehr Canal which is in the West. The border guards peppered the ship with about 200 rounds of gun-fire, from two patrol boats as well as from a nearby bridge and landing-stage, but nobody was hurt. The refugees, eight men, five women and a baby, ran the ship ashore in the canal while West Berlin police gave them covering fire. They were all brought to safety, but the captain and engineer were arrested when they recovered sufficiently from their carousal to take the vessel back to the East.

There were, too, various forms of aerial escapes. Just after Christmas 1962 a tightrope artist named Horst Klein chose to practise his skill on a high-tension electricity cable crossing some fifty feet above the lighted and patrolled 'death-strip' below. He believed all along that the wire was charged, but in fact it carried no current. In an icy wind he jumped from the mast to the porcelain insulator, then eased himself sideways in sitting position along the wire above the heads of the sentries. 'Thank God the floodlights pointed downward,' the fugitive said later. 'They couldn't see me.' But the thirty-six-year-old circus performer, known to Big Top audiences as 'Mister Quinn', was on his most dangerous stunt. With the temperature well below freezing, his hands were soon numb with cold. Every ten yards he stopped on the unsteady wire for breath. He came to another mast, located between the barbed-wire fences, and had to steel himself for two more dangerous jumps. Another thirty-five yards was all he could manage before his strength failed. He threw a rope over the wire, planning to lower himself gently. But he caught hold of only one end and crashed to the ground, breaking both arms. How long he lay there unconscious he does not know. But finally he must have moaned loudly enough to attract a dog, who woke his mistress, a seventy-two-year-old woman, at 5 a.m. She in turn alerted police, who saw that he was taken to hospital, where he was treated for exposure and multiple injuries. 'Mister Quinn' said later that he decided to flee from East Germany because he was considered there as politically suspect and therefore unable to work.

This was not the only high-wire act. As late as July 1965 a family of three managed to escape by breeches-buoy across the Wall from the House of Ministries in East Berlin, Göring's former Air Ministry. They could hardly have chosen a more exposed or closely-guarded area. But Heinz Holzapfel, then thirty-four, knew the building inside out, since as an economist he often visited it on business. After eighteen months of planning he chose the night of July 29 for his daring attempt, having tipped off friends in the West. Somehow he managed to smuggle his wife Jutta and son Günter, aged nine, into the government building without the usual formalities. They hid in an upstairs lavatory until nightfall, hanging an 'Out of Order' sign on the door. Then they shed their shoes and crept on to the roof, carrying a long nylon cord with a hammer attached and three home-made harnesses with hooks to hang over the cable. Holzapfel hurled the hammer with all his strength and fortunately it crossed the Wall. His Western friends tied a heavy 160-yard wire to the nylon line and Holzapfel hauled it with some difficulty up to the roof, making the end fast to a nearby flagstaff.

Young Günter was the first to go. He had been promised a visit to his uncle in the West, but his father told him: 'first you must pass a bravery test.' As a reward he would also get a bicycle, and after he had been so quiet during the long wait his parents said: 'You have already earned the handlebars and the bell.' They hooked him on to the line, the lower end of which was attached to a heavy trailer. He slid safely down without a sound, braking his descent with heavy gloves to protect his hands, and was caught in the West by Holzapfel's friends. Next went Jutta, the mother, aged thirty-two. She made a rough landing and was taken immediately to hospital. But she was found to be suffering from nothing worse than cuts and bruises.

Meanwhile the father waited vainly on the roof for an answer to his frantic light signals. He did not dare attempt the descent until he knew his friends were waiting to catch him. It was a whole hour after the boy's escape before he got the all-clear signal at 1.30 a.m. Meanwhile he kept looking anxiously at a lighted window near the flagpole, afraid he might be spotted. His fears, as he later discovered, were well founded. For behind that window sat a Russian guard. But all went well and Holzapfel landed safely in the West to join his family. It was not until daybreak that Communist patrols saw the tell-tale cable and tore it down. Asked why he had fled, Holzapfel said he had become disillusioned in his Communist belief. As a Party official he was supposed to defend the 'anti-Fascist Wall' and explain why East Germany was no longer advocating a peace treaty. 'I had to be a hypocrite to keep my job,' he said. 'But I decided I would be a hypocrite no longer.'

More recently there was the tale of the Trojan Cow. This was a genuine stuffed and mounted cow, prepared by a taxidermist. Its owner cut an invisible opening through which a refugee could climb into the animal's belly. Loaded on a truck, the Trojan Cow passed through the Berlin Autobahn checkpoints as a 'Display Exhibit' for a dairy show. Twice the ruse worked, as the truck picked up refugees in East Germany and delivered them to the West. But the third time, on July 7, 1968, the frontier guards gave the cow a thorough examination and found a twenty-eight-year-old girl who had been waiting for four years to join her fiancé in West Berlin. The girl and the two helpers in the truck were arrested but the organizer of the escapes, who was following the truck in his car, was not caught. The standard sentence for convicted 'escape helpers' in East Germany is three years' hard labour.

Less classical but equally clever was the invention of a submersible motor to haul a man across the Baltic. This was the brainchild of Bernd Böttger, a twenty-eight-year-old chemical engineer, who managed to convert an auxiliary bicycle motor into a snorkel engine that weighed only 22 lbs. The first such engine took him a year to build. But when he went to the seaside at Boltenhagen and started examining the coastal defences he was picked up by border troops. After they found both the engine and a diving suit in his car he was given an eight-month suspended sentence. The motor was confiscated, but he managed to get the frogman outfit back. Undeterred by this setback, he set about building a new underwater motor and subjecting it to exhaustive tests on inland lakes. He then camped for two weeks beside the relatively deserted beach at Graal-Müritz, near Warnemünde, waiting for the weather to clear. On the night of September 8, 1968, he set out on a northerly course using the Pole Star as a beacon. His motor worked fine, but he took a rolled-up air mattress and iron rations just in case. After a while he could see the regular flashes from the Gedser Lightship off the southern tip of Denmark. This was his goal. Chilled and aching from the strain of holding on to his faithful motor for five and a half hours, he was finally pulled aboard the lightship in the small hours of the morning. Next day he was brought to the Danish mainland and then to West Germany. Now working in Hamburg as a plastics expert, Böttger has patented his underwater motor in the hope that it will find a ready market among sportsmen and lifeguards. The original motor that hauled him across the Baltic may be seen in the exhibition run by the 'Working Community 13th August' close to Checkpoint Charlie.

Thirteen months later, in October 1969, a young East Berlin engineer emulated Böttger's feat. Manfred Burmeister, twenty-eight, built a similar craft and took it to the beach near Rostock

There he waited in hiding until nightfall and set out when the coast was clear. He remained submerged at first, breathing through his snorkel tube until he was past the radar surveillance zone. Then he surfaced and steered, like Böttger, for the Gedser Lightship. During his six-hour journey he navigated with the aid of a compass built into the goggles of his diving suit.

Such were some of the most spectacular escapes. But by far the largest number of refugees used less dramatic methods to reach the West. Often a Westerner, even a foreigner, was willing to lend his passport to an 'escape helper' who would take it to East Berlin to enable someone resembling the passport's owner to cross to the West. A West Berlin student group which called itself the 'Travel Bureau' claimed to have rescued 400 people from the East during the early post-Wall days. It specialized in false Western passports and identity cards, many of which were forged in a shed behind a Grunewald villa by a man who went by the code name 'Rembrandt'. The student counterfeiters in those days were amateurs acting purely from altruistic motives. They were saving their friends, relatives and their friends' friends. But soon the border guards learned to detect the cruder forgeries. Checkpoints began using secret markings and other means of ensuring that nobody could leave East Germany on a passport that had not been used to enter. These markings, as well, had to be found and imitated by the counterfeiters. Gradually the student amateurs were replaced by professionals, by escape organizations which had the resources to outwit the increasing sophistication of the Communist inspectors. One such organization alone brought a reported total of 386 East Germans to the West between March 1962 and November 1964. It employed skilled counterfeiters in several European countries and maintained a fleet of eleven German and American cars. This group's speciality was false diplomatic passports: it could provide even United Nations and East European identity papers on demand. But its services were not exactly cheap: it charged between DM 3,000 and 5,000 (roughly £300–500 or $750–1,250) for each refugee. The would-be refugees, or their Western relatives, were glad to pay. But some operators in the escape business acquired a dubious reputation. One nicknamed *Der Dicke* (The Fat One) collected a reported DM 12,000 (over £1,200 or $3,000) for each refugee brought out of East Germany in a 'blister' underneath a courier's car. Some other unscrupulous operators were no more than confidence tricksters. They would merely pose as escape helpers until they had extorted large sums from trusting victims, and then disappear. Sometimes the shadier characters were caught and prosecuted: often they got away.

A favourite dodge used by people operating on the fringe of legality was to dress up in Allied military uniform, usually Russian or American, and drive unhindered with false number plates through the Wall crossings. There was one Russian-built car in particular that regularly passed Checkpoint Charlie with a driver, a lieutenant and a major in Red Army uniform. The major would interrupt his reading of *Pravda* to return the salute of the East German soldiers as they raised the boom. Only after the car was safely in the West did the refugee emerge from hiding. He or she would have been lying on the floor at the 'major's' feet. As late as 1965 the American garrison in Berlin was embarrassed by the number of impostors masquerading as G.I.s. Sometimes the uniforms were genuine, sold by American soldiers or stolen; sometimes they were tailored from similar material. Obviously the Americans could not approve this kind of activity despite their sympathy for the refugees' cause.

Indeed, West Berlin's ruling Senate was placed in a difficult position. On the one hand it certainly did not want to obstruct the activities of genuine escape helpers, like Fuchs and his idealist students. On the other hand it could not support illegal methods: illegal, that is, by Western standards. It turned a blind eye to the forgery of passports but it had to restrain young people who wanted to blow up the Wall with explosives. Provocations of this sort could do no good: they would only increase tensions and the risk of a shooting-match. The Senate had to decide, too, where to draw the line between the escape organizations which charged no more than a fair price for their services and those that were extortionate in their demands, capitalizing on human misery. At times the police were instructed discreetly to help escape projects, such as Tunnel 57. But when, in 1964, Fuchs wanted to use a mobile crane to hoist five refugees over the Wall in a bullet-proof box, the police foiled his plan by towing away the crane at the last minute. The reason on that occasion was political: East–West negotiations for Christmas passes allowing West Berliners to visit relatives in the East were about to begin, and the Senate did not want to risk an ugly incident which might spoil the atmosphere.

Nowadays the dilemma exists no longer. Frontier incidents seldom occur, nobody tries to blow up the Wall. Flight from East Germany by any method has become so hazardous that the escape organizations have gone out of business. On the rare occasions when some refugee finds a loophole, like Eckhard Oborny at the Harbke opencast mine, his escape is due to exceptional circumstances or exceptional luck. To all intents and purposes, the Wall and the Wire have become invincible.

5

The Modern Frontier

HARDLY had the Wire and the Wall been completed before East Germany's rulers recognized that in their haste to erect the new border fortifications they had created a monstrous eyesore. They had anticipated and were willing to ride out adverse reaction to the sealing of the last loopholes. But they were evidently taken aback by the additional world-wide outrage caused by the sight of miles of sloppily strung, rusting barbed wire, of crude wooden posts and jerry-built road barriers. So the 'modern frontier' was devised in an effort to mitigate at least the visible impact of the new measures. It consisted of a new-style array of obstacles, less ugly than their predecessors—but simultaneously more effective.

In Berlin, pioneer troops were set to work in the second half of the 1960s to strip rusty barbed wire off the top of the Wall, which itself was given a sleek new look. Higher and smoother than the original untidy pile of concrete and cinder blocks, the New Wall is crowned by a wide pipe too slippery to afford a grip to clawing fingers. Its eastern face is whitewashed to ensure that any climbing fugitive is readily visible to Communist sentries. In places, close-mesh fencing is used instead of the Wall.

Other standard features of the 'modern frontier' in Berlin include an array of steel spikes cemented into the ground, followed further east by a strip of lawn or cinders up to forty yards wide. There are believed to be no mines alongside the Wall or elsewhere in built-up areas. The new-model anti-vehicle ditch is up to eight feet deep and reinforced by concrete slabs. Next to it runs the traditional sanded strip to reveal footprints, and a paved road for military patrol vehicles. Further back stand watch-towers, bunkers, trip-wires, dog runs and low fences to mark the eastern boundary of the 100-yard border strip. There are local variations: a massive concrete anti-tank barrier runs parallel to the semicircular Wall at the Brandenburg Gate: steel-girder tank-traps infest the Potsdamer Platz. Sewers are blocked with gratings and electric warning devices, canals contain underwater barriers, and underground railway tunnels are equipped with movable portcullis gates.

Along the line from the Baltic to Bavaria many of the same 'modern frontier' defences are being installed. Even the eleven-foot Berlin Wall has been copied in divided communities such as Hirschberg and Mödlareuth in Bavaria. Mile after mile of barbed-wire fencing through open countryside is being replaced by the close-mesh wire, though even this screen turns rusty over the years and appears black and forbidding to the onlooker. Power drilling machines, like the borers used for planting telegraph posts, are used to make deep holes for the supports. The working parties engaged in this fence-mending operation are always watched by armed guards. A thin red cord, visible from a low-flying helicopter, is sometimes laid on the ground to mark the western limits of the construction site. Should any man venture across it he is liable to be shot as a deserter. Unless, of course, he can choose a moment to sprint for the West when the guards are all looking the other way, as sometimes happens.

Take the obstacles along the 'green border' one by one. A visitor approaching the East–West German frontier may not find the spectacle at first sight particularly sinister. Before reaching the line he will have seen warning signs in English (for the Allied troops) as well as German, cautioning that it is only 50 or 100 metres to the zonal border. But on arrival at this point he will usually face nothing more alarming than a line of white marker stones and, at 500-yard intervals, the six-foot red, black and gold concrete posts bearing the GDR symbol. The fences and watch-towers or bunkers lie still some distance away. On the western side of the line stand white signs erected by the Federal Frontier Defence Force saying 'Halt! Zonengrenze' (zonal boundary). This is the actual boundary. Under no circumstances should a visitor pass beyond; it could be very risky to trespass upon the strip of waste land lying between the signs and the fences, for this is already East German territory. Here and there may be seen the decayed remnants of the original barbed wire fence put up in 1952. Often these are within arm's length of West German soil, but Westerners may not approach to remove these unsightly remains and Easterners have not bothered to do so. Only the old ten-yard ploughed strip, nick-named 'Pieck Allee' after Wilhelm Pieck, late president of the GDR, has totally disappeared in the

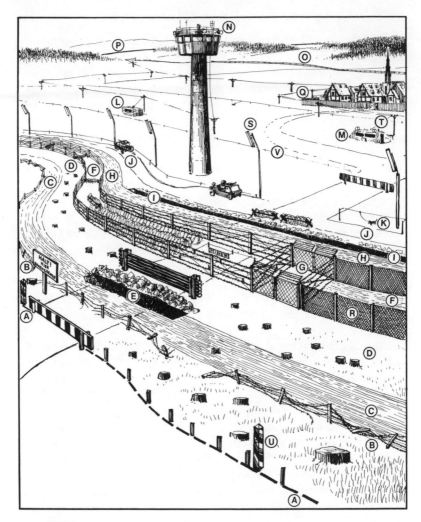

KEY

A. *Actual border line*
B. *Old Barbed wire*
C. *Original 10-yard ploughed strip, now overgrown*
D. *Clear-felled area*
E. *Vehicle trap*
F. *Mined strip flanked by barbed wire*
G. *Way through double fence*
H. *Second ploughed strip*
I. *Barrier trench*
J. *Track for heavy vehicles and footpath*
K. *Guard dog on sliding lead*
L. *Concrete bunker*

M. *Earth bunker*
N. *Watchtower with searchlights, phones, infra-red aids and possibly radar*
O. *Barrier cordoning off hinterland*
P. *Barrier of 5km forbidden zone, with police control*
Q. *Wall round village*
R. *Tall stamped metal fence*
S. *Floodlighting*
T. *Field telephone*
U. *Border marking stones and striped obelisk*
V. *Trip wires*

undergrowth. The new-style fencing lies on the far side of this no-man's-land. The tall close-mesh wire is normally used where there are no minefields. It is a tough obstacle: made of heavy-gauge material resistant to wire-cutters, its holes are too small to afford a hold for a climber's fingers. Inspector Gebhard Glania of the West German Customs displays at his 'museum' in the border information-centre at Philippsthal a pair of wooden sandals equipped with projecting metal bolts at the front which one ingenious refugee devised to gain a toehold in the narrow interstices of the fine-mesh fence.

Where the mines exist—and they cover more than half of the 858-mile border—they are enclosed between twin lines of barbed wire mounted on concrete posts only about five feet high. Sometimes one may see a squad of *Nationale Volksarmee* (NVA) pioneers laying new Russian plastic anti-personnel mines to replace the old wooden box mines used in earlier days. The box mines laid in the early 1960s rotted in the ground and proved singularly ineffective. Glania tells visitors to Philippsthal that in his twenty-five mile frontier sector refugees used to come unscathed through the minefields in the first half of 1968 at the rate of more than two a month. But that was in the days of wooden mines; the newer plastic mines represent a deadly hazard. They are laid in two or three rows, one and a half metres apart, in a zigzag pattern. Since the twin fences guarding the mines are often as much as twenty yards apart, no refugee can tell where the danger belt lies. A false step and his leg may be blown off. NVA guards are not renowned for rapidity in coming to the aid of an injured refugee. Sometimes a fugitive will bleed to death: in November 1968 a sixteen-year-old boy lay for two hours with wounded legs in the minefield before the People's Army took him to hospital. (He, as it happened, was not a refugee from East Germany but a youngster heading eastward to escape an unhappy home life in Bavaria.) Occasionally the mines present a hazard to bystanders on the western side of the border. For although they are usually set well back from the actual boundary, there are places where people pass within range of flying fragments if a mine should accidentally explode. Western visitors to sections of the border where mines lie dangerously close at hand are warned by *Achtung* signs put up by both West and East German authorities. Quite a number of mines have been set off by deer, boars and hares. Horrified visitors sometimes watch innocent deer grazing peacefully between the mines, cooped up between the double fencing. In the neighbourhood of Buch in the Harz Mountains, foresters counted over fifty dead deer in the border minefields during the years 1962–68, plus two wild boars and sixteen hares. They estimate that the figures may be at least twice as large, since many animal fatalities go unnoticed.

Behind the fences and the minefields comes the anti-vehicle ditch reinforced on its steep western side—as in Berlin—by concrete paving-stones, flanked by a six-yard ploughed strip and parallel access road. Overlooking the border stand the watchtowers and bunkers. Often it is hard to tell whether they are manned. The narrow firing-slit windows of the bunkers do not show the occupants. On occasion, People's Army border guards have been known to lie on the floor of their watchtowers to create the illusion that the towers are empty, while keeping vigil through small holes bored in the planks. Further back, usually invisible from the West, stand similar rear-echelon obstacles to those found in Berlin: Alsatian dogs attached by leads and pulleys to 300-yard overhead wires, thin tripwires stretched a few inches above the ground to set off sound or light alarms, and a communications network enabling People's Army soldiers to plug in their portable telephone hand-sets to sockets located at convenient intervals. Modern infra-red aids to night vision are also reportedly in use.

Altogether the area embraced by the three-mile zone along the entire East–West border is larger than the Grand Duchy of Luxembourg. Only part of this is lost to agriculture, since farmers are allowed, by daylight, to work the fields quite close to the frontier minefields. But the actual no-man's-land between and alongside the fences covers forty-five square miles. It lies permanently fallow and represents a loss to the East German economy. Prof. Wilhelm Seedorfer of Göttingen University has tried, with the help of building and military experts, to calculate the total annual cost of the border to the East German taxpayer. Including the waste of land, he came up with a figure of DM 1,000 million (£104 m. or $250m.) a year, of which three-quarters is accounted for by the 50,000-man Border Command of the People's Army with its equipment, and the rest by the expense of physical obstacles. For instance, he reckoned the cost of the mines alongside the Lower Saxony border alone at DM 48m. (roughly £5m. or $12m.), the price of the close-mesh fencing at

DM 30 a metre and the total expense of the ninety dog-runs opposite the same stretch of border at half a million marks. Projecting these and other costs over the entire border, Prof. Seedorfer estimated that the total cost of the physical obstacles must be DM 300m. (about £31m. or $75m.) a year. Since the war, he judges the cumulative expense of the border fortifications and their guarding must be about DM 100,000 million (£10,433m. or $25,000m.) which is no small burden to a nation of 17 million people.

The GDR is not entirely insensible to the revulsion aroused by the frontier devices it has built at such great cost. Visitors to the 'modern frontier' concede that it is less repugnant than the utterly forbidding picture of earlier years, but repugnant it is nevertheless. Official East German literature and briefings, given to visitors to the 'modern frontier' information centre by People's Army spokesmen, seek to overcome this feeling. Far from admitting that the Wire and the Wall were needed to halt the exodus of able-bodied workers to the West, People's Army lecturers claim that they were erected to protect the GDR from the depredations of Western spies, black marketeers and provocateurs.

Only privileged guests are admitted to this centre, in a room adjoining the Brandenburg Gate. It is blocked off from the West by the Wall, and to the East there is a frontier boom on Unter den Linden which nobody may pass without permission. But occasionally a Western journalist is afforded a glimpse of the Communist view of the frontier. It is an experience worth recounting in detail since it is the only opportunity Westerners ever get to study the other side. All efforts by Western correspondents to obtain permission to visit East German border areas are refused; the three-mile forbidden zone has been out of bounds to West Germans since 1952 and to foreigners as well since 1961. Furthermore, Western journalists are not allowed to visit People's Army barracks and installations. So the nearest one ever gets is the Brandenburg Gate centre, where the official briefing naturally stresses the situation in and around Berlin. The stairs leading up to the small lecture-room are hung with pictures of NVA Border Command soldiers who were killed in defending their country against 'provocateurs'. One of them is Egon Schulz, the non-commissioned officer killed when the tunnel dug by Fuchs' group under the Wall was discovered in October 1964. The People's Army claims: 'The murderer of Egon Schulz continues to live free and unhindered in West Germany—he can appear on the cover pages of papers and magazines with the caption: "I shot the Vopo!" '

One wall of the lecture-room is hung with a map of Berlin displaying alleged 'nests of spying and militarism' in the Western sectors. Espionage centres are depicted as spiders, military bases as steel helmets illuminated with yellow and white lights. The uniformed briefing officer cites with some accuracy the strengths of Allied troop garrisons and of West Berlin police. He goes on, more controversially, to claim that there are—or were—almost eighty 'spying and terror organizations' in the Western sectors devoted to revanchism, militarism and the Cold War. He points out several on the map with his baton. The visitor notices that there are no lights, spiders or helmets on the other half of the map, in East Berlin, and interrupts to ask what is the strength of People's Army forces ringing West Berlin. The briefing officer replies that this is a 'military secret'. He proceeds to recall the days before the Wall. The following quotations are taken partly from the lecture, partly from an English-language official booklet distributed at the information centre and entitled 'A Wall of Peace'.

Right along the border in West Berlin, fifty so-called *Grenz-kinos* (frontier cinemas) were built in which especially chosen films were shown to GDR citizens. It is interesting to note that GDR citizens, after showing their identity cards, had to pay only one mark in GDR currency to enter these cinemas. . . . Trashy and filthy literature, like war comics, in which German fascism and militarism were glorified and perverse and cruel crime stories were sold in West Berlin at specially manipulated prices. . . . They pursued their aim of infiltrating as much as possible of this literature over the border into the capital of the GDR in order to influence youngsters above all.

Secondly, this open frontier was used to try with the most unscrupulous methods to bleed the GDR to death economically. This economic interference was responsible for damage estimated at more than 30,000 million marks over the GDR frontier in Berlin alone. A not very minor role in this was played by the *Grenzgänger* (border-crossers) who lived in the capital of the GDR but sold their labour in West Berlin. As a rule, they were specialists who were desperately needed for the construction of the capital. In this way the GDR was doubly harmed by West Berlin. Not only was labour short in the GDR but these people exchanged their earnings at the phoney exchange rate of 1 West mark for 4·5 GDR marks (the rate just before 13 August, 1961). Thus, a *Grenzgänger* earning 500 marks in West Berlin came back home in the capital of the German Democratic Republic at the end of the month with 2,000 marks and more, according to how the rate stood. This phoney rate of exchange between the two German currencies was principally used to corrupt the people in the GDR, induce them to go to West Berlin and earn their money there more easily at the cost of the workers of the GDR. The phoney rate was also used to give racketeers and speculators the necessary incentive similarly to misuse the frontier with West Berlin. In this way valuable manufactured articles were smuggled into West Berlin. From one good pair of Zeiss binoculars or a good camera, racketeers and speculators not seldom made 500 marks and more. We estimate that we suffered 120,000 million marks losses from the cold economic war.

Much of this is certainly true, but it is noteworthy that at no point in the official lecture or the sixty-three-page booklet justifying the Wall is there any mention of the refugee exodus. The emphasis throughout is on resisting 'provocations', ranging from tunnellers to people in West Berlin who throw stones at People's Army border guards, or at lamps illuminating the Wall. The briefing officer claims that there were 40,000 such 'provocations' in Berlin during the first six years after the building of the Wall. He shows slides including one alleged photograph of a West Berlin prostitute disrobing beneath a Communist watchtower to distract the attention of the guards. The contention is that such incidents, including twenty-six bomb attacks on the Wall, occur with the complicity of West Berlin police. The booklet charges:

In almost all cases of serious border incidents commandos of West Berlin police had taken up position beforehand in order to give provocateurs covering fire. In most cases photographers and television people were already on the spot in order to film the criminal actions against the GDR. . . . In some cases West Berlin police actually equipped provocateurs. In a tunnel discovered in the Strelitzer Strasse on 5 October, 1964, GDR border guards found protective masks of West Berlin police officials in which their names were still marked.

West Berlin Senate officials merely smile and shrug their shoulders when confronted with these Communist charges. There is no pretence that the West is entirely blameless. Indeed, senior West Berlin officials speak with amusement and apparent approval of a party of Baden-Württemberg schoolchildren who came to Berlin soon after the Wall was built. The children were so incensed by what they saw that they collected money for explosives and produced a bomb which blew a small hole in the Wall. On the other hand, the West Berlin police foiled Wolfgang Fuchs's attempt to rescue five refugees by means of a mobile crane and bullet-proof box.[1] But there is no doubt that much of the money for tunnelling and other Western rescue efforts came from the Christian Democratic Union and other West German political parties; the attitude of the West Berlin Senate was ambivalent.

West Berlin police statistics on the number of refugees killed at the Wall are disputed by the Brandenburg Gate briefing officer. In December 1967 the year's death toll, displayed in black figures on a Western placard facing East across the Wall, was given as sixty-three. The People's Army insisted at the time that the true figure was nearer twenty-five. Its spokesman claims that there is no trigger-happy use of firearms. Orders to People's Army border guards are to challenge illegal border-crossers with the words: 'Halt! Stehen bleiben!' (Halt! Stand still!) If the fugitive continues to run, guards could fire in the air. Only as a last resort could they take direct aim. 'Our job is not to kill but to stop,' the spokesman says. 'Dead men don't talk.' The sub-machine-gun carried by Communist border guards is not, he admits, a precise weapon like a rifle. The standard firearm carried by People's Army border command patrols is the Russian-designed Kalashnikov carbine with an effective range of 300 yards and a magazine containing thirty rounds. Patrols normally move in pairs for mutual protection rather than to minimize desertions, the spokesman contends. Men of the Border Command are mostly unmarried youngsters eighteen to twenty years of age; they do not include a disproportionate share of Communist party members.

[1] See Chapter Four, p. 68.

After the Brandenburg Gate briefing the visitor is taken out into the open to be shown the Wall and the masonry anti-tank barrier. It is a strange sensation to stand on an East Berlin observation platform overlooking the Wall and to see familiar Western lookout stands only a few yards—but a whole world—away. It is like a view through the looking-glass. The People's Army officer proudly describes the way in which the 'modern frontier' obstacles were tested in an East German army barracks. A mock-up of the new-style Wall and all its concomitants was erected on open ground and some of East Germany's best athletes were told to try to negotiate the course from end to end. 'Not one of them made it undetected,' he says. The officer does not say in which direction the athletes were ordered to move. Vehicle ditches and anti-tank barriers, too, had been tested and found effective.

However, the most formidable barriers would be useless without the National People's Army. For all its desertions and defections, the People's Army has become a considerable military force. Its reliability is always open to doubt, but its units are so disciplined and permeated with informers that the individual soldier has little opportunity to display any resistance to the system. The first thing that strikes any visitor to East Berlin is the outward similarity of Ulbricht's army to Hitler's *Wehrmacht* (armed forces). To watch the changing of the guard at the 'memorial to the victims of fascism and militarism' on Unter den Linden is a chilling sight for any spectator who lived through the Second World War. There are the old uniforms, with the high-collar tunics and jackboots reminiscent of Nazi days. Only the insignia and the steel helmets are different. Worst of all, the People's Army uses the goose-step on ceremonial parades, an arrogant stride which will for ever be associated with the Third Reich. The contrast with the collar-and-tie, citizens-in-uniform army in West Germany is startling. Thomas Forster, a West German authority on the People's Army, writes that the choice of the 'traditional German uniform' was designed to cultivate the illusion that the NVA was a national force rather than an army under Russian command. He quotes Willi Stoph, then East German Minister of Defence, as arguing in favour of the old uniform in a speech to the People's Chamber on January 18, 1956:

There are important progressive traditions in the military history of our people which found their expression in the uniform. German imperialism and fascism, however, degraded the uniform as a symbol of military and national honour. . . . In the National People's Army, the German uniform will have a true patriotic meaning as an expression of a resolute readiness for the defence of our democratic achievements.[1]

The East Germans not only took over the *Wehrmacht* uniform; they also did not hesitate to use old *Wehrmacht* officers who had turned Communist while in Soviet prisoner-of-war camps. Among the four former generals who helped set up the Communist army in the post-war Soviet zone was Lt. Gen. Vincenz Müller, who became the NVA's first chief of staff when it was set up in 1956. Hctually a start had been made toward building military forces in the Soviet zone within weeks of the end of the war. They were disguised as police, but in course of time the disguise wore very thin. Otto Opitz, a leading Communist official, wrote in 1959 that the 'birth of the armed forces of the German working class' was as early as October 31, 1945, when the Soviet military government in Germany permitted the People's Police to bear arms. This Russian decree, and a further order two months later, violated Allied agreements on decentralization of police forces by placing the *Volkspolizei* throughout the Soviet zone under the Communist-controlled 'German Interior Administration'. By the end of 1946 the '*Vopos*' numbered 45,000 men.

The build-up continued with the establishment of *Deutsche Grenzpolizei* (German Frontier Police) in late 1946 and *Transportpolizei* (railway police). But the true military cadres which formed the kernel of the People's Army were created in 1948. These were 'police' formations quartered in barracks and led by former *Wehrmacht* officers and NCOs. Russian military advisers headed by Gen. Petrakovski were attached to these units, which grew from 8,000 men at the end of 1948 to 50,000 by early 1950. Training was conducted on Russian lines, with infantry weapons, artillery and tanks. The Frontier Police meanwhile continued their separate existence and were transferred from the Interior Ministry to the Ministry of State Security in May 1952. Successive reorganizations followed, and the pretence that East Germany had no armed forces was dropped. In 1952–53 the GDR established Combat Groups of reservists and the Sport and Technology

[1] Thomas M. Forster, *The East German Army*, English edition, London: George Allen and Unwin, 1967, pp. 28, 142.

Association, an organization designed to prepare young people for military service.

When the National People's Army was formally established by a law of January 18, 1956 nothing changed but the name. The first unit to be transferred from the 'police' garrisons to the Army was sworn in on the Marx-Engels Platz in East Berlin on April 30. By the end of 1968 the Institute of Strategic Studies in London estimated the total strength of East Germany's land forces as roughly 150,000 (Army 58,000, Border Command 70,000, security police 20,000) plus a quarter of a million Combat Group reservists. The Border Command of the People's Army is the former German Frontier Police, renamed in 1957 and subordinated to the Ministry of National Defence. Every military unit down to battalion size is reported to include political officers wearing NVA uniform but directly responsible to the Ministry of State Security. These in turn have informers among the troops who submit written reports on the reliability of soldiers. Deserters from the People's Army testify that the reports cover such matters as friendships outside barracks, private political views and participation in Communist activities. A careless word can blight a man's army record, and this in turn may spoil his chances of good civilian employment after the eighteen-month conscription period.

Thus the pressures on every soldier to show at least apparent enthusiasm for the Communist system are constant and powerful. Nowhere are these pressures stronger than in the Border Command, where desertions have been so frequent. Forster claims that men volunteering for frontier duty are carefully screened by security officers and subjected to intensive political indoctrination during their six-month special training course. He quotes Gen. Heinz Hoffmann, East German Defence Minister, as telling an audience of Border Command officers:

> In all your military activities you must always bear in mind that the frontier troops have to be an elite formation of the National People's Army. The comrades of the frontier troops who stand guard on the dividing line between socialism and capitalism are every day exposed to ideological influence of the enemy. . . .
>
> In the showdown with the class enemy our political work must radiate such a strength that every soldier shall become

convinced that socialism will be victorious and that anyone who bets on capitalism is preparing his own downfall. For this work one needs great political experience and knowledge.[1]

Political instructors tell Border Command troops that they are defending the GDR against aggression from an 'enemy who operates just below the threshold of the hot war'. But defectors report that this official line is hardly credible to the soldier who sees nothing more 'aggressive' on the Western side of the border than Customs or Frontier Defence Force guards, or an occasional Allied military patrol. The allegedly 'revanchist' West German armed forces never appear within sight of the East German watch-towers at all. The fact that the Border Command's chief task is to prevent refugee escapes is only obliquely mentioned in the military manuals, which say that frontier troops must 'allow traffic to cross the frontier only at the official crossing points'.

A touchingly sympathetic account of look-out duty in an East German watchtower was given by the Communist *Sächsische Zeitung* of Dresden in its issue of September 20, 1968. It described how Private Hans-Jürgen Naumann mounted the ladder for his first day's watch, accompanied by Corporal Ralf Schillig as chief sentry.

> Hans-Jürgen Naumann had imagined his first frontier duty would be more exciting. The landscape in front of him looks calm. Yet this calm is deceptive. Over there—the chief sentry points it out as if he had sensed his thoughts: 'Down there, where the border makes a bend, at the allotments—it was exactly at the hedge. Seventeen years ago it is now. Werner Schmidt was bestially slaughtered. Heinz Janello was shot in the back.' They show the spot to every new man who comes. They must know about it.
>
> As if by command their eyes turn in the same direction. A grey Volkswagen bus is approaching the border. How often has the chief sentry seen it before, a hundred times or more? He does not know exactly. But he registers every movement of the vehicle as if it was the first time. The bus halts, its occupants climb out. They are West German Custom officials. With rapid movements the corporal opens communication with his Company Headquarters and reports every observation as though he had never done anything else in his life.

[1] Forster, *op. cit.*, p. 186.

Mutatis mutandis this might be an account of life in an American observation post in Bavaria, or of a typical patrol by Customs or Frontier Defence Force men in the West. It goes on:

A goods train rolls by. Did something move back there? Yes, there is somebody walking there. Corporal Schillig has seen it too: 'I know her, she is going to her allotment.' Nevertheless he checks back by telephone. His assumption is confirmed. Ralf Schillig feels silently pleased with his colleague for his alertness.

Six Border Command brigades cover the frontier from the Baltic to Bavaria, three surround West Berlin and one is assigned to the Baltic coast. East Germany's borders with Poland and Czechoslovakia are guarded by one regiment of frontier troops apiece. Central headquarters of Border Command is in Pätz, a small town south-east of Berlin. The frontier troops get extra allowances and rations in recognition of their special status. In a pamphlet issued by the East German Defence Ministry, the task of protecting state frontiers is called 'a particularly responsible service in all states'.

All the more so in the GDR whose western frontier at the same time marks the line separating the two great world camps and on whose territory the special area of West Berlin is to be found.

The peace, order and security along that frontier may to a great extent be attributed to the disciplined and prudent conduct of the frontier guards of the National People's Army.

The booklet, entitled *Soldiers of Peace*, does not mention mines and killings. Nor does it divulge the secret order requiring frontier patrols to shoot if necessary at 'frontier violators'. This Regulation DV–30/9, now known to Western intelligence, describes the 'ambush sentry' as an immobile, camouflaged guard posted in the probable path of a would-be frontier violator. Then Paragraph 64 lays down:

The seizure of frontier violators is to be organized by the sentry leader in the following way:

Frontier violators who move in the direction of the neighbouring State and are discovered before the line of the forward delimitation of the frontier sentry are to be requested to stop. If they do not comply with this request the sentry has to act in accordance with the regulations on the use of firearms and not to allow them to cross the frontier.

This order is in line with the explanation given by the Brandenburg Gate briefing officer for the shootings in and around Berlin. In West Germany, the order to shoot given to People's Army guards is always singled out for special attack. Official Bonn leaflets display gruesome pictures of dead refugees riddled with bullets. But however monstrous it may be that Germans are ordered to shoot Germans, these directions are an integral part of the GDR's frontier control system, as indispensable as the mines and the barbed wire. Yet from the standpoint of the East German border guard, the demand that he shoot to kill refugees can arouse an acute conflict of conscience. Many deserters from the NVA have testified that it was this anxiety which, above all other reasons, led them to flee. It is not easy to miss on purpose and get away with it. Shooting prowess is encouraged by granting extra leave to recruits who do well on the training range; but once they are recognized as good marksmen their officers will seldom excuse a misplaced shot on the border. Soldiers who wound or kill refugees are normally rewarded with medals or promotion. Men who refuse to shoot could, in theory, rest their case on the provision in the 1962 East German military penal code that no soldier may be punished for disobeying an order if its execution would violate the 'recognized norms of international law'. He could point out that Article 13 of the United Nations Declaration on Human Rights of 1948 laid down that every person had the right to emigrate from his country if he wished. He could argue in other ways that the order is illegal. But in practice he would be wasting his breath. The GDR Constitution of 1968 explicitly confines freedom of movement to the area 'within the State frontiers of the German Democratic Republic', eliminating the provision for free emigration contained in the earlier constitution of 1949.

The effectiveness of Ulbricht's Wall and Wire—and of their People's Army guardians—may be measured from the following figures. They show the annual number of refugees who have risked life and limb to leave East Germany—illegally by GDR standards—since the Berlin Wall was built. The statistics are not

complete since they list only those escapers who registered at the
official reception camps.

Year	Registrations
1961 (after 14.8.61)	8,507
1962	5,761
1963	3,692
1964	3,155
1965	2,329
1966	1,736
1967	1,203
1968	1,135

The steady downward trend is apparent, but the curve is
flattening out. The cumulative total of 27,518 is impressive, and
Western border guards are frankly surprised that any fugitives
risk the present-day hazards at all. The Refugees Ministry in
Bonn (which produced the figures) has analysed the ages and
occupations of these refugees and found that in every year since
1962 between fifty and sixty per cent of them were unmarried
persons under twenty-four years old. The twenty-five–forty-five
age group was represented by only twenty-three per cent of the
total, and people aged over forty-five comprised less than six per
cent. By far the biggest proportion of escapers (47·8 per cent of
the total) came from the ranks of industrial, technical and craft
workers. Relatively few farm workers—only 6·7 per cent—made
the crossing, and students accounted for only 2·6 per cent of the
total. Other 'intellectual' occupations were also only lightly
represented, possibly because they can find other ways of crossing
to the West.

This, then, is the 'modern frontier' today—an increasingly
refugee-tight barrier between East and West. How does it com-
pare with other parts of the Iron Curtain? Recently a visitor
approached the Czech border in north-west Bavaria at a point
only a few miles from the south-eastern end of the East–
West German frontier. He fell into conversation with two West
German Customs men standing beside a frontier boom and asked
whether there was much difference between the Czech and East
German borders. The Customs officials looked at each other and
smiled before replying with heavy irony: 'Yes, there is a crass
difference. Here we face a foreign country. Up there'—the speaker
jerked his head towards the East German frontier—'it's Germans

on both sides.' From his tone the meaning was clear: the border between the two Germanies is much worse.

One characteristic difference is that there are no mines along the Czech frontier. True, the Czechs originally installed a refinement of their own on their frontier with Bavaria: electrified fences carrying 6,000 volts sandwiched between barbed wire barriers. But since the mid-1960s, according to the Bavarian Border Police, these electrified fences have not been turned on. Like the barbed wire beside them, they have been allowed to fall into disrepair. Instead, the Czech border guards have been erecting fences further back which carry a low electrical charge and convey an alarm signal. These six-foot fences are always built out of sight from the West, anywhere from 100 to 2,000 yards back from the border, depending upon the lie of the land. Refugees from Czechoslovakia report that this wire can be sometimes avoided altogether; the main deterrent to escape is the alertness of Czech Army patrols.

Long before the 'Prague Spring' of 1968 the Czech border began to show signs of relaxation. It was not just that the high-tension current was turned off; Western border patrols noticed that the Czech guards were more friendly. In their report for the year 1967 the Bavarian Border Police recorded: 'The heads of the Czechoslovak passport control offices, the border commissioners and senior administrative officials including representatives of the Prague Interior Ministry were seeking to increase still further the contacts and co-operation which had improved visibly in recent years.' When the liberal reform movement reached its peak in the summer of 1968 its warming influence was felt throughout the 245-mile Czech–Bavarian border. After the Warsaw Pact invasion of August 21 the Czechs tightened their border controls 'in order to prove', as a Bavarian Border Police report put it, 'that they were fully able to protect their own borders themselves'. They did not want to give the Russians a pretext to take over border policing in Bohemia. But even after August 21 this improved relationship between Czech and West German frontier guards was maintained; they continued to exchange friendly greetings and to settle frontier problems at the local level. Through the media-tion of the Bavarian Border Police it is even possible for local communities on each side of the border to co-operate in such matters as water supplies and roadbuilding. Czech border officers usually speak good German and their relations with their Western opposite numbers, despite occasional frontier incidents when

Czech guards pursue refugees on to Western territory, are correct and even cordial.

By contrast, contacts between the NVA and Western border guards along the East–West German border are generally frigid. East German soldiers often turn their backs when photographed. They are under orders not to talk to Westerners. Only very rarely will they return a wave. When a local problem occurs along the border—a stray cow or a clogged stream, for instance—the Western patrols will usually shout across the border proposing a date and time for a meeting with an NVA officer. Sometimes the People's Army officer turns up at the suggested rendezvous, sometimes not. When he does not, the West sometimes retaliates by failing to keep the next Communist-proposed appointment. There are also occasions when two passing patrols of East and West will exchange a few surreptitious words. But they speak as quietly as possible, and the NVA soldier often dares not risk stopping for fear of being seen by his colleagues.

In general, however, this statement from the Bavarian Border Police report for 1968 sums it up: 'The conduct of the Soviet zone border troops continued unfriendly and unco-operative, even at times provocative. Officers and officials only sought contact to obtain information about refugees or to influence the border population with their propaganda.' Civilians living and working in the three-mile forbidden zone seldom respond to Western greetings. Like many of the soldiers, they may wish to wave back but they dare not for fear of being labelled 'unreliable'. The effect of this attitude upon Western border visitors may be imagined. It makes the GDR and its citizens look much more repulsive than they are in reality.

6

The Border-watchers

IT was pitch dark in the little wooden hut except for the glow of a candle in the back room, shaded by a torn paper cup. Little was to be seen through the window of the observation post except some street lights in an East German village a mile away. The American sergeant handed over an instrument which felt like a bulky hand-telescope, its eye-piece emitting a ghostly green light. 'Take a look through the starscope,' he said. The effect was startling: the distant street-lamps became dazzling in their magnified intensity, and neighbouring village buildings could be seen quite clearly. Far off on the horizon a watch-tower stood distinctly silhouetted against the black sky, and close to it the starscope revealed a round white blob of light resembling cotton wool. 'That's their guardhouse,' the sergeant explained. 'You wouldn't be able to see it at night without the starscope.'

This was Observation Post—O.P. for short—30, on the Bavarian border with the East German province of Thuringia. The vantage point is not a tall watchtower but a rudimentary hut squatting on high ground overlooking the frontier. It is manned twenty-four hours a day by men of the U.S. Second Armoured Cavalry, a regiment based at Nuremberg which is responsible for keeping nearly 500 miles of border with both East Germany and Czechoslovakia under surveillance. It had taken over half an hour to reach O.P. 30 from the north-east Bavarian town of Hof. The driver of the Army jeep had taken two wrong turnings in the darkness; the last part of his journey had to be made with black-out lights to avoid attracting attention among the unseen Communist watchers across the border. An American sentry challenged as we stepped from the jeep into the mud, then guided us to the hut past a barbed-wire coil. Stepping over the threshold, one finds oneself in a tiny room containing a sleeping soldier on one of the two bunks. In a corner lie boxes of ammunition. Passing through the open doorway, one emerges into an equally small space where two men stand watch with binoculars by day and starscopes by night. The starscope, an officer explained, was developed for use in Vietnam and was a secret device until quite recently. It has the capacity of detecting and magnifying faint traces of light at considerable distances, such as the glow from a lighted cigarette. If a house seems to be in darkness, the starscope can pick out any light from a window on the far side which may be invisible to the naked eye. As its name implies, it can also make the most of any starlight or moonlight. In addition, the watchers at O.P. 30 have a small radar set which can detect movements of vehicles and even men at ranges of up to 8,000 yards. This is evidently no secret to the People's Army guards across the border, who sometimes jam the usual frequency and force the American operators to switch to an alternative channel. On the map-table and above the window are sketch-maps giving the compass bearings of various landmarks ahead, while on the walls hang charts displaying the various ranks and uniforms worn by East German soldiers. Close to hand stands a radio-telephone, a log-book containing entries every half-hour through the night, and a pile of arms including a formidable machine gun.

Each four-man crew at an O.P. in the Second Armoured Cavalry sector is relieved after 24 hours on watch, in which the men serve one and a half to two hours on look-out duty alternating with four hours off. Standards of efficiency vary considerably; at O.P. 20 near Coburg, further westward along the same Bavarian–East German border, the sergeant in charge seemed to have very little idea of what lay across the border. He did not know which of the slit-window bunkers beyond the minefield was occupied or when the last People's Army patrol had come down the line. His sketch-map was untidy, and although the weather was fine he had neglected to use the camera issued to every O.P. Yet such sloppiness is unusual. Normally the men in their flimsy shacks along the Bavarian border are keen on their job, which they find more worth-while, despite its tedium, than the usual military round of drill and exercises.

Such is one small element of the massive Western border surveillance operation which continues day in, day out, along the entire 858-mile frontier. No less than six agencies are involved: the Customs Frontier Service, the Federal Frontier Defence Force, the Bavarian Border Police, the British Army of the Rhine, the United States Seventh Army, and last but not least the British Frontier Service. In different ways and in different places up and down the line these organizations work more or less harmoniously together in a well-established routine.

West German Customs men in their distinctive green uniforms are the true eyes and ears of the frontier along more than two-thirds of its length. In Bavaria, which covers 262 miles of the border, they share this function with the Bavarian Border Police. If an incident occurs anywhere, if a refugee comes across, a mine goes off or an East German labour gang starts replacing fences, the chances are that these Customs men will be the first to spot it. Everywhere outside Bavaria they carry the prime responsibility for border patrolling. Within their area, about six miles deep, they have police powers to arrest and search. They normally move in pairs, either on foot or in Volkswagen buses, and carry side-arms, carbines, walkie-talkie radios, torches, and perhaps a Very pistol. Sometimes they take a trained dog instead of a second man on foot patrols.

The Customs Service is run by the Finance Ministry in Bonn, with a chain of command through provincial and local head-quarters down to key officials on the border who are known as Customs commissioners. Each of these is a responsible officer with a section of frontier under his charge. His 'foot soldiers' consist of Customs men organized in local frontier observation posts. These officials live in a border community with their families and patrol a few miles of the line. They know their terri-tory and its inhabitants better than any other frontier organization and there are enough of them—about 1,100 men on the 340-mile Lower Saxony stretch of border alone—to keep the line under close scrutiny. They patrol according to a secret pre-arranged schedule whereby they must visit certain points marked in letters on their large-scale maps. Nobody knows when they will appear at any particular spot. Frequently they can be seen in small wooden shelters overlooking the border only a few yards distant.

On the River Elbe, which accounts for nearly sixty miles of the border, the Customs Service maintains a fleet of some sixteen patrol boats of which six are normally on patrol at any time. East Germany has about thirty military patrol craft on the same stretch of river, many of which are faster than the Western vessels. Whenever a Western boat puts out from the Elbe's left bank a People's Army launch will normally roar away from the opposite shore to investigate and take close-up pictures of any unusual passengers. There is always the chance that a Western boat will rescue from the water a swimmer who is trying to escape from East Germany. The Customs crews have a simple rule of thumb: once a refugee is in the water he can be picked up even if he is close inshore to the Communist bank. At that stage he is fair game for both sides; if he is unlucky he will be spotted first by an East German boat and dragged back to a Communist jail. The one thing that the Western boats cannot do is to take a man off the eastern bank or one of the projecting groynes on the far side. For that would constitute a clear violation of East German territory. The true borderline along the Elbe is disputed, with the East Germans claiming alternately that it runs down the middle or along the zigzag navigable channel and the West Germans contending that it follows the eastern shore.

Customs crews say that the Elbe is a difficult obstacle for would-be refugees to cross. True, the People's Army watchtowers close to the eastern bank have been empty for years since too many of their previous occupants have fled to the West. For the same reason, soldiers no longer patrol the eastern bank. But the river itself is a formidable barrier even to strong swimmers: it varies from 300 yards to half a mile wide according to the season and it runs a $2\frac{1}{2}$ knot current which carries swimmers far downstream. In addition, it contains tricky undercurrents. Many fugitives have drowned while attempting the crossing; only fifteen succeeded in 1968, just half as many as in the previous year. Often bathers and picnic parties come down to the western bank, but the opposite shore is normally totally deserted. Far back among the trees can be seen a glimpse of barbed wire or the rooftop of a People's Army billet in the no-man's-land forbidden zone. The only sign of life is on the jetties used by East German patrol boats and aboard the launches themselves with their armed crews. In 1965 a People's Army helmsman unloaded his colleagues as usual on the eastern bank and then astounded them by opening up his throttle and escaping alone in his boat to the West. The man got political asylum but his boat was returned to East Germany. Next year an East German soldier was picked up from the river; he had spent half an hour arguing with his companion—who kept pointing a gun at him—on the bank before taking the plunge. Fortunately, the fugitive's colleague did not pull the trigger. In 1957 the Elbe froze solid from bank to bank and fifteen East German border guards were among those who seized the opportunity to

dash across. On that occasion there was trouble; a Frontier
Defence Force man was shot in the leg.

Western Customs boats on the Elbe are controlled from a
central headquarters at Hitzacker, where a map with coloured
markers shows the location of river and shore patrols. Each such
patrol is in radio contact with Hitzacker, and the boats can also
speak directly to the British Frontier Service. Thus the Western
authorities claim that they know within a matter of seconds if any
serious incident develops on the river. But river patrolling, like
any other form of border surveillance, breeds boredom and in-
attention. Escapes are so rare nowadays that the Customs boat
crews often lose interest in scanning the surface for a bobbing
head or watching the tall reeds on the bank for any tell-tale movement of a fugitive in hiding. Most escapes occur by daylight
although a crossing at night might be safer; the East German
launches have searchlights but their surveillance at night cannot
be very effective. There is no camaraderie between the boat crews
of East and West—they pass one another without waving or
greeting. The estrangement is just as complete as between their
shorebound colleagues.

It is a curious paradox that the prime responsibility for watching
the East–West border—at least the two-thirds of it outside
Bavaria—should devolve upon the Customs service. For they
have no Customs task nowadays except at the road, canal and rail
checkpoints. Along the rest of the border, the so-called 'green
frontier', they perform strictly a policing function. The East
Germans, by building the frontier minefields, effectively halted all
smuggling through the fields and forests. It was not always so: Paul
König, the official entrusted with rebuilding the post-war German
Customs Service, now retired, recalls that when his men took over
the job of guarding the East–West border in 1949 they had to cope
with massive smuggling of coffee and cigarettes from the Soviet
zone. He believes that this was deliberately encouraged in the
East in an attempt to earn hard currency and undermine Western
economic recovery. Brandy, textiles and glassware also were
smuggled to the West in later times, often with forged or falsified
papers. Already in those days the Marienborn checkpoint close
to Helmstedt on the Berlin Autobahn was manned by People's
Police, the so-called *Vopos*, as well as by Russians.

'There was no personal relationship with the *Vopos*,' Herr
König has written.

But our contacts with the *Vopos* were somewhat more human than in subsequent years. Negotiations occurred on the frontier bridge. Despite a strict ban, it occasionally happened that one of our men crossed to the other side to clear up some doubt about documents. In reverse, some *Vopos* used to come over to us at the beginning for the same reason. At Christmas, 1949, the *Vopo* detachment at Marienborn sent our people a message of greetings which we reciprocated. On New Year's Eve the Marienborn crew appeared at the frontier boom headed by an —albeit tipsy—police chief and asked to speak to me. I went there with some of my officials. Good wishes were exchanged for the year 1950 and we had a round of drinks at the barrier. Such scenes were unthinkable a little later.[1]

Today the Helmstedt Autobahn crossing has 117 Customs men working in three shifts to handle the ever-growing volume of traffic. (In 1968 they counted 1,784,079 vehicles in both directions, or nearly 5,000 a day.) The presence of these Customs men at Helmstedt and all the other border checkpoints is a living refutation to the arguments of all the purists in Bonn and elsewhere who maintain that no East–West German frontier exists in any legal sense. True, West German imports from the GDR are duty-free. But Customs officials check every truck-load at Helmstedt against the quotas laid down in the so-called Interzonal Trade Agreement between the two parts of Germany. Even lorries plying between the Federal Republic and West Berlin have to carry documents issued and stamped at the border checkpoints. 'Foreign' vehicles, i.e. those which are not West or East German, are checked through Customs at the East–West German border in just the same way as at any international frontier. Private car occupants are asked whether they have anything to declare. Travellers are also given certificates proving that they have crossed East Germany; documents which when presented at a West German post office entitle the bearer to recover the DM 5 or more that he has had to pay at the Communist checkpoint for an East German visa. For a 'non-existent' frontier, this adds up to considerable Customs activity! In addition, the visitor to Helmstedt will find representatives of the police, the Frontier Defence Force, the British and American armies and the British Frontier Service. The buildings these

[1] From the Customs Service journal, *Die Zollpraxis*, July 1966: author's translation.

organizations use are mostly wooden and temporary, in line with the theory that the border is only provisional. But it is surely only a matter of time before these unsuitable structures give way to bricks and concrete.

Down on the Bavarian sector of the 'green frontier' the Customs Service has never been able to obtain the police powers it enjoys in Hesse, Lower Saxony, and Schleswig-Holstein. Alone among West German states, the proud province of Bavaria maintains its own police for frontier duty. Federal officials in Bonn often complain that the Bavarian Border Police (BBP) are—as one Customs source put it—totally unnecessary. But the Bavarians retort that their 2,500-man Border Police fulfil a vital function. They argue that the Customs Service has no business trying to arrogate to itself police powers in frontier regions where there is no true Customs duty to be done. The task requires trained policemen, they say, and the Federal Constitution of 1949 vests police powers in the hands of the states, not the federal government. The dispute rages chiefly at the higher official levels in Bonn and Munich; Bavaria has even threatened to sue the federal government, but among the men actually on patrol along the border these jealousies cause more amusement than ill-feeling. Nevertheless, to a detached observer the existence of four different frontier surveillance agencies side by side along the Bavarian border, (the BBP, Customs, Frontier Defence Force and U.S. Army), does seem rather absurd.

My first real contact with the Bavarian Border Police was on the famous *Saalebrücke* close to Hof, the bridge which carries the Munich–Berlin Autobahn across the border. This high arched viaduct was blown up by Hitler's retreating armed forces to check the American advance during the last days of the war. Police Superintendent Herbert Brunner recalled that for twenty-two years all traffic had to follow a long detour by way of Töpen over roads never designed for trucks and trailers. He recounted the curious story of how the bridge came to be rebuilt after years of negotiation between East and West Germany. The problem was that the viaduct actually spans the border, which runs down the centre of the River Saale. It was agreed that East German workers would do the work while West Germany would pay the entire costs. But how were the East Germans to be prevented from escaping to the West? The Communist side at first demanded that the entire construction site be guarded by armed People's Army troops. But this was refused by the West because one end of the bridge was on Bavarian soil; there could be no question of allowing the East German soldiers on Federal territory. So eventually a compromise was reached: the East Germans were allowed to build a high fence around the building site at the Bavarian end of the bridge to shield their workmen from the West. But their guards supervising the rebuilding operation must carry no arms. Most intriguing of all was the provision that the tall screen fence should contain a door. If any East German workman already on Bavarian soil wanted to seek asylum in the West, he should be allowed to do so. 'We had a key to the door—that was part of the agreement,' Superintendent Brunner said. 'If a man had called through the fence to us that he wanted to escape we could have opened the door and gone to his assistance in case anybody had tried to stop him.'

The bridge was completed in 1967 and now the traffic runs smoothly over the second-busiest Autobahn crossing (after Helmstedt) between the two parts of Germany. Beside the Bavarian end of the bridge the new buildings used by the Bavarian Border Police look as if they were made to last.

Altogether the BBP maintain some 600 men on the East–West German border, working in liaison with the American Army and other agencies. Wearing distinctive uniforms with Bavarian insignia, the BBP patrols duplicate the functions performed by the Customs men elsewhere. They watch, they listen, they report all unusual occurrences along the Communist side of the line. They receive and interrogate refugees who manage to escape to the West; they deal with persons expelled by the GDR as unwanted citizens, they investigate any suspicious characters on the Western side of the line who may be criminals trying to escape by crossing to the East. But they find the East German police totally unresponsive to requests for co-operation. For instance, when the BBP tried to find out the names of West German victims of a car crash on the Hof–Berlin Autobahn, they were referred to the Interior Ministry in East Berlin.

Backing up both the Customs Service and the BBP is the *Bundesgrenzschutz* (BGS), or Federal Frontier Defence Force, a paramilitary body comprising about 16,000 men and subject to the Interior Ministry in Bonn. It has nothing to do with the West German armed forces, which have no peacetime border function: indeed, they are not allowed to approach within three miles of the border. The BGS has a volunteer, select character which is bound to be diluted by the decision to introduce conscripts to enable the force to reach its full authorized strength of 20,000 men. Its personnel are quartered in barracks set some distance back from the border; they run motorized patrols to the frontier but in general they do not know it as intimately as the Customs and Bavarian Border Police men who live in villages and hamlets along the line and patrol it on foot. Unlike the Customs Service, the BGS is equipped with armoured cars, anti-tank guns, helicopters and trucks as well as jeeps. Its function is to deal with any local threat to the security of West Germany's borders—the international frontiers as well as the boundary with East Germany—as a kind of mobile reserve. Needless to say, these lightly-armed troops are not intended to repel a full-scale invasion. But within a twenty-mile belt on the Western side of the frontier they hold limited police power. They could not intervene to suppress ordinary crime, however serious, in a border village. This would be a matter for local police. But if an agitator should attempt to lead a protest march of Western farmers to the border with the aim of tearing down Communist fences, this would pose a security threat which the BGS would have to prevent. Similarly, the BGS comes into play when frontier security is threatened by any Communist action. Sometimes the BGS responds to an East German challenge with excessive zeal. When in the spring of 1968 the People's Army—apparently inadvertently—planted a white border marker a few yards on the Bavarian side of the line near Kronach the BGS brought up seven armoured cars and demanded through a loudspeaker that the offending stone be removed. In another instance in Schleswig-Holstein the BGS telephoned David Mackie, the local British Frontier Service officer, one Saturday morning and urged him to bring up a British Army detachment because the East Germans had placed a marker just one and a half inches on the Western side of the line. Mackie retorted: 'Do you want to make me the laughing-stock of the entire British Army?' and nothing was done. The stone stayed put. But it is incidents like this which give the BGS a reputation for over-reacting to any incident, no matter how trivial. The usual technique of the Customs Service and the BBP on these occasions is to seek out the responsible East German officer and quietly point out his map-reading error. Usually this works and the intruding stone is withdrawn without any danger of full-scale confrontation. Mackie and other veterans of the frontier are convinced that the East Germans do not want to provoke trouble in their border-marking activity.

To charges of showing excess enthusiasm the BGS replies, in the words of one lieutenant, 'we think that the language of power is the only one the other side understands—we believe in showing a firm and strong response to any challenge, and in betraying no sign of weakness.' This officer added that the post-war history of the border justified this policy. Not surprisingly, the BGS is singled out in Communist propaganda for especial attack, being compared to the Nazi SS. There is no love lost between the BGS patrols and the People's Army troops across the border. Nor, for that matter, is there much affection on the Western side between the BGS and the Customs Service. Their respective police powers overlap in the six-mile border zone where the Customs men patrol; their spheres of responsibility have never been exactly defined, their methods are different. As with any government agencies operating in adjoining fields, they tend to tread on each other's toes. The situation is similar to the feud between the Customs Service and the Bavarian Border Police, except that it is not limited to Bavaria. Sometimes it gets to the point at which the Customs Service will report an item of border intelligence to Allied liaison officers without telling the BGS. Often a BGS officer lecturing visitors on the problems of the frontier contrives to avoid all mention of the Customs Service. There was even an incident in Schleswig-Holstein when an armed BGS man jumped from behind a bush to challenge two Customs officers on patrol. The Customs men laughed at the eager BGS man who, it turned out, had never been told of their existence.

Such blind spots and mutual jealousies apart, the BGS performs with every sign of keenness and efficiency. Its barracks and vehicles appear spick-and-span, its helicopter pilots first-rate and its general *esprit de corps* above the average. Its men enjoy a close working-relationship with the American Army in Bavaria, whose jeep patrols they accompany. The BGS maintains a flotilla of four patrol boats on the Baltic, due to be replaced by eight new craft by 1971. These boats run four or five patrols weekly between the seaside resort of Travemünde and the straits dividing Fehmarn Island from Denmark. It is a moot point whether the eight new craft, which will each have a speed of up to thirty knots instead of the present twenty-one knots, and carry two 40 mm. Bofors guns instead of two 20 mm. Oerlikons, are really necessary. Small motorboats could, in the view of some experts, do the job as well at less expense. Incidents in the Baltic are rare these days. Seldom if ever does a GDR vessel intrude in West German territorial waters; seldom today does a refugee from East Germany jump overboard at sea or attempt to cross the Bay of Lübeck in a small boat. Most Baltic escapes occur in Scandinavian harbours or along the Kiel Canal. So it is doubtful whether the BGS needs to choose this time to double its maritime strength. In case of a serious incident it can always call for support from the Federal Navy, which also maintains a standing patrol in the Baltic. Indeed, at the Neustadt base the Navy and the BGS use the same barracks and their officers share the same mess.

Behind all these West German frontier surveillance agencies, ultimate responsibility for the security of the East–West German border lies with the United States and Britain. Each ally guards the sector flanking its post-war occupation zone, with the link-up point close to Witzenhausen, just south of the Harz Mountains. They operate very differently. The Americans have two regiments permanently assigned to their stretch of the frontier: the Second Armoured Cavalry already mentioned and the Fourteenth Armoured Cavalry based on Fulda. Both units have been based on the border since the early 1950s, and they alone among American forces have the front-line responsibility. Colonel Adrian St. John, commanding the Fourteenth, described his mission as three-fold. Firstly, to assist the German border organizations in frontier surveillance through observation posts and patrols both on the ground and in the air. Secondly, to help counter any border attack, and therefore to maintain combat efficiency through training exercises. Thirdly, to co-operate with the West Germans as smoothly as possible. His three squadrons, which correspond to infantry battalions, are integrated combinations of tanks, infantry and artillery down to platoon level. A platoon is made up of three M-60 medium tanks with night firing devices, five command and reconnaissance vehicles, and a 4·2-inch mortar carrier, making nine vehicles in all. Both cavalry regiments maintain at their forward headquarters so-called ready reaction forces at constant readiness to move to any scene of trouble. 'Quite a bit of fire-power can be placed on the border in short order,' said Col. St. John. His men fly daily helicopter patrols along the border, weather permitting, and run ground patrols in jeeps equipped with radios, rifles and light machine-guns.

The Fourteenth Armoured Cavalry has only three observation posts along its 140-mile frontier sector while the regiment guarding Bavaria has a dozen continuously manned, and a further thirteen which are used only part of the time. The fact that the Nuremberg-based Second Armoured Cavalry has nearly 500 miles of border—with Czechoslovakia as well as East Germany—to guard is only part of the reason for this disparity in numbers. The State of Bavaria, with its Christian Social Union government, allows the American Army to acquire land rights and install telephone connections. But the neighbouring province of Hesse, where the Fourteenth is located, looks on observation posts with a less benevolent eye. For the Social Democratic government in the Hessian capital of Wiesbaden holds that since there is no legal border there should be no frontier posts on the Western side of the line. Where Western watchtowers do exist in Hesse, as near Hünfeld in the Fulda sector, they are there strictly on sufferance. This tower, known as O.P. Alpha, is a platform raised on stilts, unlike the huts in the Bavarian sector. The Fourteenth Armoured Cavalry has been unable to secure land rights and one officer told me: 'we could be thrown out of here at any time'. There are no proper access roads, and the woodland tracks are a sea of mud in the winter. Electric power has to be taken from an army vehicle whose engine is kept constantly running, since there are no power lines. 'The Germans want thousands of dollars to lay a phone line, so we have to rely on radio,' the officer said. 'If we scratch a tree or spill some diesel oil they make us pay. Even our own Army doesn't recognize that these temporary quarters are here'—and he pointed to a row of wooden trailers where the men eat and sleep—'we had to scrounge them and fix them up ourselves.' Cooking has to be done from a mobile field kitchen. The men of the Fourteenth are naturally dismayed and puzzled by these daily inconveniences. Only some of them know the reason; and these believe that the doctrine of the non-existent border is being carried to excessive lengths.

To the crews of the Fourteenth's observation posts the border is grim reality. They estimate that there are some 2,700 People's Army troops along the opposite side of the wire and minefields adjoining their sector. But one amusing story told at O.P. Alpha concerns the 'black box'. Apparently the men of the Fourteenth got tired of hearing complaints from visiting V.I.P.s that there were never any East German patrols to be seen across the border.

So an enterprising sergeant dreamed up an impressive black box made of cardboard and sprouting mock antennae in all directions. Shortly before a visiting general was due to arrive the decoy would be placed on the watchtower platform in full view of the opposite side. 'It never failed to draw a bunch of East German soldiers with binoculars and cameras,' one G.I. recalled.

Liaison between the American cavalry regiments and German border surveillance agencies is partly direct and informal between patrols on frontier duty (although here language is a problem), and partly through Border Resident Officers stationed at intervals along the frontier. These B.R.O.s wear civilian clothes, speak good German and maintain close contact with the Customs Service, the Frontier Defence Force and the Bavarian Border Police. Their prime task is gathering intelligence; they belong to the 511th Military Intelligence Group. Relations with the civilian population on the whole appear to be cordial despite the language barrier. Marriages occur between Americans and German girls and community contacts are cultivated in the Fourteenth Armoured Cavalry sector by periodic meetings with civic leaders. For instance, at Hünfeld during my visit there was a beer-and-sandwiches evening attended by Col. St. John and his officers at which the German hosts spoke warmly of a recent experiment whereby American soldiers volunteered to spend a few days living on local farms. Few if any of the two dozen enlisted men involved spoke German, but schnapps and goodwill dispelled initial shyness and the soldiers worked so well on the land that they were invited to return.

On the British sector, which runs for more than 400 miles from Lübeck to the southern edge of Lower Saxony, the British Army of the Rhine (BAOR) does not assign specific units to continuous border duty. The three divisions of I Corps, which has its headquarters at Bielefeld, each have the responsibility of guarding a particular stretch of the frontier. But every fighting unit in BAOR takes turns in providing border patrols. 'We do it by rotation,' a BAOR spokesman at Rheindahlen headquarters said. 'We think it's important that every soldier should see at first hand what the border looks like.' Unlike the American jeep patrols which are headed by an NCO, the British Army prefers to use patrols comprising several Ferret armoured cars commanded by a subaltern or a captain. The itinerary is designed to ensure that every point along the border should be visited at least once a month. One rule is invariably observed: BAOR patrols are guided along the tricky frontier lanes by an officer of the British Frontier Service.

This unique organization is at once the smallest and the most intriguing of all Western border surveillance agencies. It totals no more than three dozen members of whom less than half are concerned with the East–West German border. (The others are stationed along the Dutch border and at other crossing-points, engaged in pure Customs work affecting British military traffic.) Yet the fifteen British Frontier Service officers stationed along the 'green border' with East Germany and at Hanover exert an influence quite out of proportion to their numbers. Their job, as one of them put it, is to be 'a little buffer state between the British military and political interests on the one side and the German agencies on the other'. In other words, a liaison body somewhat analogous to the American Border Resident Officers. But the BFS is a strictly overt organization; the information it provides on border incidents and crossings is useful to the British Embassy and Allied security agencies, but it boasts no cloaks or daggers. Its men wear naval-type uniforms, speak fluent German, live and work quite openly in border towns from Neustadt on the Baltic to Göttingen at the foot of the Harz. They are mostly picked ex-officers or warrant officers of the military services. None of them at the time of writing is younger than forty; most have lived in Germany for many years and know their German opposite numbers intimately. In return they are respected and trusted by the Germans, particularly the Customs officials with whom they work most closely. Indeed, in certain cases there is a special bond of affinity—some German Customs officers owe their jobs to the men of the British Frontier Service.

The BFS has a curious history. It was set up soon after the war when the British military government decided that something must be done to bring order out of chaos on the land and sea borders of the British occupation zone. Originally it was called the Frontier Control Service; later the Frontier Inspection Service. It only acquired its present name in 1955 when the Control Commission for Germany was wound up. Its first Director was Captain Guy Maund, D.S.O., R.N., who is remembered by his former colleagues in the service as a most engaging and colourful personality. The naval-looking uniform with silver instead of gold rings on sleeves and shoulder-badges was his inspiration; it stands out clearly from the green and khaki worn by German frontier agencies and British troops respectively. This is important whenever border incidents occur. Part of his organization's early task was to conduct mine-sweeping operations in German rivers and coastal waters, since these could not be patrolled as long as they were mined. Gradually the all-British body began training Germans to take over. But the Service had until 1949 no function on the East–West zonal border at all. Once it moved in there, with the reconstituted German Customs Service under its wing, it began to start reporting on refugee escapes and other incidents as well as performing its normal Customs work of stopping smugglers and checking passports.

When West Germany became a sovereign state in 1955, the Frontier Service was taken out of the Foreign Office's jurisdiction and placed under the Ministry of Defence. It lost much of its executive work at that time but retained its reporting and liaison functions on the East–West border as well as its customs and passport control work involving military travel, as provided under the status-of-forces agreement. Today the BFS officers in their Land Rovers are a familiar sight throughout the British border sector, leading Army patrols ('like Davy Crockett scouts', said one BFS officer), talking to Customs and Frontier Defence Force patrols and visiting scenes of unusual tension or activity. Their headquarters are in Bonn, where they come under the British Joint Services Liaison Organization, with a branch headquarters at Hanover. Not until 1967 was BFS established as a permanent civil service organization with pension rights.

When a frontier incident occurs the nearest BFS officer normally hears about it quickly from his German Customs contacts and hurries to the scene. It may be an intruding border marking stone, a wounded refugee or an attempt to block Western boats in the Elbe. The mere appearance of a BFS officer in his characteristic uniform displays Britain's 'presence' to the other side. But the BFS officer does not talk to the local People's Army commander directly; he is supposed to leave the talking across the border to the West Germans. However, he makes it very evident that he is advising the West German Customs or Frontier Defence Force officer as to what he should say. In earlier days the BFS would insist on dealing directly with a Russian officer, but latterly the Russians have been keeping in the background and leaving all border disputes to the East German authorities.

One celebrated incident occurred in 1962 when the East Germans moved a barbed-wire trestle barrier to the middle of a bridge at Bohldamm, near Lüchow in Lower Saxony. The West claimed that the entire bridge (it was a very small one, as bridges go) was Western territory. Both the Customs Service and the Frontier Defence Force protested, to no avail. The dispute began to escalate when the Communist side brought up two platoons of troops and two armoured cars and began emplacing machine guns covering the bridge. Jack Owen, the local BFS officer, told the East Germans through a Western Customs Commissioner to move it back. When the other side refused the West mustered a Frontier Defence Force platoon and a British Army section. Then Owen, the Customs officer and two British soldiers simply walked on to the bridge, picked up the offending trestle and moved it bodily back to the eastern side.

'It was,' said one of Owen's colleagues in retrospect, 'a crazy thing to do. Jack didn't have enough backing. He got the M.B.E. for it but he could as well have been court-martialled.' But Owen, a taciturn ex-Marine who has served twenty years in the BFS, has always been inclined to act independently. Aubrey Nichols, Director of the BFS, defends Owen's feat of bravery. 'He was right to do it,' said Nichols at his Bonn headquarters overlooking the Rhine. 'The British Embassy knew he would move it back. We always try to retain every foot of Federal territory and resist encroachments.'

Nevertheless, the BFS tries to play it cool as far as possible, to prevent frontier disputes from escalating into East–West confrontations involving pride and prestige. Very often the mere presence of a BFS officer tends to soothe a threatening situation. Every time the BFS has intervened to request the withdrawal of an East German border marking stone from Western territory, the People's Army has complied. British officials believe that if such disputes had been left to the zealous Frontier Defence Force to handle without any British restraining influence the record might have been different. Furthermore, the BFS officer on the spot provides the British Embassy in Bonn and BAOR commanders with an independent British view of any border situation that arises. There are occasions when their detached judgment is an invaluable guide.

West Berlin's 100-mile perimeter is guarded very differently because of the city's special status as a ward of the Western Allies.

It is patrolled by Allied armoured cars, local police and Customs officials. The Frontier Defence Force does not operate in Berlin since the city is not a state of the Federal Republic. Indeed, not even the Customs Service in West Berlin is controlled from Bonn; it is a separate organization run, like the 15,000-strong police, by West Berlin's ruling Senate. Both the Customs and the police perform their border surveillance work in Berlin in close co-operation with the Allies, who carry the supreme responsibility. The American, British and French military commandants are empowered to issue orders to the Berlin police in matters involving security. This is not a power they would exercise lightly; even when demonstrators threatened to march on the United States Mission in 1968 the Allies left the city police to handle the situation on their own. Nevertheless the Allies wield considerable influence over any West Berlin city administration, and their liaison officials are permanently stationed at City Hall. They maintain 11,000 troops in West Berlin (6,000 American, 3,000 British and 2,000 French) as a token defence against Communist attack. Every West Berliner knows that his security rests on Allied support; no Governing Mayor can afford to disregard the wishes of the Western commandants.

Such is the varied pattern of frontier surveillance in the Federal Republic and West Berlin. Now that escapes and incidents occur comparatively rarely, it is a task fraught with tedium for the thousands of border-watchers involved. Critics claim that too many organizations are involved and that there is sometimes a notable lack of liaison; they suggest that the whole operation could be conducted more economically, with fewer observers submitting fewer reports on trivial matters of no significance. There is a case for overhauling the entire system as it has developed over the years. But for all its faults the system works. It has held the line against numerous provocations without allowing any incident to escalate out of control.

7

Berlin: Cutting the Sinews

BERLINERS on both sides of the Wall nowadays take the division of their city for granted. They have become accustomed to the physical barriers, the separation of public utilities and the lack of transport links between East and West. The exciting days of the blockade and the airlift, the exchanges of spies like Gary Powers and Colonel Rudolf Abel on Glienicke Bridge, the abductions of wanted persons into the East, the post-Wall saga of hair-raising escapes by tunnelling and other devices—all these have faded into the past. Herr Ulbricht's Wall has eliminated most of the old points of friction. Today the 3·3 million people of West and East Berlin go about their business in separate worlds. Raised wooden platforms affording a view over the Wall are no longer filled with West Berliners hoping to draw a furtive wave from friends and relations in the East. The wreaths and flowers beside the Bernauer Strasse houses from which refugees jumped to their deaths are shrivelled and faded now. Only 465,000 West Berliners seized the chance to visit relations in the East when the last visitors' passes were issued at Whitsun, 1966, compared with 1·2 million visits at the time of the first passes agreement of Christmas, 1963. Few West Berliners ever visit the Wall any more; East Berliners are barred from approaching it on the opposite side. In short, the Wall has become, like the wire and minefields surrounding the rest of West Berlin, just another fact of life.

But the visitor finds Berlin even today a source of endless fascination. It represents in microcosm and yet in accentuated form all the basic characteristics of German division, spiced with a peculiar flavour of its own. It is harder to divide a city than a country; the arteries and the nerves run closer. To split a capital city is infinitely more difficult than to build a mined strip through open countryside. This is what makes Berlin at once so absorbing and so disturbing a study in municipal surgery. Nowhere else is the contrast between East and West so glaring and so immediate. Perhaps there is no other city which so excites the pulse and stirs the imagination; certainly none is so full of anomaly and paradox. For the intriguing fact about Berlin is that numerous points of contact remain despite the Wall.

Take, for instance, the underground railway or U-Bahn. It has been divided since the Wall went up on August 13, 1961, into separate networks for East and West. But the Western trains still cut through a salient of East Berlin that juts out into the West. Any visitor to West Berlin can ride through Communist territory for a forty-pfennig fare; the trip is eerie but not at all dangerous. Two U-Bahn lines cross this section of East Berlin and both are easily reachable from the Kurfürstendamm. Just before one's train enters East Berlin the station announcer calls: 'last station in the Western sector' and the visitor feels a sense of adventure. As the train plunges onward into the mysterious East, hardened Berlin commuters betray no sign of tension. They gaze into space with that vacant look of subway riders everywhere, or scan their tabloid newspapers. But the newcomer to Lines 6 and 8 peers tensely at the tunnel walls, which suddenly open to reveal the first East Berlin station: grey, dead and apparently deserted. Kiosks and erstwhile bookstalls are boarded up, hoarding spaces bare, lighting dim by Western standards. The train slows to a crawl but does not stop. Tiled, old-fashioned German lettering on the unwashed wall identifies the station as Stadtmitte (on Line 6) or Heinrich-Heine-Strasse (on Line 8). Doubtless the station looked very much the same in Hitler's day. Then the traveller notices that the scene is not quite deserted after all; one or two blue-uniformed guards stand on the platform, carbines slung over their shoulders. They eye the train with bored expressions as it rumbles slowly through. At the end of the station stands a concrete blockhouse with narrow firing-slits through which can be seen, perhaps, another guard. The tunnel walls close in, the train gathers speed and hastens onward to the next 'ghost station' before finally emerging again in the West.

The task of the East German guards on the 'ghost' stations in the Eastern sector is to ensure that nobody tries to alight from the Western trains or throws propaganda leaflets through the windows. Occasionally, perhaps once a month, a Western travel- ler will try to jump off the moving train at one of these East Berlin stations. It is often a drunk who has suddenly awakened to find he has overshot his station and leaps to the door in alarm. If the trains did not slow down at the Eastern stations such in-

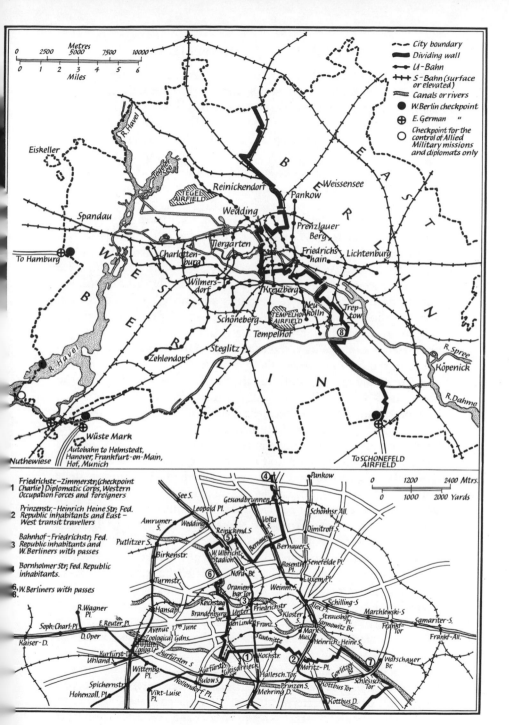

Berlin and Its Central Area

cidents would be rarer; it would be too dangerous to try to jump out. But Western experts explain that the slowdowns are due to technical factors of signalling and braking distances. Doubtless the speed reductions tempt any would-be defector among the Communist guards to spring aboard. But this has happened very rarely; a U-Bahn official said he knew of only three cases in the early 1960s and none since. It would not be easy: the guards always patrol in pairs and the train doors cannot be opened from the outside.

The Western U-Bahn pays the East a fixed sum of over DM 2 million a year for the upkeep of the track and tunnels it uses through the Eastern salient. Officials of the West Berlin public transport authority have had no meetings with their opposite numbers in the East since 1963. 'We have a telephone link to them, but we don't even know their names any more,' one expert said. 'Our relations with the London and New York public transit people are much closer—we get invited to ceremonies opening new stretches of line in Western capitals but our next-door neighbours in the East never ask us to anything.'

Among the dozen stations in the East frequented by the Western U-Bahn, only one—the Friedrichstrasse—is open to the outside world. All the others are walled off, their stairwells leading from the street bricked up or choked with rubble. At Friedrichstrasse Station the trains stop, but the platform there is a kind of neutral zone and no Communist officials come aboard to check the passengers or hinder the trains from continuing their journey. This station, situated some ten minutes' walk east of the Wall, is the sole point of contact between trains of East and West. Here one may change from the Western to the Eastern U-Bahn network, board the elevated S-Bahn trains heading in either direction or take a long-distance train to any destination. Also, of course, one may simply disembark at Friedrichstrasse and walk out on to the street. But the barriers and the passageways in this several-storied station are so designed that nobody can pass from the 'Western' platforms to the 'Eastern' ones or vice versa without submitting to checkpoint examination. The same applies, of course, to entry and egress from and to the street. The standard rules apply: West Germans and foreigners are generally allowed through the barriers whilst West Berliners are barred. However, even West Berliners frequently visit Friedrichstrasse Station to buy cigars, cigarettes and whisky at cut-rate prices in the East

German 'Intershops' on every platform used by Western trains. Goods are sold in these kiosks only for Western currency and prices are marked in American dollars. They do a thriving trade: as each U-Bahn or S-Bahn train pulls in a group of its passengers makes straight for the nearest Intershop. A bottle of good Scotch whisky, for example, costs $2·75 or DM 11, compared to roughly DM 17 in a typical West Berlin liquor store. Cigarettes on sale include most well-known American brands at prices several marks lower per carton than the prevailing rates in the West. Nevertheless this is good business for the GDR, which makes a profit in badly-needed hard currency. But West Berlin retailers— if one tobacconist is any guide—are angry at this unfair competition. They are told that Customs officers watch for 'smugglers' and black marketeers, but even at the Western U-Bahn and S-Bahn stations closest to Friedrichstrasse one never sees anyone stopped and searched. Officials of West Berlin's ruling Senate admit that the authorities turn a blind eye to small-scale purchases. As the West maintains that there is no 'Customs frontier' between the two parts of Germany, setting up Customs posts at every intersection leading to East Berlin and searching returning travellers for 'contraband' would violate this hallowed legal theory.

Unlike the U-Bahn, the above-ground S-Bahn is run in both halves of Berlin by the East. It was always operated as part of the pre-war German State Railways, and the East German State Railways of today have inherited the function in post-war Berlin. Indeed, the State Railways (as distinct from the West German Federal Railways) still operate all long-distance rail traffic through West as well as East Berlin and for this purpose maintain depots in West Berlin. Most of their employees in the Western sectors are West Berlin residents, but every day a few dozen commuters come over from the East to supervise and to perform certain high-grade technical and administrative tasks. In earlier days the State Railways buildings in West Berlin were well-known centres of Communist subversion and propaganda. Claiming territorial sovereignty over the State Railways and S-Bahn stations in the West, the East used to seize and abduct Westerners, bundling them into eastbound trains. But the three Western Allies, which have never recognized the East's sovereignty claims, promptly put Western police on duty at S-Bahn stations in their sectors.

Not so long ago, in January 1966, there occurred at Steglitz S-Bahn station in West Berlin an incident which dramatized this sovereignty issue. The West wanted to build a motorway along-side the S-Bahn tracks and to demolish the old Steglitz station building which stood in the way. The S-Bahn administration in East Berlin refused to permit this and tried to raise the dispute to the political level by demanding that the West negotiate with the East German Transport Ministry. Unwilling to follow this course, the West Berlin city fathers appealed to the Allies and secured an order demanding that the station be torn down. Armed with this fiat from the highest governing body in West Berlin, the operation was planned with the care and secrecy of a military assault. The problem was that the building contained signalling equipment and a master clock controlling others throughout the S-Bahn network. All this had to be moved to an alternative site without disrupting normal S-Bahn services. Skilled techni-cians had to be brought in to move the cables and reconnect the circuits. Although at least fifty people were in on the secret and the operation was twice postponed before being put into effect, surprise was achieved. When the 'assault' began at 10 p.m. one night, the half-dozen S-Bahn employees on duty in the station offered no resistance. They were West Berliners to a man, and if they had any doubts these were soon dispelled by the warning that they must not try to interfere with the execution of an Allied order. Four hours later, at 2 a.m., the technical manager of the S-Bahn came across in a special train from the East to voice an angry protest. He, too, was told it was an offence to obstruct Allied orders, and assured that the West had no intention of dis-turbing S-Bahn traffic. He returned as he had come, and the work of dismantling and reconnecting went on. By 12 noon, after fourteen hours of labour, the building was ready for the bull-dozer. The West had made its point: that the East's responsibility for running the S-Bahn does not involve any extra-territorial sovereignty over the tracks and installations in the West.

It does, however, involve maintenance of all S-Bahn facilities even in West Berlin. For a flat-rate thirty-pfennig fare any passenger can observe the dilapidated state of the rails and coaches. Merely to enter an S-Bahn station is instructive. Before boarding my train at the Savigny Platz I asked the station-master whether the station had ever been painted since the war. He shrugged his shoulders. I looked down the track and noticed that the rails were worn and bent. The train came rattling in and as I took my wooden seat I recalled that none of the rolling-stock has been renewed since pre-war days. S-Bahn officials do not deny that their latest coaches date from 1936, the year of the Berlin Olympics, and that many were built in the 1920s. Western experts say that the state of the track is so bad that the trains are forced to run at slow speeds, probably no more than 30 m.p.h. If the S-Bahn had to conform to West German railway safety standards it would be restricted to half this speed. Yet before the war its trains used to run at 50 m.p.h. and it was a popular sport for motorists on the 'Avus' road to race the trains running along a parallel track through the Grunewald. It is ironic that the S-Bahn slogan printed on route maps for tourists is 'Fast and Safe'.

Quite apart from any qualms they may feel about its speed and safety, West Berliners have no love for the S-Bahn. Although the subsidized thirty-pfennig fare is good value, many West Berliners avoid this elevated railway on political grounds. After the building of the Wall, the Western trade unions called for a protest boycott of the S-Bahn which reduced its takings roughly by three-quarters, according to Western estimates. Today less than one-tenth as many passengers use the network of over seventy S-Bahn stations in the West as take the U-Bahn and buses. (In early 1969 the figures were 140,000–160,000 S-Bahn travellers daily compared with a combined total of 1·6 million people carried on underground trains and buses.)

For the visitor, however, an S-Bahn ride to the Friedrich-strasse station within the Eastern sector is of interest, since it affords a close-up view of the Wall and other border fortifications. The line follows the curve of the River Spree and from its raised trestles passengers may look down on the fenced 'control strip' below with patrolling guards. The railway line itself is fenced to prevent anyone trying to reach the track in the hope of clambering aboard a westbound train. Not far away to the south lies the restored Reichstag building hard up against the Western side of the Wall, with the Brandenburg Gate beyond. As the train pulls up before the buffers barring the eastbound track, passengers are greeted by posters proclaiming 'Welcome to Berlin—Capital of the GDR'. It is as if West Berlin simply did not exist.

This 'two-cities' impression dates not only from the building of the Wall in August 1961. The Wall marked the culmination, not the beginning, of the city's division. Already as early as 1948, the year of the currency reform, the blockade and the Western airlift, Berlin was effectively split. True, hundreds of thousands of people still crossed the East–West sector border daily, commuting to work, going to schools and universities or simply paying visits. These travellers used the U-Bahn, the elevated S-Bahn, or crossed the sector line on foot or bicycle without hindrance. But they knew that when they were in the East they no longer enjoyed the protection of Western laws; that they were at the mercy of arbitrary Russian rule. By the early 1950s the former German capital had two city administrations, two different currencies and two basically different systems of economic, social, political and cultural life. No buses or trams crossed the East–West sector border. It was still possible to telephone East Berlin from West Berlin after the direct lines were cut in May, 1952, but only by the absurd device of routing the call via Hanover, in West Germany, a detour of 300 miles. One by one the Soviet zone administrators had slashed the veins and sinews linking the city: it was as if London had been split from Hampstead to Croydon, or New York from Lincoln Tunnel to Kennedy Airport.

We do not need to recapitulate in detail the familiar history of those early post-war years: the city election of 1946 in which the Communist SED party won less than twenty per cent of the votes; the progressive creation of separate, Communist-controlled administrative organs in the Soviet sector; the incorporation of East Berlin into the Soviet zone economic system and the Russian military government ban on moving food supplies across the Soviet sector boundary. Then came the first Berlin crisis in the summer of 1948, arising from the introduction of the newly-reformed West German currency into the Western sectors. The Russians blocked all land access to West Berlin, laying siege to its population for eleven months beginning in June 1948. Only the Allied airlift, which brought over a million tons of coal and half a million tons of food, saved the Western sectors from starving and freezing to death. Having failed to dominate the four-power Allied governing authority the Russians formally walked out of its meetings on July 1, 1948. They kept their place in the Allied Air Safety Centre controlling flights to Berlin and maintained their joint guard duties in Spandau Jail for Nazi war criminals, but all pretence at four-power administration of Berlin had ended.

During the blockade a series of Russian occupation directives destroyed the unity of several public utilities. The pre-war electricity concern which served all Berlin, known as BEWAG, was divided into a BEWAG (West) and BEWAG (East) following a Soviet order at the end of 1948 denying the company control over its plants in the Russian sector. At that time the power stations in the Western sectors had a combined capacity of only 132,000 kilowatts, having lost 244,000 kw of generating capacity in the immediate post-war days when Berlin power stations were deprived of their best equipment by Russian reparation seizures. Only the older generators, designed to be held chiefly in reserve, were left behind. Since these were relatively inefficient the Allies had to airlift more coal than would otherwise have been the case. During the long nights of Berlin's hungry winter of 1948–49, until the blockade was lifted the following May, citizens of the beleaguered Western sectors had to endure almost total darkness. Many city wards were supplied only at irregular hours, so nobody knew exactly when the lights would work. Candles were at a premium. Families huddled in chilly cellars or whatever habitable rooms remained in the city of wartime ruins, hardly daring to use what power there was for fear of consuming too much. When the BEWAG man came to read the meter he could punish offenders by cutting off their electricity for a month.

Power Station West, which had been left an empty shell by Russian machinery seizures, was restored with the help of air-lifted plant. Within a year the first 100,000 kw capacity had been installed. By March 1952, when the Communist authorities cut off all remaining power lines to West Berlin, the Western sectors were better prepared than at the time of the blockade. And by 1966 BEWAG (West) had well over a million kilowatts of installed capacity, much more than the entire city's prewar production.

With gas it was a similar story. All Berlin's eight gasworks were damaged and out of action when the war ended; only one of thirty-eight gas-holders was still in service. By the time of the blockade considerable capacity had been restored, but Western output suffered a setback when insufficient fuel was airlifted in. The division of Berlin led to the creation in March 1949 of two separate gas undertakings and all pipelines were cut off at the sector boundary. Fortunately two-thirds of the city's gasworks were in the West but the coke supplies which had hitherto come to the Western sectors from plants in the East were interrupted. The building of a new coking installation was started in 1957 in the American sector to obviate the need to ship coke in from the Federal Republic.

Thus the separation of electricity and gas networks in the two halves of Berlin was accomplished long before the Wall. Only a few anomalies remained in August 1961: for instance it was found that many houses close to the Wall in the Eastern sector were supplied from the West. But this 'overlap' disappeared when most of these buildings were torn down as the East established its no-man's-land to give border guards a clear field of fire. In reverse, the tiny Western enclave of Steinstücken is supplied from surrounding East Germany. The West Berlin gas and power utilities pay the East a small sum every year in recompense. The costs of Steinstücken's water supplies, which also come from East Germany, are balanced each year against the value of the water supplied by West Berlin to the East German State Railways installations in the Western sectors.

Water became a problem in the West after the Communist side cut off the bulk of its supplies in 1949. But here the separation was not so rigid; for many years the two sides exchanged limited quantities to meet temporary heat-wave shortages. The practice continued even after the Wall, but the last water pipelines were cut at the turn of the year 1966–67.

However, there is one realm of public utilities which it is technically impossible to divide: drainage. Geology and the lie of the land make it inevitable that much of West Berlin's sewage flows downhill toward East Berlin and surrounding East Germany. No Communist Canute can halt this tide and make it flow uphill. Some West Berliners fear that the East Germans could make life very unpleasant for them by simply closing off the sluices. But city authorities doubt that this is possible, and even if it were there would be suitable means of retaliation which they prefer not to discuss. Actually there is no sign that East Germany would do any such thing; on the contrary, it gets tens of millions of D-Marks annually from West Berlin on account of sewage disposal, a tidy sum of convertible currency which it must be loath to lose. In the long run, over the next decade or so, West Berlin hopes to complete its own disposal plants capable of processing four-fifths of its wastes.

Telephone connections between the two halves of the city were cut off on May 27, 1952, except for a handful of lines. The East German government claimed that the step was needed to protect the security of the three-year-old GDR in the face of West German rearmament. Today a West Berliner can dial directly to the Federal Republic, making use of the so-called Radio Bridge carrying 1,500 circuits, but he cannot telephone his friends just across the Wall. Calls to the East are simply not accepted. An East Berliner can telephone anywhere in the Communist bloc, he can even call Bonn if he is prepared to face the delays due to the shortage of lines but he cannot talk to West Berlin. Among the few Wall-crossing lines that remain is a connection between the Western Allied headquarters and the Soviet Embassy in East Berlin. Tempelhof Airport in the West is connected by a direct line to Schönefeld Airport in East Berlin. Mr. Sven Joergensen, manager of the Swedish Travel Bureau in West Berlin, has a line to his branch in East Berlin. KLM Royal Dutch Airlines have a tie line to the Tempelhof–Schönefeld connection. Besides the U-Bahn connection there are lines used by the East German State Railways to their stations and branches in the West. Certain other telephone links exist whose users prefer not to admit it in public.

There are also four or five teleprinter connections, including one used by police on both sides to exchange information on missing and wanted persons. If, for instance, a body is found floating in a river or canal in West Berlin and there is reason to believe it might have drifted across from the East, the Western police send a description to their colleagues across the Wall who can then check their missing list. When West Berlin police suspect that a wanted man has fled across the border the telex connection is used. But in recent years fewer criminals have tried this method of escaping justice. For one thing, the East Germans always interrogate new arrivals from the West and often manage to unearth unsavoury aspects of a man's past. Communist interviewers can usually determine whether an immigrant's professed enthusiasm for the GDR way of life is genuine or merely an attempt to cover up a flight from unpaid debts or a paternity suit. Unwanted arrivals in the GDR are often simply sent back to West Berlin. If they are brought to trial in East Germany, they may expect to serve their sentences in unpleasant Communist jails. In the reverse direction there are very few cases of common criminals fleeing from East to West. One well-placed official informant told me he could not recall a single recent instance of this occurring in Berlin. But in such an event the West would return the refugee to East Germany only if it was sure that he would get a fair trial in the East by Western standards. No fugitive would be returned to the East if he was liable to be accused of political offences against the Communist government. In general, police co-operation astride the Wall is strictly on a case-by-case basis rather than continuous and routine.

Of all links between the two halves of Berlin the closest and most business-like is between postal officials. It is no accident that the issuing of holiday passes to enable West Berliners to cross the Wall has always been entrusted to them. Mail crosses the Wall checkpoints without hindrance, although as a rule it takes at least two days for delivery. Postal co-operation has not always been so smooth: in December 1948 at the height of the blockade all East–West movement of mail was briefly halted on Communist orders, and in the following March ensued the so-called 'stamp war' when the East refused to recognize Western stamps and the West retaliated in kind, causing a deadlock which was only resolved by a decision of the four city commandants six months later.

Inland waterways provide another source of occasional East–West dispute in the divided city. Barges carry most of the bulk traffic upon which West Berlin's economy depends. Before the war Berlin ranked after Duisburg in the Ruhr as the second biggest inland harbour in Europe; even today the Western sectors boast ninety miles of navigable waterways representing two-thirds of the entire Berlin network. But a 1951 agreement between the Occupation Powers gave the inland waterways authority in East Berlin the right to operate the canal locks in the West. Complicated disputes have arisen over lock tolls and transit charges, with the West claiming that while the East has the right to collect the tolls this does not entitle the Communist authority to determine alone the levels at which these charges should be set. Once again there is a principle at stake: West Berlin's independence from East Germany. But broadly speaking the barges get through without difficulty.

Finally, a macabre note. Amid all the patchwork of bans and restrictions curbing movement between the two halves of Berlin one type of travel remains untouched: transport of dead bodies. Every week, sometimes several times daily, state-owned hearses of East Germany cross the Wall checkpoints bringing coffins for burial in family plots in the West and collecting corpses for interment in the East. It all works very smoothly. When someone dies in West Berlin who wishes to be buried with his ancestors in the East, a private Western undertaker will send a telegram to the City Undertakers, a people's enterprise in East Berlin. The hearse duly comes across to collect the body, for a fee of DM 99 (about £10 6s. or $24.75), payable in Western currency. Possibly at the same time the hearse brings over a corpse from East Berlin for delivery to a Western cemetery. Herr Joachim Schöne, who runs one of the largest undertakers in West Berlin, told me the price charged by the nationalized operators in the East is roughly twice the present rate in the West.

'But we are happy to see our friends come over from the East,' he said. 'After all, we know them well from earlier days when we used to work closely with them. They usually give me or one of my competitors a call when they are in West Berlin, to see if we have any more jobs for them.' Nowadays the East has a monopoly on Wall-crossing missions. 'Before the Wall we could just drive into the Eastern sector without any difficulty; in fact we lost a great deal of our regular clientele when the Wall went up,' Herr Schöne said. For a month or so after August 13, 1961, a grim exchange of coffins used to occur at the checkpoints. Hearses from both sides would meet, drive into a sidestreet or patch of waste ground and swap bodies. But the practice used to attract so many morbid sightseers and photographers that it was soon stopped. At present roughly the same number of coffins travel in each direction. The drawback about being buried in the East is that West Berlin relatives cannot visit and tend the grave. Only to attend the actual burial service are West Berliners—occasionally —given special passes by the 'compassionate office' run from East Germany. There is no hope of attending the funeral of a loved-one in East Germany; that is, outside the borders of East Berlin. And there are no 'compassionate' passes for relatives who wish to bring flowers or wreaths on special anniversaries. West Germans as distinct from West Berliners can, of course, get across to the East under the existing rules. In the reverse direction, the GDR issues no permits to its citizens, other than old-age pensioners who may travel anyway, for visits to funerals in the West.

To the question whether live East German refugees ever try to escape to the West in coffins, Herr Schöne replied that the border guards leave no coffin unopened. 'When we send bodies down the Autobahn to West Germany the caskets are opened both at Babelsberg and Marienborn,' he said. He recalled with a sense of outrage that the Communist border guards had once accused him of transporting 'living swine' in his coffins.

'I demanded that they give me proof of their charge,' he said. 'Of course they could not. Ours is a clean business and we mean to keep it that way.'

8

The Battle of Gorleben

GORLEBEN is a village on the River Elbe. It shows up on only the most detailed maps and few Germans have ever heard of it. Yet here was fought, on an overcast October day in 1966, a 'battle' which ranks as the gravest confrontation on the border since the war. To be sure, no shots were fired. But it involved physical violence, with West German boats ramming East German Army launches in midstream while British troops and tanks stood by to give covering fire. Maj. Gen. Mike Strickland, the senior British officer involved, said later: 'It could easily have started a Third World War.' He may have been overstating the case, but certainly the risks were incalculable. Yet the incident was little reported at the time even in Germany, and in the outside world it passed almost unnoticed.

The story is worth recounting because it illustrates the kind of situation which crops up on the border and the roles played by all concerned. It began in September 1966, when the Waterways and Shipping Authority in Hamburg notified the East Germans that it was sending out a small vessel to take soundings on the fifty-nine-mile section of the River Elbe which forms part of the boundary between East and West Germany. This is routine work on any waterway, and on the Elbe it must be done at least once every two years to determine the lie of the channel. Echo soundings show how the natural silting of the river bed has affected the navigable channel and where dredging is needed. Until 1966 the work had been done exclusively by the West Germans, although not without incident. On August 10 the previous year East German guards had fired four machine-gun bursts at the West German survey ship *Kugelbake* when she was taking soundings just upstream of Lauenburg. Ten bullet-holes were counted, but nobody was hurt. The East Germans claimed at the time that the *Kugelbake* had violated the 'State frontiers of the GDR'. The problem with a survey ship is that in order to do her work properly she must cross the river from bank to bank in a zigzag pattern. And this is where the *Kugelbake* ran foul of

East–West disagreement as to where the borderline runs. She could not just stick to the navigable channel, in common with the endless procession of Eastern and Western barges plying un-hindered between Hamburg and Berlin. She had to enter what the GDR claims to be its half of the river. East Germany has never been very precise as to where it believes the frontier runs: sometimes it claims that the line follows the middle of the river and sometimes that it coincides with the navigable channel. Neither definition is helpful for practical purposes since the navigable channel not only changes from year to year; it also meanders constantly across the centre line. But in any case the GDR does not accept West German claims that the border runs along the eastern bank, or at least along an imaginary line con-necting the ends of the groynes jutting out from the eastern bank into the river.

One could argue at length about the legal validity of these claims and counter-claims. Suffice it to say that Britain has never endorsed Bonn's contention that the entire width of the Elbe rightfully belongs to the West. The farthest Britain will go is to promise that British forces will support the West Germans in executing 'normal work' along the entire breadth of the Elbe where it forms the border. Surveying, dredging and buoying are all 'normal' activities by any definition, essential to keeping the Elbe open as a link in one of Berlin's main arteries to the West.

Such was the situation, then, when Hamburg informed the East German waterways office in Magdeburg of the impending 1966 survey operation. But this time Magdeburg did not reply directly. The answer came instead from the East German Trans-port Ministry in East Berlin, which cabled: 'We give you per-mission to survey'. Now the Waterways and Shipping Authority in Hamburg should have rejected this message with the rejoinder that since river conservancy work on the Elbe is a purely West German responsibility, the East Germans had no right either to confer or withhold 'permission'. But for better or worse, the message was accepted and the *Kugelbake* started taking soundings on October 3.

Two days later the East Germans sent out a survey vessel of their own, the *Lenzen*, into the same border stretch of the river. She was working near the Communist barge checkpoint at Schnackenburg, while the *Kugelbake* was operating further down-stream. The *Lenzen* was promptly halted by the West on the ground that the East Germans had no right to engage in river conservancy work along the border length of the Elbe.

Thereupon, on the night of October 6–7, the East Germans promptly sent a message cancelling their 'permission' for the *Kugelbake* to operate. Every time the *Kugelbake* sailed from then on, fast East German river patrol launches put out from the opposite bank and formed a line down the middle of the river, warning the survey ship's skipper that he would cross it at his peril. Not unnaturally, considering the *Kugelbake*'s bullet-holes from the year before, the civilian captain and his crew decided discretion was the better part of valour. They refused Bonn's urgings to ram their way through the opposing line of armed boats, contenting themselves with steaming up and down the navigable channel between the marker buoys. Finally they went on strike rather than engage in any heroics. Deadlock had developed; the lines were drawn. To Sir Frank Roberts, then British Ambassador in Bonn, and his staff, the issue was not simply one of whether or not Britain should back the West Germans against the East Germans. After all, guarding the border was and remains an Allied, not a German, responsibility. And this section of the frontier was strictly Britain's. In the British Embassy's view, the East Germans were engaged in a 'try-on' which must be resisted. They were interfering with a Western practice which had continued unchallenged since the war. If Western surveying was merely a matter of usage and tradition, it was nevertheless part of the 'case law' upon which so much of the West's position *vis-à-vis* the Russians along the zonal border was based. Here the East Germans were acting in clear breach of precedent, and the Foreign Office in London was advised accordingly. The head of the British Military Mission attached to Soviet military headquarters in Potsdam was told to make an oral protest to the Russian Chief of Staff. The Soviet officer replied predictably that this was not a Russian but an East German responsibility.

On the diplomatic level, the incident was beginning to escalate. It was clearly building up towards a confrontation which might involve the use of force. The British obviously needed to have the West German government solidly behind them—it would not do to be more forthright in defence of German interests than the Germans themselves. But the Bonn government was far from solid. At the thought of a physical confrontation the Transport Ministry began to blanch. Firstly, if there was any shooting and ramming, what would happen to the *Kugelbake* and her costly echo-sounding gear? Secondly, would the East Germans retaliate by halting barge traffic to Berlin? Since barges carried no less than 1,561,200 tons of bulk cargo to Berlin in 1965 and were in the process of carrying 1,601,300 tons in 1966 such a move would constitute a threat to the isolated city. The Transport Ministry, whose prime function after all is to keep traffic moving, began to temporize and even to argue that there was no particular urgency about carrying out the survey operation. On the other hand the Bonn Ministry for All-German Affairs under Dr. Erich Mende was strongly supporting the British position. One key official had in fact been urging Brig. Gen. Heinrich Müller, commander of the Federal Frontier Defence Force, to use force if necessary to escort the *Kugelbake* through the Communist blockade. General Müller resisted this entreaty on the ground that the political issues must first be resolved.

The issue went to the West German Cabinet, led at the time by Dr. Ludwig Erhard. It decided that the *Kugelbake* should resume her survey and endeavour to cross the Elbe from bank to bank. Britain now had the requisite German support and on October 14 Sir Frank Roberts gave his American and French colleagues George McGhee and François Seydoux an account of the position and the action Britain proposed to take. The other Ambassadors took careful note but did not react. As a matter of fact they must have known beforehand what was in the wind since whenever problems arise on the border or in relation to Berlin they are discussed in a four-power diplomatic working group comprising American, British, French and West German officials.

Sir Frank was also in touch with the heads of the British Army of the Rhine and Royal Air Force, Germany, through the so-called Commanders-in-Chief Committee. By this time the issue was not whether to assert the *Kugelbake*'s right to criss-cross the Elbe but how to break the Communist blockade.

Gen. Müller was assigned the task of working out a tactical plan. It looked more like a job for a naval officer than a former Panzer commander. But the general said later that his experience of tank battles in North Africa stood him in good stead. The Western boats must somehow break the blockade of a dozen or more Communist patrol craft and clear a passage for the *Kugelbake*. Success depended upon creating the maximum confusion in the enemy line, and this in turn depended upon close timing, sur-

prise, speed and manœuvrability on the Western side. The problem of the *Kugelbake*'s striking crew was quickly resolved: Gen.
Müller simply replaced the upper-deck and engine-room crew
with men from his coastal patrol craft on the Baltic. Technical
echo-sounding experts from the *Kugelbake*'s normal crew were
kept aboard. To beef up his mixed fleet of Western craft, he
brought in two pontoon boats by lorry to Gorleben's little
harbour, under cover of darkness. He knew that with their powerful outboard motors they could move fast and create large bow-
waves. In his conception, bow-waves and wash were essential to
break the opposing line. The plan envisaged two phases of the
operation. In Phase One the thirty-six-ton *Kugelbake*, escorted by
two West German patrol boats, would approach the blockading
'boom' of People's Army boats twice and turn back each time if
necessary. Phase Two would be to force a passage. This would be
done by dividing the Western boats, most of which would still
be in the harbour, into two 'half flotillas' each comprising one
fast pontoon, one fast rescue launch, and at least four Customs
boats.

If Phase Two became necessary, these two lines of vessels
would emerge from the harbour and approach the East German
line from the flanks, moving towards the centre, parallel and
close to the Communist boats. When the leading boats in each
Western column were close to the middle, the entire fleet would
turn towards the East German line and try to ram its way through
the gaps. The aim then would be to divide the enemy craft into
two widely-separated groupings, leaving a broad intervening
stretch of relatively calm water through which the *Kugelbake* could
steam to the eastern bank and conduct her soundings. Meanwhile a helicopter would fly low overhead, its down-draught
adding to the waves. But for the helicopter, the plan had much in
common with naval battles of the seventeenth and eighteenth
centuries! It won rapid approval from all concerned in Bonn and
London. Meanwhile the British Army of the Rhine decided to
use tanks and armoured cars from the Seventh Armoured Brigade
to provide support from the western bank. This force was commanded by Brig. Richard Worsley, whose orders were to set up
his headquarters near Gorleben, link up with the British Frontier
Service and whatever German authorities were present, and take
appropriate action to 'restore the situation'. He hid away his two
troops of Centurion tanks behind the trees so that they should be

invisible to the other side, but ranged some of his dozen Ferret armoured cars openly along the western bank. His communications with BAOR headquarters in Rheindahlen, where Edward Tomkins, Minister of the British Embassy, was assigned for liaison, was by direct radio which was entirely 'secure'.

General Müller had spent hours on October 17, the eve of the 'battle', conferring with Herr Lücke, the Interior Minister under whose competence the Frontier Defence Force lies. They met, oddly enough, not in Bonn but at the secret underground shelter in the Eifel Mountains built as an emergency headquarters for use in case of war. For the Gorleben incident happened to coincide with the so-called Fallex exercise in which most of Bonn's top officials flew to this bomb-proof hideout in an emergency drill. If the Gorleben affair *had* started to escalade into a shooting-match, the Bonn government at least would have been safe! During his talk with Herr Lücke, General Müller had been carefully briefed to use firearms only in self-defence, an order with which he thoroughly concurred. On the morning of the confrontation he flew direct from the Eifel to Gorleben by helicopter to take command of his river-borne troops and a battalion of Frontier Defence Force men ashore. He, too, had a signals truck at hand providing telephone communications with his Minister. Also on hand at Gorleben were the men of the British Frontier Service, some of whom had had very little sleep since the affair began brewing weeks earlier. Two of them were to distinguish themselves that day: Colin Ball, who provided invaluable local advice to the commanders on the bank, and Freddy Hope, who stood exposed on the wheelhouse of the *Kugelbake* in his distinctive uniform as a symbol of Britain's presence. The British Embassy's man on the scene, who also played a significant part in the day's events, was Hugh Stephenson, a twenty-eight-year-old Second Secretary who said to Aubrey Parnell, a B.F.S. officer, on the morning of the battle: 'You know, we're basing all this on your claim that the East Germans never shoot at the British Frontier Service!'

Ball said later that Stephenson would have carried the immediate responsibility for deciding whether to shoot back or call off the operation if the other side had started firing. But others agree that this onerous responsibility lay with Brigadier Worsley as the BAOR local commander. Doubtless Brig. Worsley would not have acted without taking advice from both Stephenson and

Strickland, who as a Major General was his senior. Gen. Strickland, who had only just taken over as head of the British Joint Services Liaison Organization, a body that provides liaison with the West German armed forces, had the British Frontier Service under his wing. But he had only an advisory rôle at Gorleben and could issue no orders to Brig. Worsley. He could, however, pull his rank on Brig. Gen. Müller, and this was a reason for his presence. The British felt that Gen. Müller must be held to account if the situation were to be kept properly in hand.

'Viscount Monckton, BAOR Chief of Staff, took me aside and asked if I would go up to Gorleben to sort it out,' Gen. Strickland recalls. 'I got hold of Hugh Stephenson, feeling it was no good my going up without a proper Embassy contact. We met at my house. It was at this stage—I never saw it in writing—that I was told that Britain would resist this East German challenge, restore the situation and use force if necessary.' He arrived at dawn on the 18th in Gorleben, reflecting with amazement on the speed with which London had given BAOR authority to shoot if necessary. Brig. Worsley was worried: supposing the order to shoot were given, how were his gunners to pick out the East German boats in what would doubtless become a mêlée of small craft? It was an impossible target for a sailor, let alone a soldier. Nor were there many suitable targets on the opposite bank; unlike the West, the Communist side had drawn up no armoured cars or tanks to impress their opponents. Western helicopters had been up to take a good look, but all they could see was a few machine-gun positions. Brig. Worsley was to remain a worried man all day. Not that he was the only one.

They held a morning conference in Brig. Worsley's headquarters in a barn, spreading maps on the table. 'Müller wanted to speak first, to deploy his plan,' Gen. Strickland recalls.'I said that this was Worsley's headquarters and he should speak first. Müller got rather excited and wanted to be aggressive. I had to pipe up and talk to him very firmly, saying that we all had an interest in this, using my "grade" on him, as the Americans say. After that the whole thing became much easier and the plan was finally ordered into effect. I said very firmly that everybody must stick to this plan and not do anything extra.' (Gen. Müller, now in retirement, does not recall having had any scenes with Gen. Strickland, with whom he claims to have had an excellent relationship.)

It had been agreed that in order to dispel any possible mis-understanding a BFS officer should cross to the other side to tell the East Germans from the start that the *Kugelbake* was about to resume her surveying operations and that they should cease their interference. This was done by Ron Sherrell, speaking through a megaphone to a group of East German boats moored beside a groyne. Their crews did not react in any way. Indeed, they hardly even looked up.

Meanwhile the local Press, with the exception of a television cameraman, had been told to keep back in the village. The only civilian spectators on the western bank were a few puzzled farmhands. At one stage Gen. Strickland was asked to walk about a little and display his impressive 'brass-hat' presence to the other side. An East German launch promptly put out from the far side and cruised slowly up and down close to the western bank while a People's Army officer solemnly photographed him with a cine camera. Phase One was then executed according to plan. The *Kugelbake* set out, with her two escorts, towards the opposite shore. Thereupon the fast Communist launches promptly roared into line to bar her progress, as they had so often done be-fore. Instead of trying to ram, the *Kugelbake* meekly turned back as planned, and repeated the manœuvre. A big R.A.F. helicopter and an East German helicopter were by now flying up and down the western and eastern banks.

Then, at 2.15 p.m., the critical Phase Two was put into effect. Four Ferret armoured cars carrying machine-guns took up care-fully rehearsed fire positions in full view on the western bank, while other armoured vehicles and tanks assumed firing positions behind the trees. The two columns of Western boats sailed out toward the line of waiting Communist vessels, watched with excitement and anxiety by the little knot of officers on the bank. Every West German boat had a BFS officer aboard, the 'Red Line' radio link to Rhine Army headquarters was open and General Müller's signals truck was in touch with the Federal Government in the secret bunker.

Stephenson, who had been doing much of the interpreting between the British and German commanders, recalls: 'Our plan was that each of our boats would mark an opposing boat, as in rugby football. The pontoons would make a hole through the line, and the *Kugelbake* would go through. It didn't quite work out like that. There was a ten-minute mêlée (it seemed like twenty minutes) and then the East German boats were penned in between the groynes on their side of the river.'

Colin Ball described the scene: 'The other side had fourteen boats forming a wall down the middle of the river. We routed them completely. Our boats churned up the water, aided by the Frontier Defence Force helicopter which flew so low it had to be recalled for fear of chopping off the BFS men's heads. Before the other side knew where they were their boats were locked in groyne water with our boats hemming them in. The *Kugelbake* went ahead and zigzagged across the river for twenty minutes before being recalled.'

Gen. Strickland told me: 'When the mêlée developed, that was when I expected firing to start. But I was getting reports from the boats that the other side were not reaching for their guns. Actually the crews of the opposing boats were white with fright. It was at this time that a major on the opposite bank started running around, shouting through a megaphone at his chaps. We never picked up what he said, but I believe he was telling them not to pick up their guns. In the middle of the confusion Müller's helicopter was flying very low to cause a downdraught. I was very angry because it could have ruined the whole thing—supposing its engine had failed. I shouted to Müller to order it back, which he did.' The East German boats, Strickland said, tried to maintain their line without success. He added: 'I personally am quite convinced that the Russians or someone had told them to do their best to keep in line but not do anything more than that whatever happened.' Western observers noticed that each Communist boat had an East German officer aboard, which is unusual. Instead of carrying their carbines slung over their shoulders the Communist crews were apparently unarmed. If they had weapons aboard, they must have been stowed in gun racks below decks. All this was naturally reassuring to the Western commanders. The only violence was the bumping and scraping of opposing boats in the midstream confusion. No launches on either side were sunk, but there was some rasping and splintering as the wooden-hulled Communist craft came into collision with the robust steel sides of the West's larger launches.

No watcher on the bank could have been prouder of the bloodless victory than Gen. Müller, whose plan had worked so splendidly. 'What the other side failed to recognize,' said the white-haired German general later, 'was that the wash from our boats was pushing them back towards their bank. As soon as I realized this myself I issued a change of orders. Instead of sticking to my original plan to divide the opposing force into two groups in midstream, I told my men to push them back between the groynes—and we succeeded.' He then instructed the *Kugelbake* to proceed with its surveying. The Frontier Defence Force crews had no weapons in their boats, and the German Customs men in the Customs boats had nothing more than side-arms. After the *Kugelbake* had completed her twenty-minute stint of zigzagging from bank to bank, while the hemmed-in East German crews exchanged insults with their Western 'captors', the entire West German force returned triumphantly to harbour.

It was magnificent, but was it worthwhile? There are two distinct issues here. Firstly, could the entire confrontation have been avoided if it had been better handled at the outset, before it became a test of strength? The answer is probably yes. Secondly, once the East Germans had begun blockading the middle of the river, did the West have any alternative to forcing a passage? Clearly the answer to this second question is no. If the matter had been dealt with on the lowly technical level of river conservancy officials—who continue to hold regular East–West meetings—it could probably have been ironed out without a political *cause célèbre*. After all, the original East German demand was on the face of it quite reasonable: that the GDR should be allowed to engage in Elbe surveying as well. Indeed, this demand subsequently has been quietly granted. Since the Battle of Gorleben survey ships of both sides have been calmly taking soundings in the river without incident. (Although it should be noted that the East Germans have confined their surveying to their own side of the river, mostly in order to chart and dredge the entrances to their own harbours.) If only the Magdeburg waterways authority in East Germany had not raised the political stakes by sending the routine Western notification to the Transport Ministry in East Berlin instead of answering it direct, the story would have been different. But the blame is not all on the East German side. It was surely a mistake for the West to halt the East German survey ship *Lenzen* on October 5. Why did nobody at that time try to achieve a live-and-let-live compromise whereby both sides could take soundings in the Elbe?

In any event, the chance was missed; the confrontation became inevitable. It was inescapable not only for the reasons listed above

but quite simply because Britain could not afford to appear to
back down in face of Communist pressure. For years past Britain
had been criticized in Bonn for tacitly allowing East German river
patrol boats to enter the border section of the Elbe without special
permits. Ever since 1950 these craft had been stationed on the
lower Elbe opposite Western territory, a constant source of
irritation. Now that this new dispute had arisen, British officials
were anxious to avoid giving the West Germans new cause to
complain of alleged British 'weakness'. Certainly there were wider
political considerations too. Nobody wanted to rock the boat of
Anglo-German relations at a time when London wanted Bonn's
backing against General de Gaulle's efforts to block British entry
to the Common Market.

Given the need—by mid-October—to 'face down' the challenge, it must be acknowledged that both the British and the
West German authorities played their parts with consummate
success. But they were lucky. If the crews of the East German
patrol boats had reached for their guns anything might have
happened. After the 'battle' the East German government conferred decorations upon the People's Army troops involved for
their restraint. *Neues Deutschland*, official organ of the East
German Communist party, commented with some truth that it
was only the 'prudence' shown by the GDR border soldiers
which averted 'still more serious consequences'. But the East
Germans were incensed by the slap in the face they had suffered.
Their foreign ministry warned in a statement on October 21:
'Attacks of this nature on the GDR frontier . . . place navigation
on the River Elbe, including the traffic between the two German
states and the traffic with West Berlin, in jeopardy. The GDR
Ministry for Foreign Affairs states that the authors and lackeys
of these grave frontier provocations must bear the full responsibility for all the consequences of their violations of international
law.'

Talking of international law, the legal tangle over where the
borderline runs in the Elbe remains today as confused as ever.
All three parties involved: East Germany, West Germany and
Britain, still cling to their different versions. The only tangible
change since Gorleben is, as we have seen, that both East and
West Germany now engage in river conservancy work instead of
the West alone. This looks to the detached observer more like a
victory for the East than a gain for the West. Of course, no one

can say whether the *Kugelbake* would have been allowed to operate unmolested since October 1966 if the East Germans had not been taught a salutary lesson at Gorleben. The argument is hypothetical. So in retrospect one can only conclude that the case for staging the Gorleben confrontation with all its attendant risks is unproven, to say the least. And there is much to be said for the view that the original dispute could have been handled successfully by the water-ways experts without the politicians, diplomats and soldiers becoming involved at all. The final irony of Gorleben is that the river conservancy officials of East and West actually held one of their routine fortnightly meetings on the very day of the 'battle'. They conferred at Hitzacker, further downstream on the Elbe, to discuss such matters as the location of buoys. Would it be too fanciful to suppose that at some stage they shook their heads in joint wonder and sorrow at the excesses of politicians?

9

Transport and Travel

BEREFT of its engine, the half-empty train from Bonn stood forlornly at Helmstedt station waiting for an East German locomotive to pull it to Berlin. Passengers in the dark compartments gazed wearily at the snow flurries outside. They were huddled in overcoats, for the heating was as dead as the lights. Three hours already the line of coaches had been stranded at the last station in the West; there was not even a cup of coffee to be had in the dining car. 'Sorry,' said the friendly East German attendant, 'but we are not allowed to serve a thing till we get through Marienborn.' A brightly-lit British military train bearing the Union Jack and 'Royal Corps of Transport' in large letters on its sides pulled out of Helmstedt toward Berlin. Passengers in the civilian train watched enviously. Finally a westbound train arrived in a cloud of steam, its GDR engine was uncoupled and hitched to the idle string of coaches. As if by magic, the lights came on, heating pipes crackled back to life and the long-forsaken train resumed its eastward journey. Ten minutes later it crossed a line of floodlit fencing stretching away into the night: this was the border. Drawing into Marienborn, the East German checkpoint, the train was bathed in bluish light from mercury vapour lamps. All around, the passengers noticed, the station was ringed with wire-mesh fences. Jackbooted guards carrying pistols and carbines paced the icy platform. Some came aboard with short metal ladders to search the train from end to end and top to bottom. They even opened rubbish receptacles in the corridors. Others checked passports and sold transit visas to Berlin at five marks apiece.

Yet the halt at Marienborn lasted only a quarter of an hour. The blue-uniformed guards were polite and correct, and they gave change in West-marks, not in GDR currency which cannot be used in West Berlin. The train rolled onward towards the divided city, travelling slowly because of the dilapidated track. Even according to the timetable the 110-mile distance required three and a half hours, but this time it took five. There was only one stop before Berlin, at the Griebnitzsee checkpoint on the city boundary where the Communist sentries had dogs as well as ladders. Some of the older passengers stayed aboard when the rest alighted at the Zoo station in West Berlin: they were East German pensioners returning from visiting relatives in the Federal Republic. For the train moved on to the Friedrichstrasse station in East Berlin, then to Frankfurt-an-der-Oder and Warsaw.

It was made up of mixed coaches from West and East Germany. West German *Bundesbahn* compartments contain travel pictures of Heidelberg and Cologne, East German *Reichsbahn* carriages show photographs of Rostock and Dresden. Otherwise the coaches of East and West differ in comfort and cleanliness—the capitalist seats are deeper but the Communist ones are cleaner. Signs warning of dire penalties for improper use of the emergency brake are posted in Russian as well as German, French and Italian in the Communist compartments; English is preferred to Russian in the West. It is one of the quaint paradoxes of rail travel between East and West Germany that while locomotives and train crews are invariably changed at the border, dining and sleeping car attendants may stay aboard. The reason, a dining car waiter explained, is that 'it's too complicated to hand over an inventory of all our stocks of beer and sausages at the frontier.' This waiter, encountered in a West German restaurant car attached to another 'interzonal' train, said he did not feel particularly privileged. He had to buy a five-mark visa for every journey, just like anybody else. It had to be stamped into his passport, and since he travelled the Frankfurt–Berlin route every six days his passport would soon be filled. 'Everywhere else I go, such as Holland and France, I can travel on my West German identity card alone,' he said. 'Only in going from one Germany to the other do I need a passport and visa.' Another oddity about Berlin-bound trains is that although they usually stop at every major station in East Germany nobody is allowed to get on or off until the terminus is reached. Nor, for that matter, is there any loading or unloading of parcels and letters at these intermediate stations. Westerners are mystified: the only explanation is that the halts have to be made for technical reasons to do with the schedule.

Even the military trains between Berlin and the West have to be pulled by East German locomotives. This gives rise to a traditional comedy enacted at Helmstedt each May 1 when the

East German engines arrive festooned with red flags to celebrate the Communist holiday. The Allies just as regularly protest that they will not have their trains decked with Communist banners, and there have been occasions when troop trains have waited until midnight on May Day for the removal of the bunting. But normally the changeover of engines and crews at Helmstedt and the other frontier crossings goes smoothly according to a well-established routine. Five passenger trains cross the border daily in each direction at Helmstedt alone during the winter; in the summer this number rises to nine. Herr Rolf Münch, station-master at Helmstedt since 1954, says the usual procedure is simply that crews of East and West disembark and then take the next trains back in the direction from which they came. But in the summer some of the East German crews have to stay in the West overnight; they are perfectly free to move about the town of Helmstedt if they wish, and they stay in the usual railwaymen's hostels. Once they are in Helmstedt there are, of course, no armed guards to stop them defecting.

But in point of fact amazingly few East German railwaymen have sought asylum in the West. Harry Deterling's celebrated escape with a complete train in December 1961 was one of the exceptions. Generally East German train crews remain loyal, for a variety of reasons. Many of the *Reichsbahn* crews who ply between Berlin and the border actually live in West Berlin. It must be a curious sensation for them to live in the West and work for the East. But they are paid in Western marks—albeit on the East German State Railways salary scale which is slightly lower than the Federal Railways rates. And many of them have worked for the State Railways since long before the Wall and the sharpening tensions. Even for those who do not already live in West Berlin, there are hindrances to flight. Wives and families would be left behind; a new start must be made in the West. Those who are privileged to cross the border to stations such as Helmstedt can take advantage of the Western shops, so they have in a sense the best of both worlds. Another reason for the lack of escapes is the fact that German railwaymen on both sides of the border have a certain *esprit de corps*. Traditionally the German railway guard or ticket inspector has always enjoyed a privileged status. Particularly in East Germany, he boasts a splendid uniform with gold braid and buttons. He is too proud to run away. 'Nobody has asked us for asylum for many years,' says Herr Münch. 'Nor do I know of a single case of a refugee smuggling himself across by train in the last two or three years.'

If East German railwaymen seldom flee, there are plenty of other inhabitants of the GDR who would like to smuggle themselves across by train. Some have succeeded, clinging precariously to the axle boxes beneath goods wagons or concealed within packing cases. One youngster came across from an East German factory yard in a crate just before Christmas 1968. He climbed into the twenty-by-thirteen-foot box destined for delivery to a firm near Selb in Bavaria. He thought the journey would take two days but it lasted twice as long. When Western workmen found him crouching in a corner of the crate he was half-frozen, cramped and hungry. Aged only fifteen, the boy soon recovered from his ordeal and was sent to live with his aunt in West Germany.

But he was lucky. East German checkpoint guards use Alsatians trained to sniff out human stowaways aboard westbound trains. A good view of the 'Trapos' (Transportpolizei) at work may be had from a Western vantage point overlooking the East German border station of Ellrich. One stands just above the ruined barracks of Hitler's erstwhile Juliushütte concentration camp whose fences—now replaced—once formed part of Ulbricht's border. Down in the valley lies Ellrich Station with the town beyond. A single-line track leads to the West, barred at the border by a flimsy metal gate. The GDR allows only goods trains to cross at Ellrich and each is subjected to a long, slow search. Nobody is to be seen in the vicinity of a westbound train except the guards leading their Alsatians. The silence is broken only by the dogs' deep-throated barking. Finally the train is cleared, the barrier opens by remote control and the steam train lumbers through to the West. All around, there are fences and dog runs and bunkers. . . .

Such are the outward and obvious characteristics of rail travel across the line, but they betray nothing of the planning and negotiation behind the scenes which make it possible. Four times a year technical experts from the Federal Railways headquarters in Frankfurt meet their East German opposite numbers to discuss fares, freight rates and timetables. This is the kind of meeting that railway administrators of any country hold at regular intervals with colleagues from abroad. But between the two Germanies there is a difference. Until 1964 the negotiations were more or less non-political. Since then the East Germans have been trying to use the talks as a vehicle for gaining recognition of the GDR and its government. While the East German delegations to these meetings used to consist only of State Railways experts, since 1964 they have included government representatives. They send a Traffic Ministry official as leader of the delegation, backed up by a Foreign Ministry 'adviser'. This in contrast to the Western negotiating teams which consist exclusively of Federal Railways people. For Bonn's view is that governments have no business interfering with what should be a purely technical matter to be settled between railwaymen.

But this was only the beginning. Fare and timetable conferences produce protocols—and here again the East Germans saw a chance to press for political recognition. Their delegates began to demand that the written protocols should include such phrases as 'trans-frontier traffic' which conflicted with West Germany's dogmatic refusal to regard the East–West German border as a legal frontier. Instead of the old procedure of having the protocols signed simply by the Federal Railways and the East German State Railways, the East Germans began in 1964 to insist that their Traffic Ministry official should sign as well. They got their way for the first time in a protocol signed on October 30, 1964 after a conference held in the East German city of Magdeburg. But the Federal Railways delegates fought back, and not without success. As late as February 1966 they were able to regain lost ground in the 'protocol war' by securing an agreement signed only by the two railway administrations. In the long run, however, the West was bound to lose since the East held the trump cards. At all stages of the negotiations the Federal Railways team was painfully aware that in the last resort the East Germans could always cut off the trains to Berlin. The Transport Ministry in Bonn, which was consulted whenever the political battles occurred, could only advise the Federal Railways experts to fight a rear-guard action. Slice by slice the West had to give way to Communist 'salami tactics'. In each new round of talks the East Germans refused to discuss any substantive matters until their latest political demands had been met. Sometimes they rose from their seats and threatened to walk out in a body. Yet outside the conference room all was sweetness and light; the Western delegates were wined and dined by their East German hosts and taken to the opera. When alternate meetings were held on Western soil, the Federal Railways returned the hospitality. Yet for the East Germans visiting the West there could be no unauthorized excursions. Once a State Railways official in one of these delegations took advantage of his trip to visit his son living in West Germany. The official was never again selected for a negotiating team.

Such incidents apart, the conferences continued in a routine fashion. By the end of 1967 the East Germans had won all their political demands. They obtained a protocol signed on their side by an official representing 'The Minister for Traffic of the German Democratic Republic' and no one else.

There are other ways in which East Germany has tried to use railway negotiations for political purposes, to raise the status of the GDR as an independent, sovereign state. For instance, they have been insisting in the U.I.C. (International Railway Union) that traffic between the two Germanies is not 'intra-German' as Bonn claims but international. While Bonn allows East German train crews to come to Helmstedt and other border stations on their State Railways cards alone, the East Germans insist that Federal Railways personnel produce U.I.C. international passes. Worse still, the GDR cancelled on July 1, 1965 the old all-German tariff arrangement which had been in force since Germany was unified in the nineteenth century. They claimed that West German freight arriving at East German frontier stations should be covered by international bills of lading, a demand that the Federal Republic refused. So the system ever since has been that goods trains arriving at Marienborn and other East German border checkpoints are held up while officials replace all the Federal Railways wagon tickets with new ones for the remainder of the journey.

Nevertheless, despite these political hindrances the trains continue to run and the negotiators of East and West Germany continue to meet. Indeed, the 1969 railway fare and timetable talks went uncommonly smoothly. But still there are practical problems. Take the state of the track: West Germany has often tried to persuade the East Germans to improve the condition of the rails on their side of the border, without success. In places the Helmstedt–Berlin line is single track and trains must pull off into sidings to allow traffic to pass in the opposite direction. But the East Germans derive little profit from the trains serving West Berlin. They prefer to devote scarce materials and labour to improving the north–south links between the port of Rostock on the Baltic and the industrial areas around Leipzig and Halle. West Germany's repeated offers of track material and locomotives have been rejected.

Considering the slowness of the trains to and from Berlin, considering the red tape at the Communist checkpoints, it is not surprising that the volume of railway traffic is decreasing. More and more passengers are going by air; more and more goods are carried in trucks and barges, with trains running a poor third. Bonn officials fear that if the present trend continues the time may come when the East Germans will call a halt to all passenger rail travel between Berlin and the West. In the year following the June 1968 introduction of passport and visa restrictions at the East German border checkpoints, only about 12,000 passengers chose to go by train between Hanover and Berlin. This represented a very considerable falling-off compared to previous years. But at the same time the number of people flying in both directions between Hanover and Berlin shot upwards, from 335,000 between July 1967 and June 1968 to 625,000 in the year beginning July 1968. Pan American and British European Airways, who use the Hanover–Berlin air corridor, benefit greatly from subsidized flights. For the Bonn government responded to the GDR's passport and visa curbs by granting an extra subsidy to permit a cheap air shuttle service through this, the shortest of Berlin's air routes to the West. The subsidy now represents nearly half the price of every ticket, and it was set at this level to enable the traveller to fly from Hanover to Berlin at no greater cost than the second-class rail fare.

Buses plying between Hanover and Berlin are also suffering from the air shuttle service. One bus line alone could easily handle the few remaining passengers—less than 800 a month. In former years there was enough demand to keep six bus lines at work. So here again Bonn has had to provide a subsidy.

By contrast, lorry traffic across the East–West border has increased sharply since 1962, stimulated by East Germany's efforts to save foreign exchange. Every ton of merchandise carried by rail from East to West Germany involves freight charges payable in hard West-marks for transit across the Federal Republic to its destination; shipment by road saves much of this expense. East German trucks are compelled to pay the same road taxes as West German hauliers for the loads and distances involved, but on balance such tolls are heavier in the GDR than the

Federal Republic. Altogether 48,500 lorryloads of East German goods came across the five border road crossings during 1967, five times the number in 1962, and the trend continued upward in 1968. Generally the truck traffic moves smoothly, but the East German checkpoint guards have begun turning back Western lorries carrying certain banned goods such as school atlases showing the GDR under any other name or describing the ex-German territories East of the Oder–Neisse Line as 'under Polish administration'. In March 1969 this harassment assumed potentially more serious dimensions with the repeated turnback of trucks carrying so-called 'military goods' between West Berlin and the West. Since anything from buttons to binoculars can be labelled 'military' this short-lived embargo held endless possibilities for mischief.

Almost half the bulk cargo upon which West Berlin's 2·2 million inhabitants depend is carried by barges plying Germany's extensive canal network. Two busy waterways cross the East–West border: the River Elbe at Schnackenburg and the Mittelland Canal at Rühen, near the Volkswagen town of Wolfsburg. Thus Berlin is connected to Hamburg on the North Sea and, through the Mittelland Canal, to the Ruhr and the Rhine at Duisburg. These waterways are used not only for Berlin traffic. They also carry goods moving in East–West German trade and cargoes of Czech kaolin and Polish timber. But by far the largest proportion of their traffic is to West Berlin. The barges chug slowly eastward to supply the city's daily fuel and raw material needs. Most of them return empty: in 1968 barges carried almost five million tons of cargo to West Berlin and brought only 470,000 tons back to the Federal Republic.[1] Over two-thirds of West Berlin's products come out in lorries.

Every barge, like every goods train, is closely searched at the Communist checkpoints by frontier guards with dogs. Contrary to the belief in Bonn, the East German barge skippers are allowed to bring their wives across (although school-age children normally stay behind). It would not be difficult for an East German barge skipper to defect with his family to the West, but nowadays they never do. They spend so much time in the West anyway that there is little incentive to change sides. But barge crews travelling across the border are constantly on guard against stowaways. As one West German skipper encountered at Rühen put it: 'My

[1] See Appendix C.

nightmare is that those Communist sentries will find some refugee who has climbed aboard without my knowledge—then I would wind up in jail.' Actually the Customs officers at Rühen say that not a single refugee has come across by barge for many years. Nobody knows how many have tried and failed.

Western skippers are required to moor—except in emergencies—at prescribed points in East German canals. If the weather is foggy in the morning and they cannot move, they may be stuck for the day. For even if the mist should clear by afternoon, they cannot proceed unless they are sure of reaching the next permitted mooring-place by nightfall. This of course can entail considerable delay. Canal tolls amounting to at least one mark per ton of cargo are exacted by East Germany. Western Customs men at Rühen advance the money, which may run to DM 1,000 (£104 or $250) for a single Berlin-bound barge, to skippers as they leave the West. It is collected at the Buchhorst checkpoint just across the border. Close to the wooden Customs hut on the quayside at Rühen is a bar where many of the barge crews stop for a beer and make their last purchases in Western currency before crossing to the East. Sometimes in winter the canals are closed for weeks or months on end by ice, sometimes traffic is halted by 'lock-repairs' in East Germany which have an uncanny way of occurring at times of Berlin tension. But the barge skippers take these delays and imposts philosophically. By now the system of Communist tolls and regulations has become so well established that the barge crews take it in their stride. The canal fraternity is a close-knit one: many of the skippers hail each other and the Customs men by name. Despite the toll charges, shipment by canal is still the cheapest way to move bulk goods, and the barge skippers know it.

Neither in canal traffic nor in road transport is there any East–West contact comparable with the regular railway negotiations. There is a reason for this: the railways carry many international trains across Germany from such places as Paris, Ostend and Hook of Holland to East European capitals including Moscow and Warsaw. Therefore the State Railways in East Germany cannot shut themselves off from the outside world; they must live up to international standards. But except for a relatively small number of Polish and Czech barges, all the vessels crossing the East–West German border belong either to the Federal Republic or the GDR. This means that the East Germans can operate by their own rules. They set their canal tolls and regulations by unilateral decree. They refuse to talk to the Waterways and Shipping Authority in Hamburg. The only contacts that exist in the inland waterways field are on the level of the river conservancy officials on the Elbe or the lock-keepers in Berlin. Locks in West Berlin's waterways are operated, like the S-Bahn and the long-distance railways, by East Germany. The West Berlin lock-keepers have a telephone link to their employers, the Transport Ministry in East Berlin. This connection has sometimes been used to relay messages unofficially from the Bonn Transport Ministry. The East Germans would like to deal directly with this ministry but in the past this has been generally refused. 'We are a legalistically-minded people,' a senior Bonn official observed, 'not so pragmatic as you British. Perhaps we Germans tend to be too "juridical" in outlook. But our government's view is that if ever we talked to an East German ministry we would be raising the stature of the GDR—and that, of course, is precisely what Ulbricht wants.'

Nevertheless the 'juridical' West Germans have ventured into pragmatic contacts with the unrecognized GDR government from time to time. Herr Wolfgang von Dorrer, the Bonn Transport Ministry official in charge of East–West German matters, met his GDR opposite number in East Berlin to discuss the Communist imposition of road tolls in 1955. Early in 1961 he crossed into East Berlin again to persuade the GDR Transport ministry to drop its canal tolls which had been instituted in May 1958. He went over once more in September 1969 to begin a new series of negotiations covering rail, road and canal issues. Nobody expected these talks to produce quick or dramatic results. But it is a measure of the changing mood in Bonn that these contacts could occur in 1969 without raising a political storm, even though they began at the height of the West German general election campaign. The prelude to these 1969 talks was an agreement to reopen a line through a corner of East Germany which had traditionally served a potash plant just on the Western side of the border in Hesse. The East Germans had closed this line, which goes by way of Dankmarshausen and Gerstungen, in 1967, after the West refused to meet a Communist demand for increased tolls and accumulated back payments totalling DM 6 million (£625,000 or $1·5 million). But then suddenly in July 1969 the East evidently decided it needed to exploit the line to win foreign exchange. After talks in Berlin and Frankfurt the East Germans

Typical border country, showing the double fencing with the lethal mined strip in between, and a watchtower.

Border markers on the Bavarian–Thuringian stretch of frontier near Coburg. The concrete post is painted in the black, red, and gold colors of Germany and bears the East German hammer-and-dividers symbol.

Hans Hossfeld with his daughter and wife (at window) in front of his house in the Hessian border village of Philippsthal. The far end of the house is marooned and empty, since it lies on the East German side of the line.

The wall dividing the village of Mödlareuth on the Bavarian–Thuringian border. The area to the right under the floodlights is East German.

The border where it runs across the beach into the Baltic Sea on the Priwall Peninsula near Lübeck. An innocent-looking row of red-and-white striped posts marks the boundary no bather may cross. The actual fences and minefields stand farther back.

Frau Zeh of Mödlareuth, who sells beer and picture postcards of the divided village.

Burgomaster Adolf Matthies of the Lower Saxony border village of Zicherie stands before the fences dividing his community from the twin village of Böckwitz beyond the concrete watchtower in the background. The inscription on the stone reads "Germany is Indivisible."

West Berliners wave to friends and relatives across the Wall.

A West Berlin bride waves to her mother and other relatives across the Wall in September 1961.

East German troops remove the body of Peter Fechter, who bled to death at the foot of the Wall after being shot by East German guards in an escape attempt on 17 August 1962.

13 August 1961. Bernauer Strasse, Berlin, becomes the frontier, but people still escape.

A child comes up a shaft on the lap of a helper. Fifty-seven people came through this 145-yard tunnel on 3 and 4 October 1964.

In this car a bride and mother-in-law made their escape under the barrier at Check Point Charlie.

East German soldiers (or National People's Army troops) setting up a frontier marker stone near Grossensee, watched by an armed guard to prevent any sudden dash to the West.

Erwin Schade, a West Berlin schoolboy, is escorted to school by British armored cars. After the building of the Wall Communist guards tried to stop him from using the lane through East German territory connecting his home in the western enclave of Eiskeller with the western sectors of Berlin. From then on, he was escorted daily by the British Army.

Dean Gross of Ratzeburg Cathedral is cut off from his bishop in East Germany by the frontier. The Dean, who is just over the border in the West, must communicate with the Bishop of Schwerin by mail.

agreed to accept less than half their original demand, an exchange of letters occurred in early September and the stretch of line was promptly reopened. This obviated the need to send the potash trains round by a long detour over difficult terrain. And it provided a hopeful omen for Herr von Dorrer's latest round of talks with the GDR Transport Ministry.

In these negotiations, which were expected to last some time, the West set out to secure the removal of a number of obstacles. Bonn proposed, firstly, that both sides should stop preventing each other from using their waterways for transit traffic to third countries such as Holland in the West or Poland and Czechoslovakia in the East. Secondly, there was the railway bills-of-lading issue already described. Thirdly, the West urged the creation of a joint commission on roadbuilding. This could promote co-operative planning and, for example, facilitate completion of the missing stretch of Autobahn on the border near Eisenach, where motorists have to take a long detour over country roads. If the East would complete the missing link in the highway—which connects Frankfurt to Dresden—traffic would move much more freely. But the East Germans, who would have to bear the brunt of the cost, say they can afford neither the labour nor the money at present. So the road may not be opened until the 1980s, if then.

Private motorists, German or otherwise, driving to Berlin or elsewhere in the GDR must keep to the Autobahns and follow the shortest route to their destination as listed on their visas. A British journalist who decided on the spur of the moment to turn off the Autobahn on his way home from the Leipzig Fair and spend a night in the nearby town of Weimar was roused from his hotel bed at midnight and told to get back on the Autobahn immediately. He had to forgo any further sightseeing in the town of Schiller and Goethe and head straight for the border. There is a radar-enforced speed limit of 62 m.p.h. on the Berlin–Helmstedt Autobahn. Normally the 110-mile distance takes two hours, but British military police at Helmstedt speak in awe of an unidentified British girl who broke all records by covering the distance in fifty-six minutes in her Jaguar. Either the radar was not working that day or the radar operators could not believe their eyes!

Next to motoring, flying is the most popular mode of travel between Berlin and the West. Taking to the air eliminates all the irritating and time-wasting frontier formalities at road and rail checkpoints. There is no delay at all upon arrival in Berlin, and on leaving the city passengers merely have to show their passports or identity cards. Flights run smoothly under the supervision of the Berlin Air Safety Centre, one of the two remaining four-power bodies remaining in the city. (The other is Spandau Jail in the British sector, where Rudolf Hess is the sole remaining inmate.) Located in the old Allied Control Council building in West Berlin, the Air Safety Centre controls traffic in the three Western air corridors and the forty-mile-diameter Berlin air-control zone. Russian experts continue to work well with their Western colleagues in the Centre as if the GDR with its claims to national sovereignty did not exist. Allied officials shudder to think of the trouble that might ensue if the Russians ever handed over their seat in the Centre to the GDR. But despite dire forecasts in the Western Press this has not happened. The Centre operates quietly behind the scenes, shunning publicity. It performs admirably and is largely responsible for Berlin's excellent record of crash-free flying. Yet the Centre's task is far from easy: the city is the second busiest air transport region in Germany after Frankfurt, and is unique in the world in possessing three Civil airports, Tempelhof, Tegel and Schönefeld.

Due to Berlin's special status, only aircraft of the three Western Allies fly to West Berlin—and, by an odd post-war anomaly, planes of the Polish airline Lot. Recently Air France and British European Airways pooled their Berlin operations, so the only real competition at present is between Pan American and BEA. Tegel airport in the French sector is being modernized and expanded to handle the massive increase in jet traffic expected in the 1970s. Meanwhile the bulk of West Berlin's flights, mostly medium-range jets, uses Tempelhof Airport in the American sector. Schönefeld in East Berlin has much less traffic, but the East German airline Interflug and other carriers made some 24,000 landings and take-offs there in 1966. Passengers can transfer from Tempelhof to Schönefeld by using a bus service or hiring one of the few West Berlin taxi drivers who can cross the Wall because they hold West German or foreign passports. One of these drivers, for instance, is an Israeli who is well known to the guards at Checkpoint Charlie. He treats them with a teasing familiarity which few other travellers would dare. To arrive in an ordinary West Berlin taxi at Checkpoint Charlie is to risk finding no transport on the other side. But whichever way the Wall is crossed, by bus, taxi or on foot, there is no escape from the frontier formalities.

These are fairly standardized, both at the Wall and on the East–West border. Western travellers have to alight from their cars and hand in their passports, receiving a numbered ticket in exchange. They then wait in line at a counter in the barrack building while their passports are examined in a back room. Some minutes later the passports reappear, dropped through a slot by some hidden hand. Forms must be then be filled in to declare how much Western currency is being brought in and to list details of cars, cameras and valuables. Visas must be bought at five marks (10s. 6d. or $1.25) apiece for a one-way journey to Berlin. For the same price West Germans (but not West Berliners) may obtain a one-day permit to visit East Berlin. But these one-day permits, which are also issued to foreigners at Checkpoint Charlie, expire at midnight on the day of issue. They do not permit the bearer to leave the city boundaries, which are guarded by roadside sentries. For each day's stay in East Berlin any visitor must change a minimum of five West-marks into East-marks at the official exchange rate of one to one. Travellers to East Germany, as distinct from East Berlin, have to change ten marks for each day's intended stay. Visitors to the Leipzig Fair have to change 25 marks (£2 12s. or $6.25) per day's stay. All this money must be spent; it cannot be exchanged or taken out of the country upon departure. Visas to visit East Germany cost DM 15 (about £1 11s. or $3.75) apiece. West Germans can get entry visas at the border by producing a certificate showing that they are going to visit relatives in the GDR. This certificate has to be obtained by the East German relatives from the Communist authorities and then posted to the intending visitor. On arrival at the home town of the GDR relatives, the West German visitor has to register with the People's Police. He may not leave the area without permission, and to return to the Federal Republic he needs an exit visa issued by the police.

In earlier days Western visitors used to take food parcels to their relatives in the East. Nowadays this is unnecessary since staple foods are plentiful and usually cheaper in the GDR than in the Federal Republic. But tropical fruits such as bananas are scarce in East Germany, and many visitors like to take special delicacies generally unobtainable in the East. The GDR has a detailed list of banned items. For instance, nobody may bring foods in air-tight containers. Gramophone records, tape recorders, address books, exposed or unexposed films, radios and medicines are also on the embargo list. Beyond a small free allowance, other goods may be brought into the GDR only on payment of Customs duties ranging from ten to forty per cent of the value of the item concerned in East Germany. In practice these duties can exceed the original cost of the present. A West German woman crossed into East Berlin at the Heinrich–Heine–Strasse checkpoint recently with a load of presents for her father. Among these was a nylon raincoat that she had bought in the Federal Republic for eight marks. But according to the GDR official list such a raincoat was worth 180 marks in East Germany, so she was asked to pay thirty-six marks duty. Since she had already been charged over thirty marks duty on her other presents such as coffee, chocolate, marzipan and a nylon shirt, she decided to keep the raincoat. She entered it on her list of valuables, which meant that she had to bring it out of East Berlin when she returned. The West Germans, for all their Customs officials at Helmstedt, do not levy duties on goods originating in East Germany. Indeed according to Bonn's doctrine such goods do not rate as 'imports' at all—they are simply passing from one part of Germany to another.

Many of the items on the GDR's embargo list of goods entering the country are also banned for export by departing travellers. But there are certain additions: Meissen porcelain, eels and asparagus, to name but a few. One can understand that fine porcelain is reserved for the hard-currency export trade. But why anybody should be barred from taking eels and asparagus out of the GDR defeats the imagination. Export duties are payable on goods taken out by travellers in excess of a certain minimal free allowance. Sometimes these levies can be punitive: a fifty per cent duty must be paid, for instance, on textiles and shoes.

Although West Germans can recover at any post office the money they spend on GDR visas, the other East German restrictions add up to a formidable travel deterrent. It is not surprising that the number of West Germans visiting the GDR dropped from 1·4 million in 1967 to 1,260,000 in 1968. Even if there were no red tape and expense at the Communist checkpoints, the decline is bound to continue. Relatives die, family ties weaken with the passage of years. There are fewer people in the East to arrange for Western visits. Family communication grows progressively more strained and awkward as time goes by. Living in dissimilar social systems with different sets of friendships and experiences, brothers and sisters, parents and offspring on opposite sides of the border tend to become estranged. Since individual tourist travel in the accepted sense is impossible, these family visits are the only means open to West Germans to enter the GDR—except for business trips to the Leipzig Fair and certain organized tours. On actuarial grounds alone, family visits to the GDR are doomed to become progressively rarer.

But the Ministry for All-German Affairs in Bonn and the semi-official West German organizations devoted to German unity are trying to stave off the evil day. They urge every West German who can possibly do so to visit 'the other part of Germany'. Personal links between people on both sides of the border are, they say, 'the most effective means of preventing the German people from drifting apart, and strengthening the sense of kinship here and there'.[1] They reassure nervous Westerners that travellers to Berlin and East Germany are seldom arrested. But they warn that certain categories of West Germans should never cross the border. People who left East Germany after the building of the Berlin Wall on August 13, 1961 are liable to be punished for 'fleeing the Republic'. But refugees who fled before that date can as a rule return without fear of prosecution, unless they committed some other offence against GDR laws. Leaders of West German refugee organizations should stay away from East Germany, as should anyone who held a prominent position there before his flight. Needless to say, deserters from the People's Army and the People's Police are cautioned against returning.

In its search for hard currency the GDR is anxious to promote tourist travel. But West Berliners cannot as a rule travel anywhere in the GDR. West Germans, in addition to visiting their relatives, may take daily sightseeing bus tours to East Berlin. They may not, however, travel on the bus tours reserved for foreigners that go to Potsdam from West Berlin. Besides Potsdam with its Sanssouci and Cecilienhof palaces, the GDR has a good deal to offer the visiting tourist. There is the superb Zwinger Art Gallery in Dresden, painstakingly restored at enormous cost to its original baroque splendour; the historic town of Weimar, the Thomaner Choir in Leipzig, first-rate opera and the Pergamon

[1] Ministry for All-German Affairs, *Reisen nach Berlin, Reisen nach drüben*, Bonn, 1969.

Museum in East Berlin, to name only a few attractions. A chain of modern hotels has been built by the State, and restaurants are generally cheap by Western standards. But visitors must book and pay for each night's hotel in advance, before they can get their visas. Alternatively, they can go on organized tours, such as those starting regularly from London in the summer months. In either case, travellers are bound to fixed itineraries, which in an age of free-wheeling tourism have limited appeal. As long as all this red tape persists, East Germany will be unable to attract more than a tiny share of the Western tourist trade.

Now a word on East German travellers to the West. It was not until November 2, 1964, three years after the Wall, that East Germany permitted pensioners to visit the Federal Republic. The rule is that retired men aged sixty-five and over, and women over sixty, may visit Western relatives for a stay of up to four weeks in any year. The figure of nearly 1·5 million such visits in 1968 represents an increase of more than 400,000 over the previous year. But when they come, it is inevitably in the rôle of poor relations. They can buy their train tickets in East Germany through to their Western destinations, but they may not change more than ten marks of GDR currency into Western marks. This means that from the moment of their arrival these elderly people depend upon Westerners for support. To a great extent this hospitality comes from their West German relatives. In addition the Bonn government paid out DM 87 million (about £9m or $21,750,000) to visiting pensioners in 1968, an average of nearly DM 60 (£6 5s. or $15) apiece. Provincial and local authorities and churches also contribute varying sums to pensioners visiting their localities. The Federal Railways provide rail warrants for their return journey. Not all of them go back; some stay with their families in the West, a few seek sanctuary in the Western refugee centres. In 1968 nearly 350 East German pensioners registered at Marienfelde in West Berlin alone. But most elderly people yearn to return to their cherished homes and belongings and hate to live on 'charity' when they can live independently at home. So the vast majority of visiting pensioners return to East Germany when their month's stay is up.

Much heartbreak is caused by the refusal of the GDR authorities, except in very special circumstances, to allow children or relatives of working age to rejoin their families in the West. Often parents, husbands or fiancés left family members behind, intending to send for them once they had established themselves in the Federal Republic. Now those who stayed behind are marooned in the GDR. One hears of cases involving East German girls, even those with one or two illegitimate children, who are denied permission to follow their fiancés to Western Europe. Lisbeth Märker, a widow who left her six-year-old daughter Pia behind in the GDR when she fled to West Germany in 1959, has been trying ever since to get her handed over at the border. For eight years her appeals went unanswered, while the child was growing up in a State home at Polsterstein. Finally the mother in her desperation brought a suit in the West German courts to compel the Bonn government to negotiate with East Berlin on Pia's behalf. This unprecedented case is at the time of writing still in the early stages of litigation; it may go right up to the Federal Constitutional Court. There is of course no guarantee that Pia will be returned even if Frau Märker wins her case. But the West German government has used financial and trade concessions in the past as payments for the release of people in East Germany. Sometimes East Germany tries to use unfortunate people as political hostages: it says that an East German girl may join her husband in Britain, for instance, only if Britain will recognize her East German passport. This is tantamount to a demand for British recognition of the GDR. Considering these frustrations, it is surprising to learn that as many as 1,443 refugees registered at Marienfelde in 1968 after being let out of the GDR to join families in the West. But in each case the East German authorities had their own reasons for letting the people go. Often the exit visas are granted to people who are unable to work. The heartbreak over family separations continues.

The Federal Republic exerts, officially at least, no control over visitors from East Germany. The reason, once again, is Bonn's doctrine of the non-existent frontier. Any East German who can get out of the GDR legally or otherwise is allowed into the Federal Republic provided he does not violate Bonn's laws, such as the Federal Constitutional Court ban on the Communist party. Waivers of the law are needed to permit GDR ministers and other Communist officials to visit West Germany, otherwise they would be liable to arrest. But these rules apply only to West Germany. If an East German wants to visit any other NATO country—and is allowed by his government to do so—he must apply to the Allied Travel Office in West Berlin for a special permit called a

Temporary Travel Document (TTD). This is necessary since no NATO country recognizes an East German passport. The three Western Allies in Berlin who maintain the Allied Travel Office on NATO's behalf normally issue TTDs to anybody who is not an obvious security risk or political propagandist. East German officials complain bitterly about the Allied Travel Office, to the point at which they seem to forget that their own régime with its Wire and Wall imposes incomparably greater curbs on East–West travel. What particularly annoys them is any refusal of TTDs to East German sports teams. Actually this rarely happens: the Allied Travel Office would refuse TTDs to teams calling themselves GDR players and insisting on displaying GDR national colours and playing the GDR anthem. But in practice the East Germans have often soft-pedalled these political demands and their sports teams have usually obtained permission to travel.

Although as a matter of policy the Allied Travel Office never discloses figures, informed sources say that the vast majority of TTD applications are normally approved. The word 'normally' is used advisedly: in times of Communist challenge or obduracy the Allied Travel Office provides a convenient means of applying pressure. For instance, if East Germany interferes with travel on the Berlin access routes, the flow of TTDs can be reduced accordingly. Equally, if Western salesmen, scientists or journalists are refused access to the GDR, it is easy to play tit-for-tat. But of course the East Germans and the Russians hold the trump card in any East–West test of strength. They can always put pressure on West Berlin because of its isolated position. Against this Communist advantage, the Allied Travel Office is a wholly inadequate response.

10

Communications

ONE simple statistic illustrates the division of Germany as graphically as any picture of the Wire and the Wall: there are precisely thirty-four telephone lines connecting East and West Germany. This compares with 165 lines linking the Federal Republic with Luxemburg, its smallest neighbour with a population of some 300,000 compared to East Germany's seventeen million. Calls to the GDR are liable to delays of up to four hours on an average day; at Christmas the delays run to fifteen hours or more and operators often refuse to accept private calls except at premium rates. Urgent calls cost twice the normal rate, but even these may take hours. The fastest system is to book a 'lightning' call at ten times the regular charge. For a while, the GDR allowed the number of East–West German lines to double during the period of the Leipzig Fair held each spring and autumn. The extra cables were simply hooked up at the start of each Fair and disconnected afterwards. But even this concession has since gone by the board. East Germany is willing to install twenty extra international lines linking Leipzig with such capitals as London, Paris and Brussels for the convenience of Fair visitors. But it refuses to expand its phone links to the Federal Republic even temporarily. Not only does the number of lines between the two Germanies remain grossly inadequate; the quality of those that exist leaves much to be desired. A call from Bonn to East Berlin can strain both the patience and the vocal chords. By contrast, calls between the Federal Republic and West Berlin go through instantaneously by direct dialling. There are no fewer than 2,300 channels available, mostly provided by the 'Radio Bridge' between tall masts on the Western border and at Wannsee in West Berlin. This remarkable relay link, on which construction began as early as 1956, carries over 1,500 telephone conversations simultaneously. The remaining telephone links between Berlin and the West are carried by conventional land lines through the GDR. Both systems are vulnerable to East German eavesdropping. Though the cables concerned belong to the West Germans, a small sum is paid each year to the GDR postal authorities for their maintenance and other technical costs.

Telex connections across the East–West border are somewhat less restricted. There are twenty-six lines at the time of writing and the delays are less than those involved in telephoning. But the Ministry of Posts in Bonn says that twice as many telex links are needed. Telegrams, however, move swiftly and normally, even at Christmas. Letters destined for East Germany go at domestic rates but take their time and are liable to be opened en route. Those that bear West German stamps depicting formerly German towns in the 'lost territories' of Eastern Europe are refused by the GDR. Indeed, all Communist bloc countries reject mail carrying stamps in the current West German series showing, for example, Stettin and Königsberg. (Stettin is now Polish and has been re-named Szczecin. Königsberg, the former capital of East Prussia, has fallen to Russia and been renamed Kaliningrad.) The West German Post Office could perform a useful service to its cus-tomers if it put up signs warning them not to use such stamps on letters and packets to the East—but it does not. Most mail crosses the East–West German border in sealed railway wagons. They are not unloaded at the frontier checkpoints but travel through to the sorting offices and depots on either side. Since the war West Germans have sent millions of parcels to relatives and friends in the East, first with food and then with minor luxuries. West German organizations now urge people not to send food parcels except to really needy pensioners since the reaction in the GDR is often one of injured pride. But leaflets and posters in West Ger-many appeal to the public to send regular parcels and letters to the East as a patriotic duty. 'The individual German,' says one leaflet distributed in Western post offices, 'can do nothing better and more effective for reunification than to contribute as best he can toward maintaining the human unity of our people. Certainly we cannot thereby bring about reunification before world poli-tical conditions allow it. But at least we can ensure that the German people does not fall apart in its human contacts in the meantime.' The GDR however has elaborate regulations affecting gift parcels just as it imposes close restrictions on what travellers may bring in. One of the most distressing to many East and West Germans alike is the ban on drugs and medicines. Medical care and services in the GDR are on the whole better than those in the Federal Republic, but there are many East Germans who long for certain specific drugs which are only obtainable in the West. There are other rules similar to those in force at the frontier checkpoints, but in one respect parcels enjoy an advantage over personal baggage: Customs duties do not apply.

The fact that more parcels and packets are mailed from West to East Germany than in the reverse direction means that the West German post office gets a disproportionate share of the income (from the stamps) while the GDR postal authorities have an unfair share of the work. This was bound to lead to trouble, and in the autumn of 1966 the East Germans presented Bonn with a bill totalling DM 1,680 million (£175m or $420m) for balancing the accounts back to 1948. The Federal Republic objected to the claim in principle because it was calculated by international postal accounting standards, while Bonn regards East–West German mail as 'intra-German'. It also protested that the bill was padded with compound interest and other charges. Nevertheless Dr. Werner Dollinger, the West German Minister of Posts, paid the GDR DM 16,900,000 (£1,760,000 or $4,225,000) in October 1968 for the previous year's disparity in postal services, and roughly one-third as much in February 1969 for the first six months of 1968. He coupled his payments with various practical suggestions for improving communications, suggesting quadrupling the number of telephone lines, reopening phone links between the two halves of Berlin and speeding up mail services. But so far all these proposals have been met with stony silence from East Berlin. When officials from Herr Dollinger's ministry met their GDR opposite numbers in September 1969 to discuss these matters there was no visible sign of progress toward agreement.

Such are some of the frustrations in the realm of personal communications between East and West Germany. Mass communications—television, radio and newspapers—are another matter. For they involve not just private contacts by mail, telex and telephone but the politically sensitive areas of news and propaganda, the dissemination of information and comment. No democracy can function effectively without a free flow of news; no dictatorship can be wholly successful without news censorship.

Take broadcasting first because it is the only medium of mass communication that can jump the Wire and the Wall. Its importance cannot be over-estimated. Millions of East Germans listen to Western broadcasts daily as their only escape from isolation, their only contact with the Western world, their only relief from the suffocating boredom of Communist propaganda. Television and radio transmitters in West Berlin and along the Western side of the border beam powerful signals deep into the territory of the GDR. Jamming is virtually impossible: only in a few localities such as Potsdam and Leipzig is a feeble attempt made to jam certain medium-wave radio transmissions from the West. Otherwise the broadcasts get through on a multitude of channels. Only in the extreme south-eastern and north-eastern corners of the GDR do viewers have any difficulty getting a clear picture from West German television. It is significant that well-placed East German officials admit that the density of TV sets in the GDR declines in direct proportion to the owner's distance from Western transmitters.

Listening to Western broadcasts is not encouraged in the GDR, but it is not forbidden so long as it is done in the privacy of the home. Inviting guests to watch Western TV or radio is illegal, and an innkeeper who kept the radio or TV set in his bar tuned to the West would get into trouble. Television sets are expensive in GDR shops, but they are easily available. To pick up Western programmes one needs a special aerial, called in East German parlance an *Ochsenkopf* after the name of a particular Western transmitter near the border in Bavaria. A Leipzig dentist once told me the story of his *Ochsenkopf*.

'My wife wanted to watch West German TV so she wouldn't feel so cut off,' he said. 'We had long arguments about it because the *Ochsenkopf* antenna is a dead give-away that one is listening to the West. It stands there on the roof for the whole world to see. In earlier days boys from the FDJ (the Communist youth organization) used to climb up and wreck these antennae. Eventually we decided to build a portable one which we could carry up to the roof under cover of darkness whenever there was a programme we wanted to watch, and take down afterwards. That worked fine until I had to go off on a three-day business trip. When I returned the first thing I saw was the antenna standing there on the roof in broad daylight! I was horrified and asked my wife why she had left it up—she replied that it had been too heavy to bring down without my help. But nobody said anything and indeed the thing has been up there ever since.'

The dentist's *Ochsenkopf* enables him to pick up the First Programme on the so-called ARD network, from West Germany.

A different gadget in the shape of a special tuner is needed to receive the Second Programme from the Federal Republic, properly known as the *Zweites Deutsches Fernsehen*. Importation of this tuner and its parts to the GDR is officially forbidden, but a substantial number of East Germans have these tuners anyway. They are made by radio hobbyists or dealers as a profitable sideline.

Technically, therefore, East Germany is wide open to Western TV and radio broadcasts. Since the building of the Wall it has become hard to measure the audience. But Dr. Hans Rindfleisch, Technical Director of the ARD network, has estimated that nine out of ten East Germans can receive at least one Western medium-wave station during the day, and that at night some eighty per cent of the population can hear at least three radio programmes from the Federal Republic. There is ample evidence that East Germans make full use of these opportunities. Western visitors to the GDR are often amazed to find their hosts so well informed on Bonn politics. Yet at the same time these prolific Western broadcasts induce a sense of confusion and suspicion. Once the wife of a Communist trade union official in Jena admitted to a Western visitor: 'Very often we don't believe what we hear from our GDR broadcasts. Because of this, we feel we can't believe all we hear from your side, either.' Thus the political effect of Western broadcasts is hard to measure. But the impact of West German radio and television on GDR taste and fashions is indisputable. For instance, when 2,000 East German youngsters were invited in a GDR poll to name their favourite tunes, one of their 'Top Ten' turned out to be a hit which had never been played on East German radio or TV. The children could only have picked it up from Western broadcasts. The Beatles were soon accepted and imitated in East Germany, as were mini-skirts and other Western fashions in everything from sweaters to eye make-up. East Germans write to Western broadcasting stations to request favourite tunes. The works newspaper of the GDR's large Buna chemical plant reported that nine out of ten of the tunes sung by the firm's apprentices were Western hits. An FDJ official in Dresden complained that the first programmes turned on by students in the morning were either *Deutschlandfunk* (a West German station), or Radio Luxemburg.

'If there were no TV,' said a West Berlin television journalist, 'Ulbricht's problems would be solved.' There would be no way for his population to make comparisons between East and West. 'I often think,' this journalist mused as he gazed across the roof-tops from his office in *Sender Freies Berlin*, 'that Hitler had a great advantage over Ulbricht. Apart from a few people who listened to foreign radio, nobody in the Third Reich could watch what the outside world was doing or hear what it was saying. If there had been mass television in Hitler's day he would have had a much harder time.'

Sender Freies Berlin (SFB) is in a good position to judge. One of the chain of autonomous stations which make up the ARD net-work, SFB holds a special responsibility for broadcasts to East Germany. It produces on behalf of both the First and Second Programmes a daily 'morning magazine' of television news and entertainment broadcasts from transmitters along the East–West border from 10 a.m. to 1 p.m. This is the nearest approach to a special West German programme for the GDR. Otherwise the television networks in the Federal Republic serve the same fare to their East German viewers as to their watchers in the West. This is felt to be the right approach although it often leads to mis-understanding. While advertising is severely restricted in West German television, a number of the programmes tend to present a distorted, materialist image of Western society which fits in with the caricatures of Communist propaganda. Films emphasizing sex and violence, feature programmes exposing crime and scandal, political discussions involving sharp criticism of government policies—all these are normal to television in a democracy. But the effect of such programmes upon people across the border who have known no democracy since 1933 is mixed. East Germans often write to SFB and other Western stations and complain that the self-criticism involved in many of these broadcasts is a con-fession of Western weakness. 'Why do you foul your own nest?' is the repeated refrain. It is hard at times to convince these well-meaning viewers that they are mistaken; that debate, self-criticism and exposure of shortcomings are normal and essential to demo-cracy, that they are signs of strength rather than weakness. The best propaganda, SFB insists, is to show the West, warts and all, to tell the truth and hold back nothing.

SFB is not too proud to film East German television pro-grammes for subsequent use as excerpts and illustrations in its own broadcasts. Both East and West German television stations engage in a certain amount of mutual piracy of this kind. But the

West believes that so long as it gives the East Germans due credit this does not constitute illegal plagiarism. All West German networks monitor GDR radio and television broadcasts; some record and tape more than others. For instance, the Second Programme runs from its Berlin studio a fortnightly miscellany of news and views from the GDR which depends heavily upon East German transmissions.

Every day the technicians in this studio tape two hours of GDR television and select the best material for storage in the archives. The resulting programme, which also uses other sources of film, runs for twenty minutes every second Sunday night. Called *'Drüben'* (literally: over there), it is in fact the only regularly scheduled broadcast devoted entirely to the GDR to appear on any of the three West German television channels. Ten minutes a week on the average does not seem to be an inordinate amount of time to devote to East Germany. If this is a measure of the interest shown by West Germans in their supposed compatriots East of the Elbe it is not very impressive. But *'Drüben'* is an interesting study in itself. Hanns Schwarze, its young producer, rates as a controversial figure in German TV journalism. His objectivity, his rejection of Cold War or any other clichés and his refusal to allow any vilification of the GDR in his programme have made him enemies as well as friends.

The story of *'Drüben'* is worth recounting from the beginning. Although the programme first went on the air in January 1966, Schwarze and his camera team had been at work since 1964 collecting material. In the years 1964–65 the East Germans were relatively co-operative in allowing him to film on their own soil. But then, as so often happens, the GDR began trying to use such contact for political ends. It refused to allow further filming in the East unless this were requested in a formal letter from the *Intendant* or Director-General of the Western network to his opposite number in the GDR. No such letter was forthcoming since the Western *Intendant* did not want to 'recognize' the other side. From then on there was no more filming east of the Wall. Schwarze could still go across on his West German passport and talk to people, but he had to leave his cameras behind.

Nevertheless, although so much of the material is secondhand, *Drüben* is watched on the average by about four million West Germans every fortnight. This is a good response for a political programme which often runs in competition with sport or news on competing channels. The audience generally approves of Schwarze's calm and unpolemical style of reporting on East German affairs. But there is a minority of viewers in the West which 'accuses us of being paid by Ulbricht', as Schwarze says, or 'wants us to hang a label on every programme to warn that East Germany is still a Bolshevist dictatorship'. The GDR government takes the line that Schwarze's programme is a 'particularly re-fined form of West German imperialism'.

A somewhat less refined form of Western imperialism, in the Communist view, is the RIAS radio station in West Berlin. For RIAS—the letters stand for Radio in the American Sector—sets out deliberately to burst the bonds of Communist censorship. It does not content itself, as do most West German TV stations, with enabling East Germans to overhear programmes chiefly designed for the West. RIAS has always concentrated on special broadcasts for East Berlin and East Germany. From the begin-ning, RIAS has regarded as its chief task the dissemination of news and information to the people of the GDR. It is run by the U.S. Information Agency but less than half a dozen of its 400-odd employees are Americans. The rest are Germans, including many refugees from East Germany and Eastern Europe. They are allowed to get on with the job of reporting and commenting on the news with a minimum of interference. RIAS started as 'piped radio' using telephone lines in Berlin back in 1946 when the Russians ruled the Berlin airwaves without any competition from the West. By the time of the Berlin blockade two years later RIAS had its own twenty kilowatt transmitter and became a 'fighting' station in the front line of the Cold War. When electric power was scarce in the beleaguered city RIAS sent loudspeaker cars to broadcast news at busy street intersections, laying the basis for its popularity in West Berlin which has continued ever since.

Perhaps the finest hour of RIAS's eventful history was during the East German revolt of June 17, 1953. Here was a classic case of the power of radio to influence events. It never urged East Germans to rise in rebellion: the strike that started the revolt was entirely spontaneous. Yet the rising would never have spread to towns outside East Berlin if it had not been for RIAS. On the other hand, once the Russians began moving troops and tanks to counter the disorders, RIAS was quick to warn its East German listeners of the folly of trying to fight the Red Army with sticks and stones. The revolt would have been a shortlived affair in any case; the restrained response of RIAS prevented it from turning into a bloodbath.

Gordon Ewing, the Deputy Director and Political Chief of RIAS in those days, recalls that there had been storm signals in the preceding weeks. The East Berliners and East Germans who were constantly dropping in at RIAS headquarters (the Wall was still eight years away) spoke of growing discontent. Stalin had died in March, the East German government seemed unsure of itself. But nobody believed that strikes were in the offing; strikes had never happened in a Communist country and nobody could imagine that they ever would. So when a delegation of building workers came into RIAS on the morning of June 16 with the momentous news that their mates had downed tools on a construction site in the Stalinallee, East Berlin's proudest boulevard, nobody at first was inclined to take them very seriously. Ewing himself was busy discussing RIAS administration with the visiting future head of the U.S. Information Agency. However, as the afternoon wore on the news became certainty. RIAS reporters and editors saw the strike turn into a swelling protest march through East Berlin; they heard the original demands for the abolition of a new increase in working norms develop into chants of 'Down with the government' and 'Free Elections'.

At about 4 p.m. someone came into Ewing's office and said: 'We are confronted with something that is unquestionably a revolution.' The corridors of RIAS were mayhem. More East Berlin strikers had arrived and were pleading for RIAS to broadcast the appeal they were now making for a nation-wide general strike. Younger German members of the editorial staff were excitedly demanding that RIAS rise to the occasion—the occasion that everyone had awaited. Ewing was effectively in charge. He could not reach into his office safe and withdraw a secret envelope containing contingency plans for just such an emergency. There were no such plans. His High Commissioner in Bonn, Dr. James B. Conant, was in Washington for budget hearings before Congress, accompanied by other senior American officials. Even if there had been anybody in Bonn worth asking for instructions, he would have been second-guessing from a distance without a proper appreciation of the situation. Ewing did not want that kind of advice. He was also conscious of another handicap: he had no secure telephone to the West. Anything he said to the High Commission would be overheard by the Communists.

So he was thrown back on his own resources. He knew only too well the enormous responsibility he bore. He kept thinking of a remark one of his colleagues had made when he had first arrived at RIAS: 'For God's sake be careful, Ewing. You could start a war with that station.' Ewing recognized that neither the United States nor any other Western ally was prepared to fight a war in support of an East German revolt. 'I was terribly torn,' Ewing says. 'On the one hand, we all had close connections with people in the Zone [the GDR] and wanted to help them. We certainly did not want to do anything which would recklessly endanger them. On the other hand we didn't want to look as though we were taking it easy on the Communist side.' Here was a situation that could not be simply handled by the cardinal rule of journalism: report the facts. RIAS was already reporting the facts, in its hourly newscasts and special bulletins. It was reporting the momentous news that East Berlin workers had come out on strike; that they were marching and demonstrating. Even this was enough to set the telephones ringing as American news agencies called up to protest that RIAS was showing irresponsibility and sensationalism. Ewing was not disturbed by this criticism: he had meanwhile ordered as an exceptional step that every news bulletin be submitted to him before it went out on the air, and he knew that the physical fact of the strike was undeniable. But there were two more 'facts' which had not yet been reported over RIAS. One was the call for a general strike, the other was the strikers' summons for a mass meeting to start at 7 a.m. the following morning in the Strausberger Platz in East Berlin. Ewing knew that once RIAS reported these appeals it would be entering into the arena as a direct participant: it would be allying itself to the East German rebels and rendering them a service. The delegations of East Berlin strikers were urging him and his colleagues to do just this, to make RIAS in effect the mouthpiece of the revolt. Ewing took his courage in both hands and authorized his staff to report the summons to the Strausberger Platz rally. But he refused to allow the call for a general strike to be broadcast.

Ernst Scharnowski, President of the West Berlin Trade Union Federation, challenged the second of these rulings when he arrived at RIAS late that night. He demanded to be allowed to read a script he had prepared which used the banned expression 'general strike' repeatedly. Ewing sat down with him and argued that it was unfair to urge East Germans to engage in a general strike which could so readily be smashed by Soviet troops, with punishment of the ringleaders perhaps by firing-squad. The American official was loyally backed at this encounter by his Programme Director, a German ex-Communist named Eberhard Schütz who had been an active opponent of all forms of dictatorship since serving a Soviet jail sentence in the 1930s. 'Scharnowski was terribly indignant,' Ewing recalls. 'But after a while he agreed to do some rewriting and to eliminate the expression "general strike".' The revised Scharnowski appeal went out at 5 a.m. It commended the East German construction workers for their conduct on the first day and added:

> Do not let them fight alone. Their fight is not only for workers' rights but for the human rights of the people of East Berlin and Eastern Germany. We ask you therefore to join the movement of the East Berlin building workers . . . and come to the mass rally at the Strausberger Platz. The larger the participation, the more powerful and successful will your movement be. The workers [of West Berlin] look on your struggle with admiration . . . they assure you of their fullest sympathy and believe that your fight will be upright and to a good end.

Hours earlier, Schütz had produced a RIAS commentary. He and Ewing had discussed it, agonized over it during the evening of the sixteenth. Schütz enjoyed Ewing's confidence as well as the respect of countless listeners. He had been rescued by the British from Czechoslovakia and learned the art of political reporting in the BBC during the war. He spoke carefully and calmly to the people of East Germany whose problems he knew so well. He told them they had won a victory. He pointed out that the form of their victory had disposed of the idea that resistance to terror can only be an expression of hopeless despair or martyrdom. And he concluded with this sentence: 'We would be delighted to inform you of more victories in the days to come.'[1]

The rest is history. East Germans poured out in hundreds of thousands on the seventeenth, not only in Berlin but in cities and towns over almost the whole of East Germany. Party offices were sacked and records hurled into the street, jails invaded and prisoners released. Quite incapable of handling the situation, the East German government had to let the Russians move in with

[1] Quoted by Joseph C. Harsch in an NBC/BBC commentary, June 27, 1953.

their tanks and martial law. Ewing and his senior colleagues, both German and American, knew, and warned repeatedly on the air, that resistance was hopeless. There were Americans who tried to persuade Ewing that all was not lost, that RIAS should encourage sit-down strikes in the factories. They argued that the Russians surely would not shoot women and children bringing food to striking workers. But Ewing was not convinced that passive resistance would work. He was ready to concede, having noted the amazing discipline of the Russian troops in the Potsdamer Platz and elsewhere, that Soviet soldiers would probably not shoot strikers' wives. But he believed that the Russians would have found some less brutal means of keeping food supplies away and starving the men out, and therefore decided that any encouragement to the rebels would be futile.

Those were stirring days; today RIAS operates in a lower key but still claims to reach seventy to eighty per cent of East German radio listeners. With transmitters at Hof in Bavaria as well as West Berlin it broadcasts round the clock and uses ten frequencies spaced across the medium, short and ultra-short wavebands. In its programmes beamed to East Germany it not only purveys the news from a Western standpoint but tries to fill in some of the gaps and distortions in Communist reporting of East European affairs. Czechoslovakia in 1968 was a classic case, but there are less dramatic examples. On the day I visited RIAS the Eastern desk broadcast long excerpts from a draft resolution prepared for the 1969 international conference of Communist parties—a draft which, RIAS said, had not yet been published in the Communist world. Three-quarters of the programme time was allotted to a straight-forward reading of key paragraphs in the draft, without intervening comment and without departing from the text. RIAS has changed a good deal since its loudspeaker trucks kept up morale during the Berlin Blockade. But then the Cold War has changed a lot, too. It continues in Germany, but it is fought on a more sophisticated level than in 1948.

Another powerful Western antidote to Communist propaganda is the *Deutschlandfunk*, an autonomous West German network based in Cologne. It draws nearly one-third of its funds from the Bonn government, and the rest from radio licence fees. But it categorically denies Communist charges that it takes its orders from the government's Press and Information Office. Stephan Thomas, its Current Affairs Programme Director, is emphatic: 'I would not take guidance or instructions from any government official, even the Chancellor or the Foreign Minister.' *Deutschlandfunk*, like RIAS, broadcasts twenty-four hours a day to listeners in both East and West Germany. But the Cologne network also transmits in eleven other European languages to five countries in Eastern Europe, to Scandinavia, Britain, France and the Netherlands. When it started transmitting in January 1962 its first Director-General, Dr. H. F. G. Starke, told listeners in East Germany: 'The *Deutschlandfunk* will never tire of fighting the lie with the truth, the whole truth and nothing but the truth.' Once it was suggested that the network should inaugurate a programme called 'The Lie of the Week' which would expose and denounce a particular Communist falsification. 'The proposal was rejected,' said Fritz Thedieck, the present Director-General, 'because polemics can be neither a part of our programme nor a principle of our organization.'

The *Deutschlandfunk* has its own correspondents in major capitals around the world and maintains news bureaux in Bonn and Berlin as well as Cologne. Stephan Thomas bears the immediate responsibility for news and commentaries, but he does not require scripts to be submitted to him before they are broadcast. He leaves individual reporters and commentators to work freely and use their own judgment. 'We like to think that we have become the main focus of attention (in the field of radio) for people in East Germany,' Thomas says. Every week the network broadcasts cultural programmes on books and periodicals of interest to East Germans. It engages in thorough analysis of Communist doctrine and history, and runs feature programmes on such subjects as Comecon, Tito's 1948 break with Moscow and Stalin's role at wartime Big Three conferences.

But for the *Deutschlandfunk*, as for RIAS and SFB, the prime task is not to broadcast features and comment but to get the news across. They have to repair gaping omissions in Communist news coverage. Take the official organ of the GDR Communist party, *Neues Deutschland*. Two days after the invasion of Czechoslovakia, when Western newspapers were filled with Prague developments, the East German daily led its front page with the headline: 'Economical Use of Material saves Time and Money for Construction'. Although *Neues Deutschland* had its own correspondents in Prague, they rated only twenty-two lines in the paper. Most of the Czech coverage, such as it was, appearing in the

August 23 edition consisted of quotes from *Pravda* and other Russian newspapers. A reader of *Neues Deutschland* would have looked in vain for any news of the East German troops who joined in the invasion; he would have learned nothing of the abduction of Dubcek and other Czech leaders. He would not have known that the United Nations Security Council was discussing the invasion, or that Rumania, a fellow-member of the Warsaw Pact, had raised its voice in protest. A *Deutschlandfunk* reporter noted these deficiencies in a telling broadcast from Berlin that night.

Western broadcasters not only have to try to fill the gaps in Communist reporting. They also, of course, have to compete with propaganda on GDR radio and television. The main East German radio networks are the *Deutschlandsender*, *Radio DDR* and the *Berliner Rundfunk*. *Deutschlandsender* was the name of the powerful station used by the Third Reich to spread Goebbels' propaganda all over Europe. Today the network transmits on the long, medium, short and ultra-short waves to 'all Germans, to win them for peace and unity'. It directs its broadcasts particularly to 'patriots in West Germany' with the aim of 'leading them in their struggle'. *Radio DDR* transmits two programmes for home listeners and the *Berliner Rundfunk* caters mainly for the people of East Berlin. In addition there is the *Berliner Welle*, confined to Berlin, Radio Berlin International, for transmitting abroad, and regional programmes in such centres as Leipzig, Dresden and Rostock. One television channel operates all day long, with its transmissions now strengthened by the completion of East Berlin's 1,188-foot television tower, one of the world's highest structures. Schwarze of *Drüben* acknowledges that GDR television is up to West German technical standards. Indeed in some fields such as sport it is sometimes so much better that the West Germans have imitated GDR methods.

East Germany's crack radio and television commentator is Karl-Eduard von Schnitzler, who defected to East Germany in 1947 after working for the BBC in London during the war and heading the political section of the North West German Radio in Cologne. His sarcastic, mocking style is well illustrated by a programme he broadcast at 9.30 p.m. on May 12, 1969. It was on a familiar theme—the 'neo-Nazi' National Democratic Party in the Federal Republic. He said it was no coincidence that the Bonn government had decided on the same day to forgo a ban on the NPD and to allow a 'hidden amnesty' for Nazi criminals. The

NPD belonged to the Bonn system just as Hitler's Nazi party had belonged to the Weimar Republic. In those days as today, politicians such as Hindenburg, Stresemann, Brüning and Papen, Kiesinger, Strauss, Wehner and Schmidt, had warned against the extremists of the Left and the Right, had claimed that they represented the 'democratic middle'. But, said von Schnitzler, in reality they 'crack down on the Left with all the power of the State, while they caress the Right and allow it complete freedom and publicity'. He went on to ask why West German television had given so much coverage to a current NPD convention. 'Is it to make the NPD appear as a respectable party for the September general election?' For in September a whole group of 'such people' would take their seats in the West German parliament, the parliament which claimed to represent all of Germany within the borders that existed during Hitler's Reich.[1]

East German broadcasts are constantly monitored by the Bonn government and such stations as RIAS. But very few other West Germans tune in to GDR radio or television as regular listeners. For one thing, reception of East German television is limited. Only one-third of West Germany's viewers are within range of GDR transmitters. For another, only the barest outline of East German programmes is given in Western television guides. The Bonn Defence Ministry keeps a close watch on the broadcasts of a Communist station called *Deutscher Soldatensender* which tries to undermine morale in the West German armed forces. But the general consensus in the Federal Republic is that GDR political programmes have virtually no impact among West German or West Berlin listeners. In so far as they have an effect, it is negative. East German newscasts and political commentaries are generally so biased, so loaded with propaganda that they arouse abhorrence rather than sympathy.

One form of airborne propaganda across the border uses balloons and rockets instead of transmitters. This is the 'leaflet war' between East and West Germany. Its heyday was in the 1950s, when the Federal Republic used to send millions of leaflets every year across the border, carried by small balloons floating eastward on the prevailing wind. The Eastern Bureau of the Social Democratic Party was the chief agency concerned, with the Christian Democrats also playing a small part in the operation.

[1] As it turned out, of course, no NDP members were elected to the Bonn Parliament in the September 1969 general election.

In those days the balloons used to be launched in West Berlin as well as along the East–West border and they would deposit their propaganda loads far inside the GDR. In addition, the Social Democratic Party's Eastern Bureau used to put out booklets and brochures analysing such subjects as Marxism and dialectical materialism. Since these were too bulky to be carried by balloon, they were smuggled into East Germany by courier or mail.

Herbert Wehner, the Socialist Minister for All-German Affairs in the Grand Coalition government, personally opposed this form of propaganda activity. Neither his party nor his former ministry engages in leaflet propaganda any more. But the Psychological Warfare section of the Bonn Defence Ministry is still very much in the business. It produces leaflets which are carried across by weather-type balloons and scattered over the heads of the People's Army guards patrolling the border. The leaflets, contained in bags with a clockwork draw-string release mechanism, are designed to influence the morale of the NVA troops. They cite price comparisons of such coveted items as cars and motorcycles in order to illustrate the material advantages of living in the West. They encourage desertions by giving glowing accounts of the jobs, cars and homes found in West Germany by previous defectors. These earlier defectors are named and photographed to enhance the effect. Also the Western leaflets refute Communist propaganda that anyone deserting to the West is liable to be maltreated and blackmailed into joining Western intelligence. They try to persuade East German troops that it is a monstrous crime to shoot fellow-Germans escaping to the West. Pictures of dead and dying refugees carry captions saying: 'The world knows that the overwhelming majority of the People's Army soldiers are decent young men who would not dream of committing murder.'

Just how many of these Western leaflets are launched across the border every year is a secret. But there is no secret about the fact that the East Germans retaliate in kind. Lacking the advantage of a generally favourable wind, the GDR propagandists have to use other leaflet delivery systems than balloons. Some are placed on the seats of westbound trains, some are floated down streams leading into Bavaria, enclosed in plastic or aluminium containers. But the majority are fired across by means of small rockets or papier mâché 'cannon balls'. The small aluminium leaflet canisters attached to firework-size rockets may be seen at any Federal Frontier Defence Force information centre. Each canister contains about fifty single-sheet leaflets, which are scattered by a tiny explosive charge that goes off when the rocket hits the ground. The 'cannon balls' are so flimsy that they burst open upon impact, releasing perhaps 100 leaflets. These spherical balls are fired from rudimentary mortars and have a range, like the rockets, of no more that two or three miles. The purpose of the East German operation, like that of the West, is to subvert the border guards. Communist leaflets attack Bonn government policies and demand recognition of existing European frontiers, 'normal relations between the two German states' and disarmament. Ironically, one such East German leaflet calls for an immediate end to the 'leaflet war'. It also accuses the Bonn government of exploiting 'pictures of playgirls and naked female legs' in its leaflets to attract attention—while failing to mention that East German leaflets often use precisely this technique. Meanwhile the curious duel continues. Rockets and cannon balls come over mostly at night. Sometimes weeks may pass in any given area without a single leaflet being launched, then a veritable deluge of rockets and cannon balls are shot across to the West 'as if', one Frontier Defence Force officer put it, 'the propaganda units on the other side had been given a batch of material and simply told to unload it'. In the year 1968 Westerners counted over 4,000 rocket and cannon ball shots from the GDR into Western border areas, containing some 450,000 leaflets. They also fished 600 leaflet receptacles from Bavarian rivers.

West Berlin engages in its own peculiar form of psychological warfare, using electric signs and posters instead of leaflets. The operation is run by an offshoot of the Senate Press and Information Office called 'Studio at the Barbed Wire'. It began five days after the Wall was started, using loudspeaker vans to broadcast into East Berlin and aiming its message chiefly at the border guards. But after the 'loudspeaker war' of the first post-Wall years the technique changed. Now the West concentrates instead on visual propaganda. It has three electric signs overlooking the Wall and showing running news bulletins readable at distances of up to half a mile. These are located at the Bornholmer Strasse in the Wedding district, on a tall newspaper office building close to Checkpoint Charlie and on a hill in the Rudow area at the southern end of the sector boundary. They broadcast straight news for four hours every night, until 11 p.m. In addition there is the old gantry at the Potsdamer Platz, originally built by RIAS. It is used by the

Studio today to transmit brief stationary texts which are changed every few minutes. All these electric signs are designed to be read by civilians as well as soldiers. There are also about 100 poster sites maintained by the Studio at selected points overlooking the Wall, designed to influence Communist border guards. A typical poster message says: 'Ask your officers—do they say what they think and think what they say?' At the scene of an incident in which Communist bullets killed a fleeing refugee a sign promptly appeared: 'Was there no other possibility?' The object is not to insult the soldiers or to vent Western spleen but to sow a grain of doubt which will make the Wall sentries less blindly obedient in future.

If newspapers and magazines could cross the Wall and the Wire as easily as leaflets, the gulf between the two sides of Germany would be narrower. But such is not the case; this form of communication is almost totally lacking. Since 1948, when the Soviet zone banned sales of Western newspapers in defiance of an Allied Control Council agreement, none but Communist journals have been available to East Germans. Any East Berliner in pre-Wall days who brought a Western newspaper across the Soviet sector boundary risked prosecution. In retaliation, the Federal Republic banned the general distribution of East German papers. The hope at the time was that this would induce the other side to relax its restrictions. Years passed while both sides remained adamant. The only people in East Germany privileged to get Western newspapers were trusted officials; only a tiny number of GDR publications reached the West. In April 1964 Ulbricht suggested a limited newspaper exchange between the two German States. Many Westerners thought he was bluffing, gambling on the refusal of Bonn to lift its embargo on the free sale of East German papers in the West. For four years nobody tried to call Ulbricht's bluff. Finally in 1968 the Bonn Parliament approved a government Bill to legalize the importation of East German newspapers in the hope that Ulbricht might follow suit in return. But the effects have been minimal. No Western newsagent has found a significant market for *Neues Deutschland* and other East German papers. Even if West German distributors could obtain increased supplies, which in many cases they cannot, they would find few buyers for newspapers which rate as among the dullest in the world. GDR news-stands are still as bare of Western papers as ever. Only at the Leipzig Fair does one ever see non-Communist Western journals on sale: a limited number of copies are displayed in the Press Centre.

Western correspondents attempting to visit the GDR are required to apply for permission to the Journalists' Tours Department of the GDR Travel Bureau in East Berlin. This in turn has to get clearance for any proposed visit from the East German Foreign Ministry and, no doubt, the security authorities. It was always a chancy, frustrating business for non-Communist Western reporters to try to visit the GDR. Letters would go unanswered for months, dates would be fixed only to be changed at the last minute. Permission to visit any area or installation even faintly sensitive on security grounds would be denied. Tours had normally to be made in a large hired limousine provided, together with chauffeur and guide, for a considerable fee by the GDR government. The cost naturally had to be paid in hard currency, together with hotel and fixed subsistence charges. Guides were pleasant and helpful, but they were always trusted Communists and their presence at most (but not all) meetings with East Germans tended to inhibit frank conversation. Nevertheless, these journalistic tours were eminently worthwhile. Now, since the summer of 1967, the screws have been tightened. It is almost impossible for Western journalists to get permission to travel in the GDR. Even the Leipzig Fair became difficult to visit in the immediate aftermath of the 1968 invasion of Czechoslovakia, although in the past the East Germans had been keen to attract as many journalists to the Fair as possible. Possibly on the 1968 occasion the authorities feared that instead of reporting on the Fair, visiting Western journalists would show an embarrassing interest in the views of East Germans on the Czech experiment and its suppression. If so, they were probably right.

11

The Border Regions

LÜBECK'S handsome spires rise in a beckoning cluster above the flat Schleswig-Holstein countryside as the traveller approaches from Hamburg. Lübeck is one of Germany's most appealing towns, a place of infinite charm and character. Its splendid brick Gothic buildings have been lovingly restored after the ravages of wartime bombing, its docks modernized. Today its narrow streets bulge with traffic and shoppers. To all appearances Lübeck is enjoying a resurgence of its proud Hanseatic prosperity whose relics abound on every side.

Yet less than three miles from the city's island centre lies the Ugly Frontier. Fully one-third of Lübeck's municipal boundary comprises the border with the Communist world; its airport adjoins the East–West frontier. Ulbricht's tall wire fences line the eastern bank of the Trave estuary linking the port of Lübeck with the Baltic Sea. Inhabitants of the Schlutup suburb live right up to the border, and when they extended their potato patches across the line they were called to order by People's Army guards. Bathers at Travemünde, the holiday resort at the head of Lübeck Bay, gaze across at the curving coastline of Mecklenburg with its fringe of Communist fences and minefields. The actual boundary lies not down the River Trave but across a tongue of land called the Priwall Peninsula which juts out from the Mecklenburg side of the estuary. Here a row of red-and-white striped posts runs straight across the beach to the sea; in the summer the sand to the west of this border is dotted with basking sunbathers while the beach to the east is totally deserted except for the wheeling sea-gulls. For the fences, minefields and watchtowers are set back from the shoreline to run along the dunes at the top of the beach; the beach itself is no-man's-land.

Visitors wonder how Lübeck has managed to escape the decay and depopulation that have overtaken other communities along the unnatural dividing-line. Before 1945 roughly half the city's business was with areas lying East of the present frontier; today this hinterland is almost completely cut off. But the dropping of

Germany

the Iron Curtain on Lübeck's back doorstep has not proved an unmitigated disaster. The ancient Hanseatic port was able to become a funnel for much of the modern trade between West Germany and Sweden, between the Common Market and Scandinavia. This business has grown by leaps and bounds, and Lübeck with its rail, road and canal connections has managed to corner an increasing share. Its docks handled 5·5 million tons of seagoing cargo in 1968, a forty per cent rise over 1963. Over a million passengers used the six ferry lines which operate all year round from Lübeck and Travemünde. By contrast, its share of East European trade is minimal. Czechoslovakia still ships 50,000 tons of kaolin a year to Finland by way of East Germany's canals and Lübeck. But the GDR is concentrating its seaborne trade on Rostock. Poland ships through Szczecin. Altogether Lübeck handled only 200,000 tons of Eastern bloc cargo in 1968, a one-third increase over 1963 but still only a fraction of its turnover in the burgeoning business between western and northern Europe.

Lübeck, then, is a success story. The city would naturally be better off if its traditional business with Mecklenburg and other areas of present-day East Germany had survived. But the town has been able to adapt to political necessity. Although its population of a quarter of a million includes over 90,000 post-war refugees, it has virtually no unemployed. It has attracted enough industry to occupy one-third of its work-force; there is no sign that Lübeck is being drained of its best citizens through migration to other areas further back from the frontier. So long as the Common Market and the European Free Trade Area continue to channel much of their trade and tourism through Lübeck, the city's continued prosperity seems assured. East Germany tried to attract some of this business in 1960 when it opened the road and rail crossings at Schlutup and Lübeck. The hope was that Swedish travellers and goods destined for West Germany would use the shorter Trelleborg–Sassnitz ferry across the Baltic to the GDR and then travel by road or rail to the West. But in the event these hopes were disappointed; only about 20,000 travellers cross the Schlutup road checkpoint every year and the amount of rail freight is also too small to affect Lübeck's seaborne trade.

As one drives southwards along the *Alte Salzstrasse*, the highway which used to carry creaking wagonloads of salt from the Elbe quayside to Lübeck for shipment to Scandinavia, the first sizable town is Ratzeburg. This is the capital of the *Kreis* (district or county) of Lauenburg, with its curious history as an auto-nomous Prussian duchy. One of the largest counties in the Federal Republic, it stretches southward to the Elbe; a region of lakes, woods, meadows and marshes. *Kreis* Lauenburg's fifty-mile eastern border is the frontier with East Germany, signposted in the lakes by warning buoys as well as shore-line fences. Flying over it in a Frontier Defence Force helicopter, one can see the ditches and meandering streams that mark the old Schleswig-Holstein pro-vincial boundary with Mecklenburg. 'You see,' says the pilot through the intercom, 'our side is green, theirs is brown.' He smiles as he says this because the word 'brown' has a special association with totalitarianism in post-Hitler Germany. In the literal sense he is right: the untended wasteland between the border and the Communist minefields is indeed brown by comparison with the green fields of the West.

The pilot points out a ditch along the border that is cleaned in alternate years by men of East and West. But such co-operation is rare along this stretch of frontier which, by a recent count, mustered fifty-one watchtowers and sixty-eight bunkers. Its mine-fields and fences, often flooded in the watery landscape, block twenty-four roads, lanes and railway lines. Thistledown blows across from no-man's-land, infesting Western fields. Economi-cally, *Kreis* Lauenburg is a classic case of the typical border region. Its market towns, its dealers in animal feed, seed and farm machinery lost up to three-quarters of their clients when the frontier was closed. Its industries such as shipbuilding on the Elbe were badly hit; businessmen had to find new markets and sources of raw materials to make up for those they had lost in the East. Usually this involved extra expense due to the need to trans-port over longer distances. Ratzeburg and other border towns suffer from the 'semicircle effect' of being cut off from suppliers and customers in half of the traditional area which they used to serve. Yet local officials tell visitors to the eighteenth-century *Kreishaus* (seat of district government) in Ratzeburg's Market Square that their area has managed to adjust: that it has attracted sixty-five new businesses since the war and that Lauenburg's population continues to rise despite the drift to the cities. Even the communities closest to the border have succeeded in resist-ing migration to more prosperous areas further West.

Partly this happy result is due to the natural reluctance of Lauenburgers to uproot themselves from home and hearth, partly it is a result of the special aid programme provided by Federal and provincial governments for the border regions. Bonn has long since recognized the claims of border communities to compensation for the losses caused by economic disruption. A twenty-five mile wide strip of territory adjoining the frontier has been declared the 'Zonal Border Area'. Actually it goes further than the East–West German border alone, covering the Bavarian–Czech frontier as well. Within this area, covering over 18,000 square miles or nearly one-fifth of the entire Federal Republic, farmers and businessmen enjoy various forms of financial assistance. They get freight rate concessions toward the extra cost of long-distance shipment, cheap loans and enlarged depreciation allowances for tax purposes. Villages and towns get subsidies and easy credits to finance road-building and other public works. Poorer communities in the immediate vicinity of the border can get up to four-fifths of these costs from the Federal and provincial exchequers. But the funds involved are limited: total Zonal Border Area aid tripled in 1968 over the previous year, yet still came to little more than DM 110 million (under £12m or $27·5m). Without this help many border towns and villages would be much worse off. But despite it, the frontier regions as a whole are poorer than the average in the Federal Republic. Furthermore, no amount of money can compensate for the loss of social and cultural ties or dispel the psychological effect of the minefields separating neighbour communities.

To return to Ratzeburg: the island town is dominated by its Romanesque cathedral of Henry the Lion, noteworthy not only for its beauty but for its peculiar rôle as an ecclesiastical bridge between East and West. Ratzeburg Cathedral stands, to be sure, on Western territory. But by the laws of the Church it belongs to the Protestant bishopric of Schwerin in the East German province of Mecklenburg. Dr. H. D. Gross, the courtly, silver-haired Dean, tells the story to visitors over a drink in his book-lined study.

'Until 1937 the Cathedral and its neighbouring parishes were part of Mecklenburg,' he says. 'Then the area was given to Schleswig-Holstein, but the Cathedral remained under the Bishop of Schwerin. I submit the annual Cathedral accounts to him by mail, and we correspond whenever administrative problems arise. He has been over here twice on official visits in the last few years and from time to time we talk by telephone.'

Dr. Gross gets no financial support from the East for his

Cathedral and its two parishes. But he notes that there is nothing furtive or secret about his links with Mecklenburg. The synodal law in which the Church recognizes this connection is an official document registered with—and evidently accepted by—the East German government. It says, in paragraph 3: 'The laws, ordinances and other legal and administrative regulations of the Mecklenburg Evangelical-Lutheran Church are also valid in the Ratzeburg administrative area, in so far as they do not conflict with any other provisions of this Law or . . . because of their nature cannot apply outside the territory of the GDR. In case of doubt the Supreme Church Council shall decide.'

The Dean believes that Ratzeburg Cathedral is the only important church in West Germany which is controlled from the East. It represents one of the few fragile links remaining, now that the connections between the once-united Protestant Churches of East and West have been formally broken.

Continuing down the Old Salt Road to cross the Elbe at Lauenburg we enter the province of Lower Saxony, which accounts for 338 miles of the 858-mile border with the GDR. Here at Lauenburg stands a symbolic statue of a sailor calling across the river to East Germany. All the way upstream to Schnackenburg the river forms the border, nearly sixty miles of waterway which no man may cross. Upstream near Dömitz are the broken road and railway bridges, never repaired since the war. Schnackenburg itself is a condemned village in a dying corner of West German territory jutting into the GDR. It has no doctor, no dentist, no district nurse; no large shops and only a small school. Only one bus a day connects Schnackenburg with the nearest town twenty-five miles away. Over one-third of the population consists of Customs men and their families, fated to live in Schnackenburg because it is the last port of call in the West, the checkpoint for thousands of barges entering and leaving the GDR every year. Some years ago an East German barge crew defected lock, stock and barrel to the West. The Customs men at their dilapidated riverside headquarters also recall that a West German barge once defected to the East. So the score is even, and nobody expects any more desertions either way. The only deserters at Schnackenburg today are the villagers themselves. Younger able-bodied inhabitants have given up hope that any government aid scheme will put Schnackenburg back on its feet. It is just too remote, too isolated to attract new investment regardless of subsidies and tax incentives. So one by one the younger families drift away, leaving their houses empty and decaying.

Further southward in Lower Saxony the border villages have been spared the fate of Schnackenburg, thanks above all to the 'Beetle', the phenomenal Volkswagen produced at the Wolfsburg factory, which turns out more cars per day than any other automobile plant in the world. Wolfsburg with its 100,000 people lies so close to the border that East Germans can see the VW symbol on the firm's tall administration building. Fifty-two thousand people work at the Volkswagen factory, many of them from towns and villages up and down the border. To drive to Wolfsburg in the late afternoon is to meet endless columns of VW workers coming off the day shift and returning to their homes in such places as Helmstedt. They all drive Beetles since the firm has a preferential sales arrangement for its employees. Their pay packets sustain countless thousands in other jobs; the sturdy Beetle carries much of Lower Saxony on its back. Soon it will carry even more, since Volkswagen is building another plant (its sixth in Germany) at the depressed-area town of Salzgitter some twenty-five miles to the south. It will provide 3,000 jobs and produce 400 vehicles daily. Since Salzgitter, like Wolfsburg, is in the border zone, Volkswagen is benefiting from the government's programme of border incentives. It will get one-quarter of the DM 450 million (£47m or $112·5m) total investment cost of the Salzgitter works from the State. Until now, Volkswagen has not been able to take advantage of this subsidy scheme: an official of the provincial Economics Ministry said in Hanover: 'If we had paid out to Volkswagen on the same scale as other firms, we would have had nothing left for anybody else.' The government aid that Volkswagen is getting now is a small recompense for all that the Beetle has done for Germany.

Close to Wolfsburg and benefiting from its prosperity is the border village of Zicherie, visited by hundreds of thousands of tourists a year. Its main street ends at the barricades where sightseers gape across at the twin village of Böckwitz behind the Wire. Only a hefty stone's throw away stand the houses of families who have been neighbours for centuries, now marooned in the East. Beside the Western vantage-point lies a rough-hewn stone with the brave inscription in capital letters: *Deutschland ist Unteilbar*— Germany is Indivisible. But across the road is an information centre displaying in graphic terms precisely how Germany *has* been divided.

'You are standing here,' says a wall placard, 'in the middle of the double village Böckwitz-Zicherie, which until 1945 was a single social and cultural unit. On July 1, 1945, the Soviet Army occupied Böckwitz. The inhabitants of Zicherie lost their school, their dairy, almost all their tradesmen's workshops and their connection with relatives and friends.' The sign recalls the creation of the original barrier in May 1952, a wooden wall 300 yards long and ten feet high, built of boards which were soon pierced by peepholes drilled when the guards were not looking. Burgomaster Matthies of Zicherie remembers the anger with which his villagers watched through these spyholes the forced eviction of the local publican from his inn that used to stand in today's barren no-man's-land.

'Our impulse was to tear down the board fence and go to his aid,' Matthies says. 'It was just as well that we didn't. The innkeeper, his wife and son soon managed to escape across the border. The daughter stayed behind to finish her schooling, and now she is stuck over there.' The burgomaster has mixed feelings about the proximity of his village to Wolfsburg. He used to be thankful that the Volkswagen plant was so close since it gave jobs to refugees—including neighbours from Böckwitz—and farm hands made redundant by mechanization. But now he finds that it is giving too many jobs: village tradesmen like the local bricklayer and electrician are also commuting to Wolfsburg, and this is a real deprivation. Zicherie's 250 inhabitants in pre-war days almost doubled after the influx of refugees in 1945. But since then the village population has dropped to 250 again. Only fifteen of the fifty-five families who engaged in farming before the war are still farming today. Altogether forty-five Zicherie men and women work in Wolfsburg and other neighbouring communities. Twenty-seven Zicherie families include people stemming from towns and villages in the East. Matthies himself is not a refugee; he has lived on his wife's farm in Zicherie since his marriage. But he has now lost his own farm in Böckwitz which he had continued to cultivate.

Zicherie has new buildings and well-paved streets; it does not have the decadent air of Schnackenburg. But the 200,000 to 250,000 tourists who, Matthies says, come to the village every year to gaze across the border do not bring the locals much business. They pull up in the free parking places beside the burgomaster's house, walk to the border, read the placards, take some snapshots and drive away without spending a pfennig. Perhaps some day the village will boast a souvenir stand selling refreshments, picture postcards and toy People's Army soldiers. But so far nobody has had the temerity to defy the convention that it is bad taste to make money out of German division. The inn up the road does not advertise; its main lunchtime business is selling ice-creams to local children at twenty or thirty pfennigs apiece. Matthies worries about the future of his village when these children grow up. He fears that they may choose to settle further West rather than rebuild old houses and barns in Zicherie. Older Zicherie citizens still nurture their family links with Böckwitz: they wave from the outlying fields when nobody is watching, they receive visits from Böckwitz relatives who have reached retirement age and can travel to the West. Sometimes Zicherie people get visas to visit the GDR, but they may not go to Böckwitz because it lies in the forbidden zone. So they have to make a rendezvous somewhere further from the border.

South of Zicherie the road runs next to the border, so close that for two miles the roadside ditch marks the boundary. Here one may see the cross marking the spot where Kurt Lichtenstein, a Dortmund journalist, was shot dead by Communist guards in 1961 when he jumped the ditch to talk to workers in the adjacent East German fields. Road and frontier then separate and the line of warning signs recedes into the distance, only to reappear near the Rühen bridge over the Mittelland Canal a few miles North of Helmstedt.

Helmstedt has become world-famous for its Autobahn checkpoint, the scene of dramatic confrontations and Communist hold-ups since the Berlin Blockade. People forget that the town of 30,000 with its charming market square and erstwhile university has a post-war history of its own. Shorn of its old business links with the rich Magdeburg area to the east, Helmstedt and its county lost 30,000 people to the richer industrial regions in the west and south-west. There were no jobs for them in Helmstedt's depressed economy. By the early 1950s over two-fifths of the local population consisted of retired people. One of the worst blows was the division in May 1952 of the opencast lignite workings straddling the border between Helmstedt and Offleben. Until then the giant excavators on the Western side of the line had continued to supply the Harbke power station and the Bismarck

Briquette Factory on Soviet zone territory. In return, Helmstedt and other areas in the British zone continued to draw electric power from Harbke. This was laid down in an agreement signed on January 1, 1947, between British and Russian officers. Two thousand workers crossed the line in each direction to operate the entire industrial complex as a single unit. But on May 26, the day the frontier was closed, Communist troops spread barbed wire through the middle of the lignite workings. It so happened that an excavator worth DM 2 million (about £200,000 or $500,000) had just been returned to the eastern part of the mine after undergoing repairs in the West. Border-crossing commuters found their way blocked by fences and armed guards. The power station and briquette factory were cut off from their Western raw material supplies. Access from the West to those opencast workings remaining on the Western side of the border was blocked by great earthmounds: it took a year to clear openings and get the digging restarted. Helmstedt meanwhile had lost its power from the Harbke generators, and had to buy electricity from the West German grid until a new power station could be built at Offleben. The burdens involved in this mammoth readjustment were enormous. Not until the late 1950s did the mine managers of both sides agree at least to a *modus vivendi* permitting the West to tip its waste material on to GDR territory, and vice versa.

Helmstedt officials made other mutually advantageous pacts with the East. For instance, both sides agreed to co-operate in draining a 3,000-acre stretch of marshland beside the frontier south of the town, turning it into fertile fields and meadows. But on the whole it has been hard for Helmstedt to adapt. The old contacts have dried up, the business links are gone. Until the late 1950s it was still possible for football teams and singing groups to cross the checkpoint and exchange visits with friendly towns in the East. But all that came to an end in 1961, as did most of the official contacts on such matters as river control and air pollution from power station chimneys. Again the Beetle came to the rescue: every day 1,500 people from Helmstedt town and 12,000 from Helmstedt *Kreis* commute to the Volkswagen cornucopia in Wolfsburg. A large tyre factory has come to the neighbourhood, too, and Helmstedt is recovering. But the lignite reserves will run out in the 1990s. And even today the town's wages are said to average ten per cent below the national level while its food and clothing prices are higher.

Close to the Helmstedt–Berlin Autobahn lies the burned hulk of a bus trailer athwart the old *Reichsstrasse 1*, a famous landmark for refugees in the great trek across the 'green border'. When they reached it they knew they were in the British zone. Today its rusty roof has caved in and it is overlooked by Communist watch-towers. The road itself, which used to run proudly from Aachen on the Belgian border to Königsberg (now Kaliningrad) in East Prussia, ends in fences and minefields. A few miles south at Offleben, beyond the divided lignite mines, is another favourite lookout spot for border visitors. A friendly policeman points out the site of the old village cemetery, its gravestones now torn up by People's Army guards. Nearby, he recalls, a refugee bled to death among the mines in October 1967 and he tells of the in-credible escape by a father who led his three small children safely through the same minefield in December of that year. The infor-mation centre at Offleben recounts that the town sawmill lost sixty per cent of its clients and a local butcher half his business through the building of the border. But the most impressive frontier view of all in this area is that of Hötensleben, at the end of the short drive from Schöningen. Hötensleben is a closely-packed East German town lying immediately beside the border with its tall metal screens and dog runs. Western visitors can walk for several hundred yards along their side of the stream that marks the actual boundary, searching the windows of the houses for a furtive wave (which sometimes comes) and watching the People's Army troops sunning themselves beside the entrance to their bunker.

From Schöningen it is only a short drive to the Harz Moun-tains whose misty crests stand out above the plains of northern Germany. If ever there were a cultural unit sundered by an un-natural dividing-line, this is it. The boundary runs just west of the Brocken, a mountain famous in German legend where witches riding broomsticks were said to gather each April 30 to celebrate their Sabbath on Walpurgis Night. Its summit, once the goal of countless ramblers, now stands forlorn and deserted in the for-bidden zone; since 1961 not even foreign tourists visiting the Eastern Harz can scale its easy slopes. For years after the war it was possible for yodelling groups and other typical Harz organ-izations to exchange visits. Singing contests were held, other cultural links maintained. But from about 1960 onwards these East–West visits became impossible. Older Harz residents in the

West yearn for the old days. Talking to them one realizes that they still feel more kinship with the Harz people across the border than with the lowlanders of Hamburg and Cologne.

Dr. Rolf Denecke of Bad Harzburg lives only three miles from the border. He edits the nostalgic little monthly magazine *Unser Harz* (Our Harz) which calls itself a journal for the 'entire Harz'. He shows visitors the section devoted each month to news from the East Harz, such as this item, evidently taken from an East German newspaper published in Wernigerode:

> From year to year the Harz proves more of a magnet [to East German tourists]. Although young people, especially, often prefer to spend their holidays in friendly countries abroad [i.e. Eastern Europe] rather than in the Harz Mountains, the hotels in Wernigerode are already partially booked out for the summer months. But people not only visit the Harz to spend regular vacations here. More and more just come for the weekend to this charming area. Convenient rail connections stimulate the urge to travel. Passengers from Berlin, Dresden, Leipzig, Halle and Magdeburg can travel directly to this colourful town. Express motor coaches from Erfurt, Halle and Magdeburg have set their timetables to enable people in search of recreation to arrive in the Harz in the morning and leave for home in the evening of the same day.

Tourism is the chief industry of the Harz, both East and West. In the West it is flagging badly because more and more West Germans like to go further afield, to bask in the sun of Majorca rather than hike in the cool and rainy Harz. Despite considerable investment, towns like Bad Harzburg have a dearth of visitors. Half-empty hotels stand prim and old-fashioned around the spa's modern pump room, waiting for the guests who never come. Perhaps they would be better off if the border had been drawn further West, for East Germans cannot fly to Majorca. But then, again, there is the three-mile forbidden zone on the Communist side of the frontier where only the birds and the animals can roam at will. Dr. Denecke shows visitors an East German map of the Harz: like the other GDR maps it stops short of the border so as not to betray the lie of the land to any would-be refugee.

A sad place, then, the Harz. Dr. Denecke travels far and wide showing eager audiences his lecture slides of beloved towns and villages cut off by the Ugly Frontier. Sometimes he gets contributions to his magazine from Harz residents in East Germany, writing non-politically about the silver-mines of bygone days or the old hunting lodges. He prints them as unsigned articles, or under a *nom de plume*. But all this is sentiment and nostalgia, like the signs assuring the visitor to the border amid the forest that 'The other side is Germany, too'. Today's reality is different: the Harz is divided as drastically as a tree split by lightning.

The Brocken is now called by local residents the highest mountain in the world—because nobody can climb it. Further south, near Duderstadt, is the 'longest station in the world' at the village of Zwinge, so named because to travel from one end of its divided platforms to the other one must go by way of Helmstedt or Bebra, a detour of 250 miles. Until 1966 the farmers in the West could see through the barbed wire into the brick factory beside the station. But then the view was blocked by a 500-yard concrete wall ten feet high, a slice of Berlin Wall through one of Germany's smallest villages. One farmhouse in the West, perhaps a couple of hundred yards from where the rusty rails end in a tangle of weeds, still draws its electric power from the East. But the West has installed a spare cable to provide an alternative supply if the GDR supply should fail.

Duderstadt itself is a town of timbered houses and narrow streets, so close to the border that it used to get most of its water from a rich spring at Brehme in the Soviet zone. Then the source began to dry up because nobody bothered to keep the spring clear. Only one-third of the original quantity came across and Duderstadt had to dig for alternative supplies. If the remaining flow of GDR water should fail, Duderstadt can now meet the need from the West. For many years Dr. Matthias Gleitze, the former *Oberkreisdirektor* (district commissioner) of the county of Duderstadt, was able to iron out local problems with his local government colleagues across the frontier. 'Now,' he says, 'they have evidently got cold feet on the other side. There are no more negotiations at the community level.' One of his last attempts to make contact with the GDR was on September 15, 1967, when he telephoned the county administration in Worbis, ten miles away across the border. He wanted to ask whether a missing seventeen-year-old Duderstadt boy had turned up in East Germany. The Worbis switchboard operator said nobody was available to discuss the matter and referred him to the People's Police who denied knowledge of the boy. But, in fact, Gleitze found out later, the boy was already there, and in process of being sentenced to three months' jail for crossing the frontier illegally. Only when it is in the interest of the East to respond does it follow up an approach by the West. For instance, when Gleitze reported that ten East German cows had strayed to the West, the other side was quick to send a man to fetch them back.

Duderstadt has the unusual problem for a border community of having too many children. A Catholic town, Duderstadt has twenty-five births per thousand inhabitants compared with only seventeen or eighteen per thousand in neighbouring areas such as Göttingen. 'So we have to spend large sums of money on schools,' says Gleitze. 'Yet many of our school-leavers emigrate to other parts of the country because they cannot find work here, or because the pay is better elsewhere. Duderstadt has become to some extent a training-ground—our taxpayers fork out the money but other communities reap the benefit.' Local industries suffering from the loss of their hinterland complain that the government aid scheme hardly begins to make up for the extra transport cost due to the border.

Duderstadt is full of human stories typical of the frontier. For many years the Duderstadt men's choir and brass band came up to the border on Christmas Eve to sing carols to the people in the neighbouring village of Ecklingerode, who responded by flashing a light or waving a towel from their windows. There was a Duderstadt woman who carried a wreath to the frontier on the day of her mother's funeral in Ecklingerode. She hung the wreath on the barbed wire as she watched the sad ceremony through binoculars from the West.

Here in the south-easterly corner of Lower Saxony is the Friedland refugee camp through whose gates more than two million people have passed since World War II. A commandeered cowshed, cleaned and spread with heather, was the first impro- vised shelter for Friedland refugees in 1945, supplemented by tents and hundreds of Nissen huts. The primitive camp was the gateway to the British and American zones. It was used by returning German prisoners-of-war from Siberia as well as civilians; soldiers staggered into the compound suffering from malnutrition and tuberculosis. Permanent buildings, flower beds and paved roads have replaced the rudimentary facilities of those early days. The flow of refugees has ebbed to a comparative trickle. But Friedland, like Berlin's Marienfelde refugee centre, still keeps the gates open.

Witzenhausen, near Kassel, marks the provincial boundary between Lower Saxony and Hesse, the point at which the U.S. Army takes over its frontier patrolling responsibility on BAOR's right flank. The *Hessisches Bergland* is beautiful rolling countryside, green and fertile. Across it runs the Autobahn toward Eisenach, with its unfinished stretch crossing a bulge of GDR territory and its detour over country roads.

Doubtless the most famous house along the entire 858-mile border is the home of the Hossfeld family at Philippsthal. It has the distinction of being the only building which actually straddles the frontier. The Hossfeld family printing works and most of the adjoining living quarters lie in the West. But a small section of the building stands empty and decaying in the East, walled off from the rest. Hans Hossfeld, a burly man in his early forties, relates for the thousandth time his remarkable tale. When he came back from a Siberian prisoner-of-war camp in 1948 he found his house in the Soviet zone and Russian sentries outside. He moved back in, joining his father Erich and more than twenty relatives who were already there. But they were determined to resist incorporation in the Communist world. The late Erich Hossfeld, who had lived in the house since 1903 and printed a local newspaper until the Nazis banned it, was not to be intimidated. He went to the American commander at nearby Bad Hersfeld and told him that the Russians were encroaching on Western territory. He could prove it: the old Hessian-Thuringian provincial marker stone which was supposed to show the zonal border lay right in front of his house entrance. The Americans backed him and persuaded the Russians to pull back a couple of hundred yards, thus 'liberating' several houses to the West. But still the Hossfelds had not won their battle, for the Russians took the view that since the front door lay just to the East of the marker stone the whole house and printing works rightfully belonged to the Soviet zone. Threatened with dispossession, the Hossfelds took matters into their own hands. Hans and his brother-in-law secretly began in 1951 to carry bricks and mortar into the house, lugging them in rucksacks and an old naval kitbag over the hills by night and bringing them in by a back window. On New Year's Eve in 1951 they were ready to wall off the small section of their house lying in the East. The Americans knew about their plan, but warned:

'Don't expect us to back you if it fails—we don't want a second Korea.' The Hossfelds plied the Communist sentries with schnapps and muffled the hammering as they built a framework to hold the bricks. Then they worked through the night and by daybreak the wall was finished. Taken by surprise, the Communist guards did not try to evict them. For a while the family was harassed by shots and stones from the People's Police. But since then they have lived under Western protection. Reviving the printing plant was difficult since four-fifths of their old clients lived in the East, across the River Werra bridge in the adjacent town of Vacha. Today they live mostly from government printing contracts, and wonder whether they might not have done better simply to abandon their house and claim compensation. Hans Hossfeld speaks of a 'certain bitterness' among border residents at their treatment by the government. He cites one occasion when all his windows were broken and his roof damaged by exploding Communist mines. He claims that it was a month before he got any compensation at all, and the sum was so derisory that he sent the cheque back with a rude note to the Federal minister concerned in Bonn.

From Fulda, with its baroque splendour and its exquisite St. Michael's Church dating from the ninth century, the border curves eastward into Bavaria. It follows the fringe of the Thuringian Forest which lies now in East Germany, with large fields, low hills and streams. The *Coburger Tagesblatt* caters for the yearning of its readers for news of communities over in Thuringia. Dr. Richard Wicke, its editor, says his East German column appears only irregularly, when there is something to run. Its contents come mainly from letters written from East Germany to people in the Coburg area and passed on by the recipients to him. Occasionally the paper gets material from East German visitors to Coburg or from refugees. Telephone communication across the border is useless, Dr. Wicke says, because even when a connection can be obtained the person at the other end is unwilling to speak frankly for fear of line-tapping. The main interest of *Coburger Tagesblatt* readers is in news from Thuringia, but the column also tries to satisfy curiosity about places as far afield as Dresden. The editor says his only object in running the feature is reader interest: it reports the news as it is received, covering both positive and negative aspects of life in the GDR. Most of the material is 'parish pump' news which can hardly be politically distorted.

Bavaria is full of frontier lore. Local people recall the days when whole villages adjoining the Thuringian side of the border were razed by the East German authorities to simplify the task of frontier control. When Rottenbach was demolished some of its evicted residents who had fled to the West stood weeping at the Wire as the bulldozers flattened their homes. For many years the road to Lehesten, just inside East Germany north of Kronach, was the only place along the entire border where people still commuted daily to work. As late as May 1961 some eighty Western workmen used to cross by bus and motorcycle to the Lehesten slate mines, as their fathers and grandfathers had before them. They drew their basic pay in Western marks and their fringe benefits such as children's allowances in GDR currency. Many of them bought schnapps with their East-marks in the socialized store and brought it back in their rucksacks. It all worked quite smoothly: the workers were not subjected to any political pressure in the East. Once a couple of them were re-warded for their hard work with the GDR title of 'Activists' and given 120 marks as a cash bonus. But Konrad Hoderlein, their local trade union chief, was unperturbed. 'It was all very un-political,' he said. 'Should we have made them feel bad about taking the 120 marks?'

This anomalous situation was bound to end. In September 1961, soon after the Wall had blocked all remaining commuter traffic in Berlin, the road to Lehesten was finally closed. But other oddities continue: the town of Sonneberg in East Germany still takes its electricity supply by a short-circuit route across a bulge of Bavarian territory from Lehesten instead of taking the long way round. Once every two or three years a group of East Ger-man workmen comes across to paint the pylons. Near the neigh-bouring town of Tettau the wayward frontier cuts off a section of the railway line that serves the local glassworks and other factories. The wagons, complete with their loads of coal and kaolin, must be mounted on road transporters at Steinbach am Wald and taken six miles to Tettau. The cost of this 'portage' is met by the Federal and Bavarian State governments. Also in this area there are East German farms still supplied with gas from the large gasworks at Neustadt in Bavaria. Until Christmas Eve 1967 the Neustadt plant continued to feed gas to the toy and glass factories across the border in Sonneberg and Lauscha, but the Communist authorities then ceased taking the supply.

Further east lies Hirschberg on the Saale River separated by a broken bridge from the Bavarian village of Tiefengrün. The owner of Hirschberg's large leather factory used to cross the river every day from Tiefengrün, until one morning his path was blocked. The plant is now a 'People's Factory' and the former owner has moved away with his family to the West. A Berlin-style wall runs along the East German bank of the Saale and the denizens of Hirschberg seldom return a wave from the West.

If Philippsthal in Hesse has the best-known house on the border, Mödlareuth in Bavaria is the frontier's most famous village. For it is divided by a wall 1,800 feet long and ten feet high, the latest in a series of barriers slicing straight through the valley community. It separates the large duckpond in Communist Thuringia from the village green in Bavaria. It divides families who used to meet in the early post-war years beside the frontier booms. When the border was barricaded in 1952 the East Germans erected an eight-foot board fence similar to the original barrier in Zicherie. Villagers could still climb ladders from the Western side and peek across; they could bore small holes. Five families came across from East Mödlareuth in 1952 when they were threatened with eviction and resettlement further back from the border.

In 1957 the wooden fence was replaced by thick coils of barbed wire, which in their turn gave way to the wall on the Berlin pattern that was completed in 1966. The two halves of Mödlareuth today provide the spectacle of a miniature Berlin, a microcosm of German division amid the bucolic landscape of rolling pine-woods and fields. As one walks along the stony road next to the concrete barrier the sounds of village life rise from both sides: tractors, clucking hens, barking dogs and shouting children. Where the wall reaches the end of the village it gives way to barbed wire and minefields, enabling the visitor to see into the other world beyond. Smoke rises from the chimneys of the trim houses in East Mödlareuth; the settlement looks peaceful and there are no People's Army guards or watchtowers in sight. But far back on the edge of a wood outside the village lies a concrete bunker affording a high vantage point over the extraordinary scene. And beyond it again stands a high wire fence, presumably built to mark the edge of the border zone which nobody but the politically trusted inhabitants of East Mödlareuth are allowed to enter without a pass.

Beside the village green on the Western side of the wall lives

Frau Lena Zeh, a sturdy woman in her late sixties who sells picture postcards and beer to tourists. Her sister-in-law lives only fifty yards away on the Communist side. Until the board fence went up in 1952 they could still shout across to each other at the frontier booms, or wave from their respective windows. But now the view is blocked and all direct communication is at an end. Frau Zeh recalls in her strong Bavarian accent the escape of two East Mödlareuth families on June 4 and 5, 1952. She watched one family climb out of a stable window close to the border at 10.30 p.m. and nip across to Bavaria with whatever belongings they could throw to the ground. But they had to leave their cattle and other livestock behind. Next morning another family managed to flee while the *Vopos* were busy evicting people from houses in another part of the village. Frau Zeh has seen it all; seen the Russians commandeer her house in the first year after the war, seen the children peek over the old wooden fence, seen the People's Army pioneers build the wall with its girder reinforcement, seen the village school turned into a grocery shop for lack of pupils. She has talked to countless visitors, including President Lübke of West Germany, who came in 1964. On top of a cupboard in her kitchen lies a stack of letters and postcards she has received from tourists, including a Christmas card from a family in Bradford, Yorkshire, who once made the trip to Mödlareuth. Through it all she has kept up her sardonic humour. Her picture postcards show Mödlareuth at various stages of its post-war history. She does not know how many she has sold over the years; once she told a visitor with a cheery wink: 'I'll get thousands of them printed and then one day Germany will be reunited and I'll be stuck with the lot!' On the kitchen wall hangs one of those devout religious plaques so often found in peasant homes. Some of its sentiments acquire special significance in a house so close to the wall:

> Lord, in Thy great goodness;
> Protect us from all misery.
> Watch over this our house . . .
> And spare us from all evil.

Today Mödlareuth's local affairs are managed from Töpen, a village in the next valley some miles away. Hermann Schultz, burgomaster of the combined communities, is the local baker and shopkeeper—at Eastertide he is busy making giant flat cakes for children's confirmation parties, which he loads on to a large farm wagon for delivery. He recalls that Mödlareuth was always divided into Bavarian and Thuringian administrations, and that the people of East Mödlareuth used to have their own mayor until the late 1940s. The children of Töpen went to school in the East section of the divided village until their way was blocked by the board fence in 1952. Burgomaster Schultz used to meet his colleagues of the neighbouring East German community during the early post-war years to discuss such matters as forestry and water. But all these contacts came inexorably to an end, like the electricity links that were cut in 1950. Töpen itself enjoyed a temporary boom as long as the River Saale bridge was down, for the village lay on the detour road used by thousands of cars and trucks forced to turn off the Munich–Berlin Autobahn. Petrol stations and restaurants sprang up in Töpen to cater to their needs. But since the bridge was rebuilt Töpen has resumed its quiet existence off the beaten track, and the petrol pumps have vanished from the filling stations. Farmers on both sides of the border lost fields when the frontier was closed. As elsewhere along the boundary, land belonging to farmers still in East Germany is cultivated by the West and the proceeds go into a special blocked account in the true owner's name. If ever the owner comes to the West, as a refugee or as a pensioner, he is able to draw on the nest-egg that has been accumulating to his credit.

Both Töpen and West Mödlareuth lie within the remotest *Landkreis* (district) of the Federal Republic, a corner of Bavarian territory projecting northward from Bayreuth. Bounded by the Czechoslovak as well as the East German border, the rural district of Hof is far removed from the focus of West German industry along the Rhine, the Ruhr and the Main. Its breweries and textile mills never had to compete before with Dortmund and Munich; they found ready markets close at hand in Thuringia, Saxony and northern Bavaria. Now the Thuringia–Saxony area with its dense population has been cut off and Hof has had to readjust. 'We have to face west instead of north,' says *Landrat* (district commissioner) Schulze in his Hof office. 'West-bound transport links either didn't exist or had to be improved at great expense. But you can't reduce the distance from here to Frankfurt, however good the roads are.'

Schulze says the portrayal of Hof and its neighbourhood as a 'dead corner' of the Federal Republic has been much overdone.

But he admits that the border has hurt Hof more than most places. While Munich and Upper Bavaria have enjoyed population growth, *Landkreis* Hof has taken a gradual decline of its working population over the last ten years. 'In the last year or so this out-flow has slowed down,' he said in early 1969. 'There is prosperity here, with full employment. But even full employment is not everything. Regardless of the amount of "political aid" we get, we can only hope to slow down the working of the negative factors. We can never eradicate them.' *Landkreis* Hof with its 35,000 inhabitants and forty communities has been able to get DM 3 million (£312,000 or $750,000) from the Federal government and one-third less from the Bavarian government in special border assistance. The money has helped build roads, schools and hospitals. Local industries have benefited from the special tax write-offs but, as Schulze says, 'you can only have write-offs from profits'. The government compensation for excess freight costs has helped firms using coal, for example. But there is no 'freight aid' subsidy for electric power, and this might lead some major power-using firms to build elsewhere. Schulze would like to attract the growth industries of the future, but although he can offer labour it is mostly untrained. Furthermore, service in-dustries such as banking and insurance cannot be expected to invest in rural areas far from great population centres.

The *Landrat* remembers that local border-crossing traffic con-tinued in his area until the middle of 1953, when it suffered a check. Then came a period of relaxation in 1954–55 after the shock to East Germany from the 1953 rebellion, before the cur-tain came down in 1961. Travelling in Bavaria one comes across evidence that the old co-operation across the border is not en-tirely dead. Bayreuth borrows musicians and opera singers from East Germany to perform in its Wagner Festival. Research workers can still get co-operation from East German libraries when they ask for documents and microfilms. But such examples are rare, and there is growing reluctance to talk about them for fear that they will disappear altogether.

But even when exchanges of community visits still took place the GDR groups used always to bring over Communist officials to ensure that there were political overtones. Once Schulze sug-gested to his opposite number in East Germany that they discuss mutual problems such as water. 'The Communist official started talking about the atomic bomb,' Schulze recalls. 'I told him that if he wanted to talk about the Bomb he had better go to Stalin!'

At the Upper Franconia government and Chamber of Commerce in Bayreuth the experts confirm *Landrat* Schulze's account of Hof's economic troubles and say that Hof is no exception. The whole of Upper Franconia—covering the north-easterly corner of Bavaria from Forchheim to Hof and from Coburg to the porcelain district around Selb—was hard-hit by the Iron Curtain. As one local economist puts it, Upper Franconia found itself transformed from an integral part of Central Germany's industrial area—second in importance only to the Rhine and the Ruhr—into a peripheral region on the fringe of the Federal Republic and the Common Market. It was forced to turn to new markets and new sources of raw materials located much farther away. As a result of these handicaps its prosperity grew at a much slower rate than the booming growth in more centrally-situated regions. Great efforts have been made to improve Upper Franconia's transport, electricity and gas links with the rest of the Federal Republic. But the facts of geography are ineluctable, and northern Bavaria seems fated to remain the classic example of a problem-ridden border area for the indefinite future.

This selective survey of the border regions from Lübeck to Hof has been necessarily confined to the West since first-hand reporting from the East German side of the frontier is impossible. No Western observer is permitted to enter the three-mile forbidden zone; few Western correspondents may tour the GDR. Some years ago Philip Shabecoff of the *New York Times* wrote a brilliant description of Mödlareuth as seen from the West. He recorded in his article that he had hoped to visit the Eastern side as well, and had applied for permission to the Journalists' Tours Department of the GDR Travel Bureau. His application was refused on the ground that 'the United States and the Federal Republic of Germany do not have diplomatic relations with the German Democratic Republic'.

Given this blank refusal, the Western writer seeking to portray living conditions on the Communist side of the line can only quote East German reports. Here is a portrait of the East German border village of Wahlhausen as described by the Communist party organ *Neues Deutschland* in its issue of May 24, 1957. There is no reason to suppose that conditions in this 'shopwindow' have changed very much in the meantime.

When the trains on the West German railway line from Frankfurt/Main to Hamburg travel along the bank of the Werra many passengers look searchingly out of the window for a glimpse of the 'Iron Curtain', which is so much discussed in West German newspapers and radio broadcasts. But the lovely Thuringian landscape lies exposed to view. A small village rests in the valley, red roofs crowning the bright, clean, timbered houses. Children play in the street and farmers work in the fields to exploit the timely spring.

The village of Wahlhausen stands on the border with West Germany like a shopwindow that shows the quality of everything beyond. Passing travellers are not the only people who look. When the village forester was visiting his relatives in the Odenwald [West Germany], the farmers there besieged him with questions about the German Democratic Republic. The forester told of this interest recently at a village meeting after the First Secretary of the *Bezirk* Erfurt [administrative region of Erfurt], Hermann Fischer, had described the reunification policy of our Party to the citizens of Wahlhausen. The farmer Wilhelm Stallknecht, deputy burgomaster of the village, laid emphasis on the appeal of the thirtieth Central Committee session to raise production for the market. 'That is realistic and possible,' he said, 'and all agricultural businesses in the community will do their best to fufil the demand of the Party and the government.'

Who are these people, and what does this village look like, this village with just the same number of inhabitants as the total of days in a year?

Take Wilhelm Stallknecht. He farms 3·5 hectares and is a member of the village council and the [Communist-affiliated] CDU. Although he is no longer the youngest, he plays an active role in social life. Meetings and events without him are hardly imaginable. We asked him how he could reconcile all this with his work.

'Yes,' he said, 'it would not be possible if my farm were not heavily mechanized.' And he ticks off the list: electric feed cutter, power mower, washing machine and several other machines.

'We are modern farmers,' Günther Gastrock-May confirmed. 'We use everything that can lighten our work.' Something else that can lighten life is standing gleaming in the clean farmyard: a 'Wartburg' car that the young Eichsfeld farmer was able to buy because he maintains his eight-hectare farm in perfect shape. Günther Gastrock-May, who came to our Republic only a few years ago from West Germany, is a member of the village council; this shows that he has won the confidence of the inhabitants both through his farming achievements and through his exemplary work in the FDJ [Free German Youth] group.

These farmers are not the only ones who can show successes in their work. Apart from sizeable advance deliveries for the year 1957 the village was able to send 128,586 kg. of milk, 45,000 eggs, 56 dozen beef cattle and 139 dozen pigs to the open market. The farmers managed this because they constantly employ new methods and exchange experiences. Last but not least, the small LPG [socialist farmers' cooperative] played a considerable part in this result.

New life has come to the village school, too. Four out of eight school-leavers in 1956 were able to go on to high school. This is a big achievement on the part of the teacher, Karl Schulz, who until now has had to teach all ages in one class.

The village council also concerns itself with the children. Once a month a council member takes part in the teaching, and whenever difficulties occur they are settled by general discussion. The school will soon have two classes.

The soldiers of the Border Command are inseparable from the villagers. Twelve of them are even directly related to the Wahlhauseners since they have married girls from the village. But stronger still than these family bonds is the common desire to make village life ever better. 'We get rid of difficulties jointly,' Lieutenant Günther Jahn told us. 'For example we all found it deplorable that for a long time there was no inn. We didn't go running to the *Kreis* or the *Bezirk*; we saw to the re-opening ourselves. Farmers and soldiers now often spend happy times there together.'

'The most important thing about our cooperation is the security of the frontier sector near Wahlhausen,' Lt. Jahn told us. 'Whenever there is a shortage of men, the border soldiers do not stand alone. Everyone in the village who possibly can join in any action to deal with attempted border violations does so. Nobody can enter or leave Wahlhausen unobserved.'

The reason that so many people actively join in protecting the village and thereby our Republic is that they have achieved so much unaided. Voluntary work worth 5,323 DM was rendered in 1956 for National Construction. Well over a thousand fruit trees were planted, roads improved and renewed, the fire station was built from local reserves, the church tower repaired with contributions from the villagers. Thirteen pasture feeding-places were kept supplied with food by pioneers from the school. A sports field is also being built.

In the evening we met in the village inn all those that we had got to know during our visit. The farmers Wilhelm Stall-knecht, Günther Gastrock-May, the cooperative farmer Kurt Müller sat at the village council table. Among the listeners were the teacher, the soldiers of the Border Command, the farmers of the village and their wives. It was like a big family. People discussed the problems of the village and the Plan for National Construction. It is the Plan of the farmers. And it is characteristic that the Village Work Plan is chiefly designed to ease and improve the fulfilment of the State Plan.

This is Wahlhausen, small and modest, but a convincing shopwindow of the Workers' and Peasants' State, in which creative people gear their efforts and their fate to general advantage.

Such is the view of an East German border village as seen through Communist spectacles. It speaks for itself.

12

Berlin Out on a Limb

WEST Berlin is the border area *par excellence*. It displays in accentuated form all the symptoms of frontier malaise found in communities from Lübeck to Hof. It depends upon massive transfusions of aid from Bonn. Yet it remains, for the time being, very much alive. True, the population is declining, but this is due to its disproportionate death-rate rather than to any exodus to the West. Most of the 2·2 million people in the Western sectors have learned to live as islanders in a Communist sea.

A Berliner born and bred, with his big-city mentality, dry wit and *'na und?'* (so what?) philosophy feels no more at home in Hamburg or Cologne than a London Cockney transplanted to Manchester. 'If I had to live in West Germany I'd just as soon emigrate,' a well-known West Berlin architect, Hans Müller, remarked. Nodding vigorously, a lawyer agreed. 'Everything is so conservative, even reactionary—I feel stifled every time I am over there,' he said. Neither man used the term 'provincial', but this is the feeling most Berliners have about the Federal Republic. Yet despite their disdain for 'provincial uncles', Berliners readily absorb newcomers who are willing to accept their metropolitan rules of life. The city is a melting-pot, and this has given it a dynamic quality lacking in the older, more staid towns of West Germany.

After surviving Communist threats and harassments for a quarter of a century, few West Berliners today are frightened by the bogey of a Red invasion. The faint-hearts left long ago at the time of the blockade, Khrushchev's threats or the building of the Wall. Every Berliner knows that the tiny Allied garrisons would be overwhelmed in a trice if the Russians ever made a move. But he also believes that since such an attack would touch off a Third World War, it is unlikely. There is a constant trickle of migration among Berliners seeking better jobs in the booming Federal Republic or simply escaping from the claustrophobia of Berlin. But the vast majority of citizens are content to stay on their tight little island.

Actually their island is neither so tight nor so little. Barely half the 185-square-mile area of West Berlin consists of brick and asphalt. The rest is made up of spacious parks, woods, lakes and even farms. Citizens complain that they cannot go jaunting into the hills or to the beach at weekends, like their fellows in the Federal Republic; they grumble that by now they know every blade of grass in the Grunewald. But at least these large recreation areas exist: places where Berliners can walk, swim and enjoy their bracing climate, which is the envy of every West German. They have other assets. West Berlin is rich in theatres and concerts, cabaret and opera. For lowbrows and tourists, the city is bursting with night-life ranging from restaurants with telephones on the tables to striptease bars. Its downtown streets buzz with life long after the sober citizens of Bonn have gone to bed. Street hawkers press nightclub advertisements into the hands of passing tourists ('See six stark naked lovelies for DM 10') and prostitutes frequent the Savigny Platz. Pavement cafés on the elegant Kurfürstendamm nowadays provide their glassed-in customers with a close-up view of angry young men as well as the perennial passing parade of female fashions. For after all it was Berlin's Free University which launched the German student protest movement. But this, too, is a sign of life. Building proceeds apace, with new motorways, subways and office blocks under construction. Excellent public housing schemes continue to grow, along with the developing local school system which rates as the best in Germany. Young bloods drive garish cars sporting psychedelic colours. Berlin, in short, remains an exciting city despite the passing of its heroic days as an embattled 'outpost of freedom'.

This, indeed, is one face of West Berlin, the image which a growing number of fun-seeking visitors take home with them at the end of their stay. The fact that the city raised its per capita income by 48·5 per cent in the years 1962–68, compared with an average increase of 39·5 per cent in the Federal Republic, would seem to confirm this picture.

Yet it is deceptive. Behind the mask of eat-drink-and-be-merry West Berlin is a city of complications and problems. One of the worst is its over-abundance of little old ladies eking out their existence in back streets and tenements. At a recent count there were 1,327 women to every thousand men, and a disproportionate number of them are in the older age groups. The working population has to support nearly twice as many old people as the average in the Federal Republic. There are never enough births to balance the number of deaths. The gap is widening from year to year as the birth-rate falls and the death-rate rises. As a result, the city's population dropped by 85,000 in the years 1958–68, and continues to fall by 20,000 a year despite the net influx of migrants from the West. The German Institute for Economic Research forecasts that the population of working age—between fifteen and sixty-five— will drop by 185,000 in 1967–77 unless the gap can be filled by immigration.

So the city's ruling Senate is engaged in a massive campaign to attract young people from West Germany with a variety of incentives. For instance, it pays travel and moving costs. It finances periodic trips home. It helps new settlers find homes in public housing projects. People employed in West Berlin pay roughly one-third less tax than their colleagues in similar jobs in the Federal Republic. These lures have had some effect: during the years 1958–68 over 60,000 more people came to the city than left it. But Dr. Karl König, West Berlin's Senator for Economics, reports that the results have been less than satisfactory. Despite the annual expenditure of millions of marks, the net influx is not enough even to fill the city's present shortage of labour, let alone to maintain the total potential work-force at a constant level. He urges, among other things, a bigger effort to attract foreign workers to fill the gap. But at a time when production and employment are booming in West Germany nobody supposes that it will be easy to solve this chronic problem.

The other main economic bottle-neck is capital investment. West Berlin is still Germany's biggest city and its leading industrial centre. It has managed in recent years by dint of a wide range of inducements to attract many more new industrial plants than, say, Hamburg. But here again the results have fallen far short of the need. Senator König and others have been forced to conclude that financial incentives do not suffice, that firms considering investing in Berlin do not base their decisions on economic factors alone. Even the big firms that are already in Berlin have been hedging their bets by moving their company headquarters and large parts of their production elsewhere. Dr. König complains that such firms have been expanding their capacity in West Germany much more than in their Berlin plants. He is deeply concerned that West Berlin is not attracting enough of the modern growth industries. Too much of its economy is based on banks and other service industries which cannot, as he says, 'leap the frontiers of the Berlin market' but are limited to the local consumer.

More than two-fifths of West Berlin's city budget is met every year by subsidies from Bonn. In numerous other ways the West German taxpayer helps to compensate the city for its special handicaps and burdens. But what holds true for Hof and Schnackenburg is even more valid for West Berlin: no amount of money can change the facts of geography, no subsidy or tax relief can induce either a worker or a businessman to stay in Berlin or any other border community if he feels unsafe or thinks he can do better elsewhere. The climate of confidence must be maintained; transport links must be kept open and dependable. And these in turn depend in the case of Berlin upon the goodwill, or at least the good behaviour, of the East Germans and their Russian masters. Communist blocking or harassment of the surface access routes to Berlin can undo in a day the confidence built up by a month of speeches and advertising.

So the issue comes back to politics: how can this truncated city of West Berlin survive and prosper in a divided world? How can it remain viable, not as a gigantic old people's home dependent upon Western alms, but as the thriving centre of industry and culture it is today? Can it continue indefinitely on the present basis or should it seek a new rôle, perhaps as a kind of bridge between East and West?

Heinrich Albertz, the former Social Democratic mayor of West Berlin, called for a reappraisal of the city's rôle in a notable speech shortly before his downfall in September 1967. It seemed axiomatic to him, as it does to many left-wingers in his party, that the city must become a pathfinder to coexistence, a contact point between East and West. To do this it must loosen its ties with Bonn and abandon its old 'fortress' image; it must set out to cultivate ties with the Communist world. Radicals of the extreme Left go further: they envisage West Berlin as a more or less autonomous area under the protection of the four wartime Allies, the two German states and the United Nations; they see it as a laboratory for synthesizing social systems. Some of these latter ideas come close to the 'free city' concept long advocated by the Soviet Union. Andrei Gromyko, the Soviet Foreign Minister, said to the Supreme Soviet in April 1962 that normalization of the situation in West Berlin meant 'abolishing the occupation régime there and replacing the occupation troops by troops of the neutral states or the United Nations for a definite period'. Thus, he went on, 'West Berlin would be converted from NATO's military outpost and a centre of subversive activity against the German Democratic Republic and other states into a free city of peace and tranquillity.'

Moscow's free-city proposal can be ruled out from the beginning, if only on the ground that no prudent West Berliner would accept any plan involving the withdrawal of Allied (especially American) troops. They cannot defend him effectively, but they stand as a visible symbol of Allied determination. However, some of the 'bridge' thinking holds considerable appeal. It seems at first sight entirely reasonable and natural that West Berlin should come to terms in some manner with its Communist surroundings.

Obviously in order to meet East Germany half-way West Berlin would have to show a certain independence from Bonn. This raises the whole question of West Berlin's ambiguous position in relation to the Federal Republic. Britain, France and the United States, as the three wartime Allies which still rule West Berlin in the last resort, have never accepted the claim that the city is a *Land* or State of the Federal Republic. For in legal terms West Berlin is still under Allied occupation. Federal Republic laws do not apply automatically to the city: they must be extended to West Berlin by legislation of the local House of Representatives which in turn is subject to veto by the Allied Commandants. From time to time the three Commandants do indeed veto certain clauses and paragraphs, particularly in international agreements which treat Berlin as part of the Federal Republic. The twenty-two Berlin delegates who sit in the Bonn Parliament cannot vote in plenary sessions, although they take a full part in committees. West Berlin is fully integrated into the financial and economic system of the Federal Republic, but the Western Allies do not recognize the jurisdiction of the Federal Constitutional Court in Karlsruhe over the city.

Berlin's special status as a ward of the four victorious Allies of World War II was laid down in a joint statement by the governments of the United States, Britain, France and the Soviet Union on June 5, 1945:

> The administration of the 'Greater Berlin' area will be directed by an Inter-Allied Governing Authority, which will operate

under the general direction of the Control Council, and will consist of four Commandants, each of whom will serve in rotation as Chief Commandant. They will be assisted by a technical staff which will supervise and control the activities of the local German organs.

Legally, this agreement remains valid despite the Russian walk-out from the four-power Allied governing authority in July 1948. The three Western Commandants still hold regular meetings, leaving an empty chair. Indeed, absurd as it sounds, the Commandants still observe the custom of waiting two or three minutes at the start of every session for their Russian colleague to arrive. In a subsequent declaration dated May 26, 1952, the Western commanders said that they 'retain the right to take, if they deem it necessary, such measures as may be required to fulfil their international obligations, to ensure public order and to maintain the status and security of Berlin and its economy, trade and communications'. But at the same time the Allies said they wished to grant the Berlin authorities the maximum liberty compatible with the city's special position. The aim was to encourage the economic and financial links with West Germany upon which the city's prosperity depends.

Problems arise, however, concerning the political symbols of West Berlin's solidarity with the Federal Republic. Various Bonn Ministries employ over 20,000 Federal civil servants in Berlin. The Federal President maintains a residence there. The Bonn Cabinet holds occasional sessions in the city, although these are called 'ministerial conferences' rather than Cabinet meetings. The West German Parliament has not held a plenary session in Berlin since April 1965, when its speeches were punctuated by sonic booms from Russian fighters flying low in protest against this 'provocative' event. But many of its committees regularly hold meetings in the restored *Reichstag* building beside the Wall. When the Federal Republic followed tradition by choosing to elect its new President in Berlin in March 1969, the East Germans showed their indignation by blocking the Berlin Autobahns for hours on end. The Western Allies usually approve these gestures of West German support for Berlin. But they turned thumbs down on Bonn's proposal that the World Bank and International Monetary Fund be invited to hold their 1970 meeting in West Berlin. Copenhagen was chosen instead as a less controversial site.

When Russia and East Germany protest that the Federal Republic is engaged in an 'illegal' drive to grab West Berlin they display brazen hypocrisy. For their own violations of Greater Berlin's four-power status have been glaring and consistent. One need only mention the Wall, the establishment of East Berlin as the GDR capital and the presence of East German troops in the Eastern sector. But the Communists are not the only critics of Bonn's efforts to display kinship with West Berlin. Many West Berliners and many West Germans saw the decision to elect President Lübke's successor in Berlin as an unnecessary irritant to East–West relations which could do West Berlin no good. Few Germans would bet today that the next such election—in 1974— will be held in Berlin. But there is no sign that the Federal Republic will be prepared to reduce its other, less demonstrative, activities in West Berlin. *Bundestag* (Federal Parliament) committees will continue to meet in the city. The Bonn Cabinet will go on holding sessions there. The Federal President will hold court there. All these things have become traditional; a body of precedent has been established and few people in the West believe that it should be abandoned.

Certainly nobody would suggest abandoning such gestures without a suitable *quid pro quo* from the other side. There was much discussion of just such a deal at the time of the last presidential election. Moscow let it be known through its ambassador in Bonn that if West Germany would call off the planned election in Berlin and hold it somewhere else then Russia would use its influence in East Berlin to allow an early pass agreement enabling West Berliners to cross the Wall and visit relatives. But Ulbricht wrote to Willy Brandt in the latter's capacity as leader of the West German Social Democratic Party offering to allow passes for Easter 1969 only. This, as he probably knew, was not enough for Bonn, which wanted a long-term pass agreement covering Whitsun and perhaps Christmas as well. Negotiations between Horst Grabert, West Berlin's official representative, and Michael Kohl, the East German government delegate, came to a sudden halt. The GDR insisted, in a message transmitted over the telex line linking police in East and West Berlin, that further meetings between the two negotiators would only be acceptable if the West declared in advance that the election would not be held in Berlin. True, there was a sudden switch on the very eve of the poll. The GDR offered Easter passes and also promised negotiations on subsequent pass agreements. But this came too late, and the election duly occurred in West Berlin regardless of Communist protests.

The upshot was a blow to Ulbricht's prestige. He had promised to 'prevent' the poll and failed. Moscow sent its emissaries to East Berlin to restrain the GDR from rash reprisals. The Auto-bahn hold-ups that ensued were expected; they did not constitute the kind of retaliation which would provoke an Allied response. The West felt justified in its belief that the Russians did not want a Berlin crisis.

Holiday pass agreements now appear to be a thing of the past. Practically the only human contact between East and West Berlin now remaining is the arrangement enabling citizens of the Western sectors to visit Eastern relatives on compassionate grounds. The Communist regulations permit West Berliners to visit close family members across the Wall in the event of births, weddings, deaths and critical illness. Actually the number of 'compassionate' passes issued is substantial—over 70,000 people were able to make use of this loophole between October 1964 and the end of 1967. Moreover, the East Germans have been issuing the passes more liberally of late. But otherwise there is no evidence that the GDR is prepared to expand its dealings with West Berlin in any direction. Klaus Schütz, the present West Berlin mayor, has been trying without success to persuade the GDR to stop its dis-crimination against West Berliners, who think it unfair that West Germans can cross the Wall for one-day visits at will while they cannot. East Germany argues that the Wall was built to protect the GDR from West Berlin 'subversives', and that therefore the discrimination must be maintained. But this is illogical since any 'subversives' could just as well come from the Federal Republic. Trade between West Berlin and the GDR is small. East Germany takes barely one per cent of West Berlin's exports. True, the Western sectors of the city provide a useful outlet for East German milk and lignite briquettes, but apparently neither side wants to become economically dependent upon the other.

In short, the idea that West Berlin should become an East–West bridge looks more like wishful thinking than practical politics. Few West Berliners take it seriously; as one observed: 'To build a bridge you need two pillars, and there is no pillar at the eastern end.' Indeed, from the GDR standpoint it is hard to see what use-ful purpose would be served by opening up channels of communication with West Berlin. Why should the East Germans punch holes in the Wall that they erected at such risk and expense as recently as 1961? As long as West Berlin remains a ward of the Western Allies, as long as it keeps up its intimate ties with the Federal Republic, it must be Ulbricht's interest to keep the city's boundaries hermetically sealed. Talk of newspaper exchanges, scientific and cultural contacts, official links between East and West Berlin and reviving telephone connections across the Wall sounds unrealistic in the face of the GDR's present intransigence. Brandt tried hard for such 'small step' relaxations during his years as mayor of West Berlin: all he could achieve was the pass agreement. Now even that is gone. Ulbricht has evidently decided that a relaxation of tensions in and around Berlin would not serve his purpose. For the existence of West Berlin as an outpost of the West gives him a ready instrument for applying pressure on Bonn and NATO. 'We are sitting on the long end of the lever,' he says. Subject only to Moscow's restraining influence, Ulbricht can apply pressure to West Berlin's access routes whenever he feels disposed. So long as the squeeze involves only an increase of traffic tolls or a temporary blockade due to 'manœuvres' or on some other pretext, the West is helpless. It can only accept the Communist decree under protest, grit its teeth and carry on. From long experience the Russians and the East Germans know where the threshold of forcible response lies. They do not dare to interfere with Allied military convoys on the Autobahns or planes in the air corridors. Such moves would be too risky, but any harassment short of this is fair game.

The more the harassments continue the more determined West Berlin will be to cling to Bonn's political and economic coat-tails as well as to Allied military protection. The city cannot afford to strike out on its own, to chart a more independent course between East and West, as long as the East is so threateningly hostile. So West Berlin finds itself in an impasse. Only the GDR can break the vicious circle—and it will do so only when it believes that the advantages of better relations with West Berlin outweigh the disadvantages. That time is not yet in sight.

Meanwhile the anomalous situation of West Berlin will persist. The exposed city, with its vulnerable access routes, will remain an embarrassing liability to NATO: the one place in the world where a direct clash between Russian and American troops might occur at any time. It will also remain a liability to West Germany, which must pay so many millions of marks for its upkeep. Actually this burden is not so onerous as some critics claim: it amounts to only 0·8 per cent of the West German Federal budget. Last but not least, a continuation of the *status quo* is bound to sap the self-respect of West Berliners. Already there are firms in the city which seem to assume that Bonn owes them a living, that the West German taxpayer will bail them out of all their difficulties. To live indefinitely on outside aid is degrading and corrupting; West Berliners will need to resist these influences. But despite these dangers and drawbacks, there is no definitive reason why the *status quo* should not continue for the foreseeable future. Except that some means will have to be found of meeting West Berlin's shortages of labour and capital investment. Otherwise it will decay into a depressed area, a city of pensioners and idle factories.

13

The Wider Perspective

WHAT holds true for Berlin also applies to Germany as a whole: the East German government is no more interested in opening up the Wire than in punching holes in the Wall. Perhaps the chasm dividing the two Germanies today would be narrower if Bonn political leaders had been less stiff-necked and legalistic. But the prime responsibility for the lack of contact lies indisputably with the GDR. This is evident not only in the physical creation of the Ugly Frontier and the deliberate reduction of technical and local contacts to a minimum. It is also to be found in the unhappy history of links at more exalted levels, both official and unofficial.

Attempts to organize direct meetings at government level and between political parties have been failing more or less consistently since 1947. In fact the last ministerial conference between East and West Germany broke down in that year almost before it had started. Germany was still in rags and ruins, the Occupation was in full force. Hans Ehard, the Bavarian provincial premier, invited all his colleagues from the other states, including those from the Soviet zone, to a conference in Munich. His circular letter said the meeting should discuss measures to 'prevent the German people from sliding further into hopeless economic and political chaos'. But when the sessions opened on June 6 the five provincial premiers from the Soviet zone insisted that they did not want a pragmatic discussion of economic survival. Their interest was political; they wanted to talk about the 'creation of a German central administration to establish a united German State on the basis of understanding between the democratic German parties and trade unions'. On this disagreement the conference collapsed. The East German premiers left Munich in a body and their Western colleagues conferred without them.

With the establishment of the Federal Republic and the GDR in 1949 the prospects for intergovernmental talks became even worse. Bonn refused to recognize the Communist régime; it

insisted that there could be no talks with a government that had
not been democratically elected. Any West German Minister who
exchanged the time of day with a GDR official was risking his
political neck. For instance, Fritz Schäffer, Justice Minister in the
government of Dr. Adenauer, came under fire in 1958 for allegedly
meeting senior East German representatives. He conceded that
he had waited in the East Berlin flat of Vincenz Müller, the deputy
GDR Defence Minister, for a meeting with the Soviet Ambassador to East Germany. During the wait he had not exchanged a
single 'political word' with Müller. Revealingly, Schäffer added
that Chancellor Adenauer had known in advance about this East
Berlin trip and had warned: 'If anything comes out of it, I'll back
you, but if it fails I'll deny all knowledge of it.'

An attempt was also made in the 1950s to establish contact
between the liberal Free Democratic Party and its 'sister party'
in East Germany, the LDP. The LDP, like the East German
Christian Democratic Union, belongs to the 'block of anti-
fascist democratic parties' in the GDR and has nothing in common with its West German namesake except the claim to be
'liberal'. This was demonstrated when three Free Democratic
leaders, Erich Mende, Walter Scheel and Thomas Dehler, went to
the East German town of Weimar in October 1956. They debated with their opposite numbers of the LDP in the Hotel
Elefant on ways of promoting reunification 'through co-operation
of both parties'. But they got no nearer agreement, and Mende
refused the suggestion that he talk to Ulbricht.

Much excitement was generated in the spring of 1966 by the
prospect of a meeting between leaders of the Socialist Unity Party
(SED) of East Germany—the official Communist party—and the
Social Democratic Party (SPD) of West Germany. For a while it
seemed that East Germany was actually prepared to allow Willy
Brandt, the SPD leader, and his senior party colleagues to speak
in a public debate which would be televised on both sides of the
border. Two debating encounters were tentatively arranged, one
in Karl-Marx-Stadt (formerly Chemnitz) in the GDR, and the
other in Hanover. It all began on February 7, 1966, when the
Communist SED addressed an open letter to the SPD suggesting
that the two German workers' parties should try to get the
German problem out of its blind alley by discussing ways of
normalizing relations between the two German states. On
March 19 the SPD replied welcoming the idea of an 'open poli-

tical discussion' and challenging East Germany to publish the correspondence of both sides in its newspapers.

Sure enough, the official SED organ *Neues Deutschland* did publish the SPD letter a week later in a startling break with its controlled tradition. East Germans rubbed their eyes to read such SPD questions as: 'How can there be an open and unprejudiced discussion in Germany when shots are fired at persons who wish to break out of one part of the German Fatherland, divided from the other by minefields, wall and barbed wire?' Copies of the newspaper sold at prices of up to eighty East marks—about £7 or nearly $20—to eager buyers. The GDR government tried to counteract the effect of the West German letter by simultaneously publishing an answer of its own. This devoted considerable space to justifying the Wall and the Wire, recalling that the open frontier that had existed previously 'was utilized to rob the GDR and its citizens of sums running into the thousands of millions'.

'We cannot forget,' the SED letter said, 'how, with the support of the West German government, deliberate attempts were made to disorganize the health services of the GDR by luring away medical specialists. This disruptive work was systematically concentrated in various areas, and did us great damage.' It added that thanks to the 'measures taken on August 13, 1961'—i.e. the building of the Wall—

> the economy and the standard of living in the GDR have greatly improved; this is acknowledged even by our enemies. . . . We have frontiers, just as all other states have. Like other states, we demand that our frontiers and laws should be respected. No harm comes to anyone who respects our law and order. But anyone who acts in accordance with criminal appeals to infringe our frontiers and our laws, anyone who believes the stupid propaganda that the GDR does not exist and that its frontiers need not be respected, risks his head. . . . In West Germany and in West Berlin there are repeated attempts to negate our frontier and to disregard our laws; and this naturally makes it necessary for the GDR to take measures accordingly. These measures protect our state and our people, and prevent dangerous conflicts. For this reason we do not intend to change our guarded frontier into an unguarded frontier.

If the GDR authorities thought that this counterblast would nullify the effect of the SPD letter they were mistaken. In factories throughout East Germany workers took up the cudgels and held teach-ins on the issues raised by Brandt and the SPD. Now that *Neues Deutschland* had published them, the sixty-four dollar questions concerning freedom of travel, freedom of the Press and so forth suddenly became respectable and permissible topics of open debate. Alarmed by signs that a wave of public heresy was sweeping the country, the GDR government took fright. It realized that if the open debates took place as scheduled, with full news coverage, political unrest at home might get out of hand. So the Karl-Marx-Stadt and Hanover meetings were postponed from May until July, and finally called off altogether. Albert Norden, the chief East German government spokesman, delivered the *coup de grâce* at a press conference on June 29. His pretext was that East German speakers would be discriminated against when they came to Hanover. But the excuse did not hold water; most Western analysts believe that Moscow and Ulbricht combined had decided that the experiment was too risky and must be abandoned with minimum loss of face.

Since then East Germany has not allowed itself to be drawn into similar ventures by the SPD or any other Bonn political party. But with the entry of the SPD into the Grand Coalition government that took office in December 1966 there was a marked change in Bonn's methods. Traditional refusal to have any direct dealings with GDR leaders was dropped. When Willi Stoph, the East German premier, wrote to Chancellor Kiesinger on May 10, 1967, his letter was accepted at the Chancellery. This in itself was a singular break with precedent. Apart from an exchange of letters in November 1951 between the then Presidents Pieck of East Germany and Heuss of West Germany, the Bonn government had ignored official letters from the GDR. They were either returned unopened or dropped into the wastepaper basket. But in the spring of 1967 Dr. Kiesinger not only accepted the Stoph letter, he answered it. His reply was taken to Berlin by a Chancellery official on June 13. As it turned out, the correspondence proved barren and shortlived. After a further exchange of letters in September it was abandoned. In essence, Stoph offered to meet Dr. Kiesinger either in Bonn or East Berlin to discuss 'normalizing relations' between East and West Germany—a euphemism for some degree of recognition; accepting existing frontiers—meaning the Oder–Neisse Line and the Lübeck–Hof border; halving arms spending and creating a Central European zone free of atomic weapons. The Federal Chancellor, for his part, replied that a much more promising field of discussion would be small steps to improve contacts across the Wire and the Wall such as easier travel, expanded trade, improved communications and newspaper exchanges.

If Dr. Kiesinger's letters had been printed in the East, as Stoph's messages were publicized in the West, there might have been some point in continuing the correspondence. But they were not, and it became clear that further debate was useless. The two sides were talking at cross-purposes, just as they had in Munich twenty years earlier. The agenda had changed, but the West still wanted to be pragmatic and the East still wanted to be 'political'. The West wanted to chip away at the division of Germany and the East wanted to solidify and codify the *status quo*. In content if not in form, the Kiesinger-Stoph correspondence left the two sides as far apart as before. There would be no purpose in a meeting at the summit or any other official level as long as neither side was interested in what the other wished to discuss.

The only bright spot in the field of official contacts between Bonn and East Berlin is trade. Since Bonn does not recognize the GDR it employs a middleman to avoid the appearance of direct dealings between governments. The present intermediary is Willi Kleindienst, who heads the so-called Interzonal Trade Office in West Berlin. But the ruse deceives nobody: Kleindienst is an official of the Bonn Economics Ministry and takes his instructions directly from the Minister.

In pre-war days it is estimated that the area which is now the Federal Republic used to deliver fifteen per cent of its industrial production to the provinces that now comprise East Germany, which in return used to sell thirty per cent of their output west of where the border is today. These traditional economic patterns were rudely disrupted by the division of Germany: during the Berlin Blockade of 1948–49 trade between the Soviet zone and the West practically ground to a halt. When it resumed the East Germans set out to make their economy as independent of West German supplies as possible. For in those Cold War days the Bonn government regarded trade as a convenient weapon: Western deliveries could be cut off in reprisal for Communist provocations. Gradually the weapon has become blunt. East Germany conducts seventy-five per cent of its foreign trade with the Communist bloc and only ten per cent with West Germany. There has been no recent attempt by Bonn to use trade embargoes as a means of applying pressure; any such move nowadays seems certain to fail. On the contrary, West German policy is to cultivate 'interzonal' trade as one of the few remaining links between the two Germanies.

'We are not trying to wrest East Germany from its close economic relationship with the other socialist countries,' Kleindienst says. 'We are seeking to improve the structural composition of our trade such as befits two highly industrialized countries. Bulk deliveries of raw material such as East German lignite are giving way to the mutual exchange of sophisticated goods.' Thus the GDR is supplying West Germany with increasing quantities of machines, precision instruments, chemical products and textiles. West Germany in return sends chemical goods, machinery, iron and steel products and non-ferrous metals. There is also a major exchange of farm produce, with East Germany supplying some of West Berlin's needs.

The outlook for East–West German trade looked better in 1969 than for years past. It picked up by six per cent in 1968 to a total turnover of DM 2,909 million (£303m or $727m) and showed a massive thirty per cent rise in 1969.[1] Several factors were responsible: the growing quality and competitiveness of East German products, various trade concessions by West Germany and the GDR's tacit acceptance of West Berlin's integration into the West German economy. The bottleneck in East–West German trade during preceding years had been the lack of demand for GDR products in the Federal Republic. The resulting imbalance could not be righted by transactions through third countries, since trade between the two Germanies is essentially bilateral. It counts for West Germany at least as internal German trade, involving no Customs duties. This is recognized by the Western world by protocols to the General Agreement on Tariffs and Trade and the European Common Market Treaty. But it is unique in other ways. There is no official rate of exchange between the West-mark and the East-mark. The East German mark is a purely internal currency which may be neither imported nor exported. The East Germans cannot bring themselves to accept the West-mark as the medium of exchange, so the agreements reached through the Interzonal Trade Office are officially registered in 'accounting units'. But since each 'accounting unit' is equal to one Western Deutsche Mark (DM) this is a thin disguise.

[1] See Appendix E.

Trade is conducted on the basis of the Berlin Agreement of 1951 which avoids mention (and therefore recognition) of the GDR by calling itself an agreement between the 'currency areas of the DM-West and the currency areas of the DM-East'. Use of the plural word 'areas' in each case has political significance: it takes account of the special status of Berlin—East and West—as an area of four-power Allied administration. Kleindienst's Interzonal Trade Office negotiates on behalf of West Berlin as well as West Germany, despite Communist claims that West Berlin is a 'special entity' distinct from the Federal Republic. Meetings are held weekly, alternately in West and East Berlin, between Kleindienst's team and officials of the East German Ministry for Foreign Trade. Participants in these negotiations say that they occur in a pleasant and business-like atmosphere which belies political differences. But then both sides have a common interest in keeping the trade flowing, just as the East and West German Railways have a joint interest in keeping the trains running across the border. Businessmen of East and West Germany exchange visits without harassment on either side. Any East German buyer or salesman allowed out by his own government is permitted to enter the Federal Republic without hindrance. West German businessmen have to obtain visas like anyone else to visit the GDR, but this normally presents no problem. The only people who have difficulty in this respect are West Berliners.

All in all, trade is one of the very few effective bonds linking the two parts of Germany. Some people say it is the only one that counts. To be sure, there are numerous difficulties, and the economic importance of this trade is marginal for both sides. East–West German commerce accounts for only about two per cent of the Federal Republic's total trade. Thus West Germany could do without it altogether at a pinch. But the ten per cent share that 'interzonal' trade takes in East Germany's total is still regarded by Bonn as significant. Kleindienst is trying to maintain this ten per cent stake as the GDR economy grows.

Legal co-operation astride the border fairly bristles with difficulties. In civil law there are countless ties and obligations spanning the frontier, concerning everything from wills to support payments. Generally cases involving these cannot be settled without obtaining legal documents from the other side. But when a West German court writes to an East German court requesting co-operation, only a few GDR judges reply direct. In most cases the correspondence is referred by the Eastern court to the Ministry of Justice in East Berlin. Even when the Justice Ministry approves the request, East German courts never supply original files from their archives. They will, however, pass on extracts and copies of documents, provided that the case is, in the GDR view, a valid one. East Germany does not accept Bonn's doctrine that the laws of the Federal Republic apply to the GDR as well as West Germany. East Germany refuses to help West German courts trying to determine whether a refugee from the GDR is entitled to (Western) compensation under Bonn laws for property destroyed or confiscated in the East. No help can be expected from an East German court in any case involving someone who in GDR laws counts as an illegal fugitive. Such a person forfeits all his or her civil rights and property in the GDR.

Suppose, for example, an East German girl has fled to the West, bringing an illegitimate child but leaving the father behind. She sues the father for support payments to maintain the child. But the GDR replies, in effect, 'If the girl comes back to us she will recover all her civil rights, but until then—not a pfennig.' In the reverse direction, the West German authorities would require the Western father of an illegitimate child to pay for its support even if the child were in East Germany. But the money would be paid to a Youth Authority in the West, not to the GDR. And the Youth Authority would then spend the funds on supporting children who are not getting the maintenance funds due them from the GDR.

Whenever an East German has a claim on a person living in the Federal Republic, or on the Bonn government, the claim is handled in West German courts like any other. The resulting payment goes into a blocked account to the credit of the claimant. Citizens of the GDR are only allowed to make use of such funds with the permission of their Central Bank; in practice most of them prefer their credits to accumulate in the West as a nest-egg against the day when they will be able to travel as pensioners to the West. This blocked account system is the same as that used to safeguard other funds accruing to East Germans, such as farmers who still own fields on the Western side of the border. The GDR government naturally does not like this system; when it recently tried to get the frozen money transferred it gave the total as DM 5 million (about £500,000 or $1,250,000). The transfer was refused, but occasionally *ad hoc* payments are made. When, for instance, it was found in 1968 that there were 4,500 illegitimate children of West German fathers in the GDR, twice the number of offspring in the West of East German fathers, Bonn paid a substantial sum to the GDR youth authorities.

Co-operation in the realm of criminal law also presents a varied picture. West German criminals often flee to East Germany in hopes of escaping punishment for crimes committed in the West. Every day, according to Justice Ministry officials in Bonn, debtors skip across the border because they cannot meet their instalment payments. Once in the GDR they declare their loyalty to the Communist régime and frequently are given sanctuary there as 'victims of capitalist exploitation'. They escape jail in the West but they are put to work in the East—and this, for some defectors, is a shock. When really serious offenders such as murderers and rapists run away to East Germany they are promptly handed back to the West. East Germany is no more interested in harbouring dangerous criminals than any other country. When West German police seek East German co-operation in tracking down offenders of this kind the request is usually met. There may, however, be delays if the request is not routed through the 'proper channel'— namely the State Prosecutor in East Berlin. In reverse, West Germany does usually hand back common criminals who flee from the GDR to the West. It goes without saying that political offenders who have only sinned in Communist eyes are invariably given sanctuary in the West.

An operation which is now conducted in secrecy is the 'ransoming' of political prisoners from East Germany. The operation began in 1964 when freedom was bought for 800 prisoners. The Bonn government paid in goods such as coffee, citrus fruit and fertilizer rather than cash. Up to the end of January 1966 a further 1,800 prisoners were freed in return for West German payments, which by that time had reached a total of about DM 100 million (£10,400,000 or $25 million). West German officials used to discuss the scheme openly, but now prefer to treat it confidentially for fear of imperilling future releases. The GDR government is naturally sensitive to charges that it is 'trading in human beings'. But the operation continues on a much reduced scale. Releases are arranged semi-privately through two well-known lawyers in East and West Berlin. These lawyers have also been instrumental in arranging prisoner swaps and in pressing for the release of tourists and others who have been jailed on spy charges.

Less clandestinely, the West German Trade Union Federation (DGB) and its member unions have tried to make contact with labour unions throughout Eastern Europe including the GDR. But this was always a delicate business, highly charged with political dynamite. The explosion came on August 28, 1968, just after the invasion of Czechoslovakia. The West German Federation decided to break with unions in all the countries—East Germany included—which had joined in the Warsaw Pact intervention. Karl Hauenschild, a member of the Chemical, Paper and Ceramics Union executive, wrote later: 'Certainly it was not the unions in the countries concerned that ordered the invasion. But we have not so far heard of a single union in a single country participating in the invasion that has let it be known that it wished to dissociate itself from the action of its government.' This, he said, did not mean that contacts with East European unions were pointless. It just meant that they could not be cultivated at all costs.

The most recent example of ruptured ties between East and West Germany is provided by the Protestant Church. Since 1945 the Evangelical Church of Germany (EKD) had existed as an umbrella organization linking the Protestant majority of East Germany with their fellow-Protestants of the West. It worked under increasing difficulties, and separate synods for East and West had to be established when the Wall prevented personal contact. But the Protestant churchmen of both sides still owed allegiance to the joint organization: although they met in separate conferences they discussed the same agenda and usually arrived at the same conclusions. Finally in May 1969 the East German member churches broke away to form their 'Federation of Evangelical Churches in the GDR'. It was small consolation to the West that Article 4 of the new federation's constitution spoke of the 'special communion of the entire Protestant Christendom in Germany'. The EKD was left as a rump grouping representing the Protestant churches of West Germany alone. The sole remaining link between Eastern and Western Protestants exists at a lower level through a body called the Evangelical Church of the Union (EKU). This includes Lutheran and Reformed churches in certain provinces on both sides of the border.

What are the chances that the Wire and the Wall will come down? What are the prospects that East Germany will transform the

Ugly Frontier into a normal border with reasonably free travel and communications?

The answer of Germans on both sides of the boundary is unanimous: the outlook is bleak. Even if Bonn were to recognize the GDR and to accept the border as an international frontier, this would not necessarily reduce the Wire and the Wall by a single strand or stone. For the Ugly Frontier was not built because Bonn refuses to recognize the GDR; it was erected to halt the outflow of refugees and provide the framework for East Germany's economic recovery. The great debate in Bonn over whether and to what extent to recognize the GDR is therefore largely irrelevant to this question. What counts is whether and when the East German government will decide that its frontier controls can be relaxed. And this, in turn, depends on the likely outflow of refugees, the probable loss of useful workers if East Germans were allowed to travel. It also depends upon the Ulbricht régime's assessment of the effects upon the East German population of increased exposure to the West.

Clearly the GDR government does not believe that the frontier can be safely 'normalized'—to use a favourite Communist word. If it thought that the barriers could be reduced in the near future it would not be spending so much money and manpower on constructing the semi-permanent 'modern frontier'. But what of the more distant future: are there trends afoot in East Germany which might make the frontier fortifications obsolete and unnecessary? The question is an intriguing one.

It is easy as a Western visitor to meet East Germans, even to strike up political conversation with complete strangers. Curiosity about the West is such that everyone seems willing to talk: professors, building workers, trade union officials, actors, students, civil servants, waiters, schoolteachers, factory managers. Once one gets behind the iron mask of the Wire and the Wall, the true face of East Germany is surprisingly open and frank. People do not look over their shoulders as they talk: they criticize their régime and crack political jokes in a way which would have landed them in concentration camps in Hitler's days. Until comparatively recently even political cabaret was allowed remarkably free rein.

The first question that one asks, once mutual confidence has been established, is whether there would be a stampede for the West if the Wall came down. The answers vary according to the age and occupation of the person involved. The wife of one well-placed Leipzig professional man told me she would 'walk barefoot to the border' if only she could leave the country without having to wait until she was sixty. Refugee statistics show that this longing to escape is still shared by many others, especially youths in their late teens and early twenties. Yet there is ample evidence that the urge to flee is diminishing. Some years ago there was a saying in East Germany that one had better climb a tree when the Wall came down or one would be 'trampled in the rush'. This was undoubtedly true once; it is less true today.

The reasons for this change are often cited. Living standards in the two Germanies are much closer today than in the early 1960s. Since then the GDR has experienced its own Economic Miracle. It ranks as the second industrial nation of the Communist bloc after the Soviet Union; its products are becoming more and more competitive in world markets. East Germans are proud to see Czechs, Poles and even Russians buying goods in GDR shops. National income rose three-fold between 1950 and 1967 and foreign trade gained eightfold in the same period, placing the GDR thirteenth among world trading nations. All this has been achieved despite wartime devastation, despite East Germany's lack of almost all raw materials except lignite, despite massive post-war dismantling and reparations exacted by the Soviet Union and despite the lack of any Marshall Plan. East Germans have every right to be proud of this 'operation bootstrap' achievement, particularly the middle-aged people who played the main rôle in it.

Many GDR citizens take pride also in their country's social gains. They claim that their schools and medical services are generally ahead of those in the Federal Republic—and West Germans agree. Less tangibly, many East Germans contend that their society is less materialistic, less corrupt and more 'decent' than that of West Germany. The moral comparison, like other comparisons, is always with West Germany rather than any other Western country. This for obvious reasons: the relationship is a love-hate one fed by West German television, Communist propaganda (heavily loaded with attacks on the Federal Republic) and contact with West German visitors. An 'admass' show of sex and violence on West German TV or a tactless remark by a patronizing West German visitor can play into the hands of Communist propaganda. East German news-stands are not festooned with 'girlie' magazines, East German cinemas do not show sex films, East Germans are spared the slick commercialism of glamour advertising. On the whole, they seem to prefer it that way. It does not occur to East Germans that such excesses are inevitable in a free society, that they are the price that a democracy pays for freedom from censorship. But then the people of East Germany have known nothing but dictatorship since Hitler came to power in 1933.

None of this should be taken to suggest that the majority of East Germans are uncritical devotees of Ulbricht and his system. They were not in 1953 when they staged their revolt in the streets, they were not in the pre-Wall years when they 'voted with their feet' by coming to the West and they were not in 1966 when they responded so excitedly to Brandt's letter in *Neues Deutschland*. But even if they were so minded, East Germans know that rebellion is futile. A liberalization movement along the lines of the Prague Spring also appears unthinkable. To be sure, the demand for liberalization is there, particularly the yearning to travel to the West. But unlike the Czechs in the spring of 1968 the East Germans already have the Russians within their gates: over twenty Red Army divisions are based on GDR soil, garrisoned in barracks across the country and screened from view by high wooden fences and watchtowers. If the Russians could invade Czechoslovakia in August 1968, how long would they hesitate to use their troops to crush any budding reform movement in East Germany? They have already intervened once with troops and tanks—in 1953—and they would doubtless do so again at the drop of an uncensored newspaper.

Given this Soviet straitjacket, given also the traditional German respect for authority, it is only natural that many of East Germany's 17 million people should bury their misgivings and try to make the best of the system. It is a system which many regard, rightly or wrongly, as basically superior to that of the West. To this extent, two decades of Communist indoctrination have had their effect. But even the staunchest supporters of 'the system' recognize many of its faults.

It was a student at East Berlin's Humboldt University who summed up the views of many of his contemporaries most neatly. He had been asked to say where and when he would most like to have lived, given a choice of any country and any period. After some thought he replied: 'In the GDR at a time when we could travel everywhere, read everything and be able to learn everything at first hand.' It was a wistful plea for the removal of the Wire and the Wall. Yet he was a convinced Communist and he saw the present necessity of these barriers to his country's economy. He knew that the GDR with its top-heavy proportion of pensioners needed every able-bodied worker; he, too, feared that if the Wall came down East Germany would lose too many people. He believed that most of those who long to travel to the West would return to East Germany after satisfying their curiosity. But there might still be an unacceptable loss, a renewed brain drain which would jeopardize the GDR's future.

In short, the Ugly Frontier will become less ugly only when the East German government of the day considers that the risk of opening it is bearable. Of all East European governments the GDR is the most loyal to Moscow, the most resistant to East–West détente. It looks as though it will remain inflexible in the years to come: Erich Honecker, Ulbricht's heir-apparent, has been called 'a younger Ulbricht without a smile'. Meanwhile the long separation will continue to erode human relationships across the border. Honecker himself stems from the Saarland in West Germany. His father, sister and five nephews live in the West; his father visits him every year in the GDR. Even Ulbricht has Western relatives: he has a sister and a daughter by his first marriage in West Germany and his brother Erich lives with his family in the United States. These are just two prominent examples; a recent survey showed that eleven per cent of West Germans still have parents, grandparents, brothers or sisters in the GDR, forty per cent write letters to the East and thirty per cent send parcels. Relatives and friends often rendezvous in other East European countries such as Czechoslovakia or Rumanian holiday resorts beside the Black Sea. An East Berlin girl who lived only one kilometre from her West Berlin fiancé met him on a Black Sea beach after both had journeyed over 2,000 kilometres. Yet their reunion could only last a few precious weeks.

German families feel an acute sense of loss if a beloved brother or sister, uncle or aunt, is absent from such occasions as baptisms, confirmations, weddings and funerals. But there is a worse agony than this: the realization that even when Uncle Fritz can come to the West for Christmas—because he has reached sixty-five—he may be a stranger in his habits and thinking. For instance, Westerners notice that many visiting East German pensioners frequently ask whether they are allowed to travel to such-and-such a place or buy such-and-such an item. 'We constantly have to explain,' one Bavarian said, 'that even in our highly bureaucratic Federal Republic nobody's ever thought of trying to tell people where they should go or what they should buy.'

To repeat, the gulf between the two Germanies is widening, the divisions are hardening. There is, it seems, not much that the West Germans can do about these trends except to cling to such frail links as remain: to write letters, send parcels, keep the trains running and the trade flowing. West Germany will have to reconcile itself to the prospect that the Ugly Frontier with all its horrors and inhumanity will last indefinitely, that the GDR is a going concern and that German reunification is as remote as the crock of gold at the end of the rainbow. Many individual West Germans have already accepted these unpalatable truths. Even the Bonn government has begun to face reality: although many of its documents still speak of the GDR as the 'Soviet zone' or 'Middle Germany', leading politicians including Willy Brandt, the Federal Chancellor, now frankly call it the German Democratic Republic. The term East Germany, incidentally, still means in official Bonn parlance the former German territories beyond the Oder–Neisse Line, now in Polish and Russian hands.

Already Brandt concedes the existence of two German states; one day the time must come when Bonn will recognize the East–West German border as a genuine frontier and cease referring to it as a 'demarcation line'. Calling a spade a spade is only one of the shifts ahead. Other changes no doubt will come, including some form of recognition of the GDR. But this, as we have seen, is unlikely to remove the Wire and the Wall. On the contrary, it will merely ratify their existence.

Appendices and Index

Appendix A

Refugees from GDR 1949–68

(Those registering at official reception centres)

1949	129,245
1950	197,788
1951	165,648
1952	182,393
1953	331,390
1954	184,198
1955	252,870
1956	279,189
1957	261,622
1958	204,092
1959	143,917
1960	199,188
1961 (Wall built 13.8.61)	207,026
1962	21,356
1963	42,632
1964	41,876
1965	29,522
1966	24,131
1967	19,573
1968	16,036

Altogether 2,933,722 people registered as refugees between September 1949 and the end of 1968, of whom 124,825 came after the building of the Berlin Wall. Among the latter were 27,518 who risked life and limb to flee across the Wire and the Wall, seventy-one per cent of whom were under twenty-five years old. (See Chap. 5 p. 85 for annual breakdown.) In addition to the above, some 122,000 East Germans, mostly elderly or otherwise unable to work, have been allowed out since 1962 to join their families in the West.

Source: Bonn official statistics.

Appendix B

East–West German Border Fortifications

(As of June 1 1969)

Length of double fencing	899 miles
Length of minefields	498 miles
Length of close-mesh fencing	121 miles
Length of vehicle ditch	327 miles
Length of parallel access road	494 miles
Pillboxes and dug-outs	999
Observation towers	496
Observation platforms in trees	150
Dog runs and number of dogs	317 and 441
Number and length of floodlit stretches	88, 74 miles

Source: Federal Frontier Defence Force, Bonn.

Appendix C

Inland Shipping Mittelland Canal
Border Crossing Rühen/Buchhorst
(West–East)

Loads in thousands of tons

| | Nationality of Vessels | | | | |
	FRG	GDR	Czechoslovakia	Poland	Total
1965 to:					
Berlin (W)	2,566·4	5·0	—	20·6	2,592·0
GDR	305·2	175·2	2·7	—	483·1
Czechoslovakia	—	—	0·4	—	0·4
Poland	—	—	—	22·9	22·9
1966 to:					
Berlin (W)	2,716·6	5·3	—	0·3	2,722·2
GDR	360·0	167·8	1·4	—	529·2
Czechoslovakia	—	—	0·5	—	0·5
Poland	—	—	—	56·7	56·7
1967 to:					
Berlin (W)	2,873·1	6·7	—	0·2	2,880·0
GDR	257·3	160·2	—	—	417·5
Czechoslovakia	—	—	—	—	—
Poland	—	—	—	59·2	59·2
1968 to:					
Berlin (W)	2,778·0	10·9	—	0·2	2,789·1
GDR	156·1	152·6	—	—	308·7
Czechoslovakia	—	—	—	—	—
Poland	—	—	—	98·2	98·2

Appendix C

(continued)

*Inland Shipping Mittelland Canal
Border Crossing Buchhorst/Rühen*
(East–West)

Loads in thousands of tons

	Nationality of Vessels				
	FRG	*GDR*	*Czechoslovakia*	*Poland*	*Total*
1965 from:					
Berlin (W)	264·1	—	—	—	264·1
GDR	317·7	216·2	—	—	533·9
Czechoslovakia	—	—	33·7	—	33·7
Poland	—	—	—	47·3	47·3
1966 from:					
Berlin (W)	263·6	1·1	—	—	264·7
GDR	284·8	281·5	0·3	0·7	567·3
Czechoslovakia	—	—	36·7	—	36·7
Poland	—	—	—	74·0	74·0
1967 from:					
Berlin (W)	295·9	—	—	—	295·9
GDR	389·6	299·8	—	—	689·4
Czechoslovakia	—	—	29·1	—	29·1
Poland	—	—	—	85·2	85·2
1968 from:					
Berlin (W)	294·5	—	—	—	294·5
GDR	222·5	238·2	—	—	460·7
Czechoslovakia	—	—	36·1	—	36·1
Poland	—	—	—	111·6	111·6

Appendix C

(continued)

Inland Shipping Elbe
Border Crossing Cumlosen/Schnackenburg
(East–West)

Loads in thousands of tons

	Nationality of Vessels				
	FRG	*GDR*	*Czechoslovakia*	*Poland*	*Total*
1965 from:					
Berlin (W)	146·1	0·1	—	—	146·2
GDR	2·0	205·8	2·4	—	210·2
Czechoslovakia	—	—	304·9	—	304·9
Poland	—	—	—	5·5	5·5
1966 from:					
Berlin (W)	131·5	—	—	—	131·5
GDR	3·3	313·9	1·3	—	318·5
Czechoslovakia	—	—	354·1	—	354·1
Poland	—	—	—	3·2	3·2
1967 from:					
Berlin (W)	166·2	—	—	—	166·2
GDR	24·6	414·1	0·2	—	438·9
Czechoslovakia	—	—	367·8	—	367·8
Poland	—	—	—	0·9	0·9
1968 from:					
Berlin (W)	174·8	0·2	—	—	175·0
GDR	10·5	396·3	1·2	—	408·0
Czechoslovakia	—	—	465·0	—·	465·0
Poland	—	—	—	—	—

Appendix C

(continued)

Inland Shipping Elbe
Border Crossing Schnackenburg/Cumlosen
(West–East)

Loads in thousands of tons

	Nationality of Vessels				
	FRG	GDR	Czechoslovakia	Poland	Total
1965 to:					
Berlin (W)	1,561·2	—	—	—	1,561·2
GDR	75·9	219·9	8·6	—	304·4
Czechoslovakia	—	0·6	404·1	—	404·7
Poland	—	—	—	6·1	6·1
1966 to:					
Berlin (W)	1,601·3	—	—	0·7	1,602·0
GDR	164·5	329·2	2·0	—	495·7
Czechoslovakia	—	0·6	510·7	—	511·3
Poland	—	—	—	2·6	2·6
1967 to:					
Berlin (W)	1,969·8	2·2	—	—	1,972·0
GDR	31·9	377·8	—	—	409·7
Czechoslovakia	—	—	386·4	—	386·4
Poland	—	—	—	1·0	1·0
1968 to:					
Berlin (W)	2,160·4	10·6	—	—	2,171·0
GDR	90·9	571·6	4·8	—	667·3
Czechoslovakia	—	—	432·9	—	432·9
Poland	—	—	—	—	—

Appendix D

Number of Passenger Trains travelling daily between West and East Germany

Border Crossing	1964 Terminus	1967 Terminus	1968 Terminus	1969 Terminus
Lübeck Herrnburg	1 Stralsund 1 Rostock	1 Stralsund 2 Rostock	1 Stralsund 2 Rostock	1 Stralsund 2 Rostock
Büchen Schwanheide	3 Berlin	3 Berlin 1 Dresden	3 Berlin 1 Dresden	2 Berlin 1 Dresden 1 Schwerin
Wolfsburg Oebisfelde	4 Leipzig	1 Zwickau 1 Dresden 4 Leipzig	1 Zwickau 1 Dresden 4 Leipzig	1 Zwickau 1 Dresden 4 Leipzig
Helmstedt Marienborn	4 Berlin 1 Moscow 1 Warsaw 1 Magdeburg	4 Berlin 1 Moscow 2 Warsaw 1 Leipzig 1 Görlitz	4 Berlin 1 Moscow 2 Warsaw 1 Leipzig 1 Görlitz	3 Berlin 1 Moscow 2 Warsaw 1 Leipzig 1 Görlitz 1 Brest
Bebra Gerstungen	2 Berlin 3 Leipzig	2 Berlin 2 Leipzig 2 Dresden 1 Cottbus 1 Stralsund 1 Warsaw	2 Berlin 2 Leipzig 2 Dresden 1 Stralsund 1 Frankfurt/Oder	2 Berlin 2 Leipzig 2 Dresden 1 Stralsund 1 Frankfurt/Oder 1 Warsaw
Ludwigstadt Probstzella	1 Berlin 1 Saßnitz (Malmö)	2 Berlin 1 Saßnitz (Malmö) 1 Leipzig	2 Berlin 1 Saßnitz (Malmö) 1 Leipzig	2 Berlin 1 Saßnitz (Malmö) 1 Leipzig
Hof Gutenfürst	1 Leipzig 1 Karl-Marx-Stadt (Chemnitz) 1 Dresden	2 Dresden 1 Rostock	2 Dresden 1 Rostock	2 Dresden 1 Rostock
Total:	26	38	38	38

Number of Goods Trains travelling daily between West and East Germany as of June 1, 1969

Border Crossing	West–East regularly scheduled, daily or weekdays	West–East additional, on demand	East–West regularly scheduled, daily or weekdays	East–West additional, on demand
Lübeck/Herrnburg	2	3	3	2
Büchen/Schwanheide*	10	13	10	7
Vorsfelde/Oebisfelde	6	6	15	5
Walkenried/Ellrich	3	4	3	4
Helmstedt/Marienborn*	13	1	4	1
Bebra/Gerstungen*	6	6	7	7
Ludwigsstadt/Probstzella	4	5	5	7
Hof/Gutenfürst*	5	5	6	2
Total:	50	43	53	35
Total May 1968	50	42	54	34
Total May 1967	52	40	57	33
Total May 1966	52	36	55	31

* Lines serving Berlin.

Appendix E

East–West German Trade, 1959–68 (in millions of DM-West)

	Federal Republic deliveries to GDR	GDR deliveries to Federal Republic	Total
1959	1,063	935	1,998
1960	1,030	1,007	2,037
1961	911	917	1,828
1962	902	899	1,801
1963	907	1,029	1,936
1964	1,193	1,112	2,305
1965	1,225	1,249	2,474
1966	1,681	1,324	3,005
1967	1,490	1,255	2,745
1968	1,459	1,450	2,909
1969 (1st 6 months)	914·8	753·8	1,668·6

Travel Across the East–West German Border (*in thousands*)

	1961	1962	1963	1964	1965	1966	1967	1968
A. From West Germany to the GDR:								
West German visitors		No Count Made				1,500 (app.)	1,424	1,261
West German emigrants	20	9	5	5	6	4	4	3
Returning E. German pensioners	None	None	None	664	1,219	1,055	1,072	1,047
Other East Germans	738	9	18	301	1,063	812	87	118
B. From West Germany to West Berlin:								
1. By surface transport:								
West Berliners	2,402	2,242	2,281	2,486	2,302	2,493	2,409	2,323
West Germans			No Count Made			1,484	1,588	1,346
Foreigners	170	174	251	300	320	335	376	349
2. By air:								
West Berliners ⎫ West Germans ⎬ Foreigners ⎭	728	959	1,124	1,212	1,511	1,626	1,825	2,083

Source: Federal Ministry of All-German Affairs, Bonn.

Index

A Note About the Author

David J. A. Shears was born in London in *1926 and
studied at Christ's Hospital and Oxford University.
He began his career in journalism as a trainee on the*
Bristol Evening Post, *1949–50. The next ten years
were spent as a correspondent for the* Reuters News
Agency: *first in Pakistan (1951), then in the Netherlands (1952–5) and in Washington, D.C. (1955–
60). He has worked for the* Daily Telegraph *since
1961, serving in that paper's Washington bureau
through 1965 and since then as bureau chief in Bonn,
Germany. He has also written for* The New York
Times Magazine *and* The Spectator.

A Note on the Type

The text of this book was set on the Monotype in a type face called Garamond. Jean Jannon has been identified as designer for this face, which is based on Garamond's original models, but is much lighter and more open than Garamond's original form. The italic is taken from a fount of Granjon, which appeared in the repertory of the Imprimerie Royale and was probably cut in the middle of the sixteenth century.